Holy Ice

Past Lives & Crystal Skulls: The Secrets of Time

Continuing the journey of a soul...

by
Paulinne Delcour–Min

For permission, or serialization, condensation, adaptions, or for our catalog of other publications, write to: Ozark Mountain Publishing, Inc., P.O. Box 754, Huntsville, AR 72740, ATTN: Permissions Department

Library of Congress Cataloging-in-Publication Data
Holy Ice by Paulinne Delcour-Min -1948-

Holy Ice, takes you on a breathtaking journey through time, to the heart of the mystery of the crystal skulls.

1. Spiritual 2. Crystal Skulls 3. Healing 4. Metaphysical
I. Delcour-Min, Paulinne, 1948 II. Crystal Skulls III. Metaphysical IV. Holy Ice

Library of Congress Catalog Card Number: 2020935837
ISBN: 9781940265766

Cover Art and Layout: Victoria Cooper Art
Book set in: Times New Roman, Gabriola
Book Design: Summer Garr

Published by:

PO Box 754, Huntsville, AR 72740
800-935-0045 or 479-738-2348; fax 479-738-2448
WWW.OZARKMT.COM

Printed in the United States of America

Image on the back jacket, Galaxy Cluster 1E
0657-556, courtesy of NASA/CXC/M.
Markevitch et al.

For Veronica Fyland

Your deep understanding and natural affinity with the crystal skulls made you the perfect companion for this adventure. No matter into what strange territory our regression work took us, you always brought me safely back.

You showed me the secrets of Time.
Thank you from the bottom of my heart.

If you would prosper in challenging times, this book is for you.
Making sense of the chaos in the world …

Acknowledgments

A very big thank-you!

To everyone who has helped *Holy Ice* leave the world of ideas and actually manifest on the planet.

Especially my guides and Archangel Michael, Archangel Uriel, Archangel Gabriel, and Archangel Raphael, without you I would never venture into the inner world. You keep me safe, imbue my experiences with truth, make sure I know the importance of love, and bring healing. Veronica Fyland, you always found time to help me unearth the material. Isabelle Crummie, you nurtured the tender shoots of my writing and your questions were invaluable. Guy Needler, you were so generous with your time, advice, and help after the manuscript took shape, I can't thank you enough! Ozark Mountain Publishing made it happen, and special mention must go to Nancy Vernon, Brandy McDonald, and Debbie Upton, my editor, because you were all an absolute joy to work with. Bill Homann deserves thanks for his lovely photographs of the Skull of Love / Mitchell-Hedges skull / Bah Ha Redo; and Michele Nocerino for the striking photograph of Sha Na Ra. It was a joy speaking with you both. And thanks go to my husband Ye for his love and support, and to Grace and M D for all that they do for the skulls.

Sha Na Ra's website is https://www.shanaracrystalskull.com/ and Michele can be contacted on +1 925 577 3957.

The Skull of Love's website is http://mitchell-hedges.com/bill-homann/ and Bill can be contacted on +1 219 616 0886.

BOOK 2

Holy Ice: The Map of Time

*Those who forget the past are doomed to repeat it.
When we see where we've come from, it's so much easier
to see where we are going.*

Contents

The Legend: The Crystal Skulls Warn of a Coming Disaster   i

Chapter 1: Introducing the Crystal Skulls and Other Dimensions   1

Chapter 2: Chronicles of Atlantis 1   29

Chapter 3: Chronicles of Atlantis 2   58

Chapter 4: Chronicles of Atlantis 3   87

Chapter 5: Chronicles of Atlantis 4   110

Chapter 6: Chronicles of Atlantis 5   132

Chapter 7: Chronicles of Atlantis 6: Distorting the Divine Archetype   150

Chapter 8: Atlantis Had Gone, but Her Legacy and Her Children Live On   175

Chapter 9: The Legacy of Pyramid Temples   198

Chapter 10: Merlin's Children   221

Chapter 11   231

Chapter 12   243

Chapter 13: Etheric Crystal Skulls   249

Chapter 14: Three WARNINGS Extraterrestrial Perspectives   268

Chapter 15: Skulls in the Present Day   279

Meditation and Prayer for Healing the Past   285

Battle Hymn of Merlin's Children: Meditation   286

Bibliography   288

About the Author   291

Books by Pauline Delcour-Min

Spiritual Gold
Published by: Ozark Mountain Publishing

Holy Ice
Published by: Ozark mountain publishing

Divine Fire (Coming Soon)
Published by: Ozark Mountain Publishing

For more information about any of the above titles, soon to be released titles,
or other items in our catalog, write, phone or visit our website:
Ozark Mountain Publishing, Inc.
PO Box 754, Huntsville, AR 72740
479-738-2348/800-935-0045
www.ozarkmt.com

The Legend

The Crystal Skulls Warn of a Coming Disaster

This is a book about the crystal skulls, and about past lives and their stories. It is the journey of a soul, mine. I am a past life therapist and when Native American elders brought crystal skulls to England on the Wolf Song tour in 1998, I knew I had to have a private sitting with the ancient quartz skull known as Sha Na Ra. I asked the skull a question about my life and my future, and it showed me the answer in a picture that appeared deep within its crystal. The picture was detailed and sharp.

So the mysterious things I'd read about the skulls were true!

And if they were true, that meant the legend of the crystal skulls was worthy of research—using my skills with past life recall. Regression has been my passion for over thirty years now, and the legend troubled me, because it runs like this:

Native American legends tell of thirteen ancient crystal skulls, the size of human skulls, which hold information vital for the very survival of the human race at a pivotal point in time—and though they've been scattered and hidden, one day they will be brought back together to save us from disaster.

Well! That time is now—it has begun—which is why skulls like Sha Na Ra are being brought out onto the world stage by their guardians. But it's the coming disaster that troubles me deeply.[1]

1 The legends are held in common by the Mayan and Aztec descendants of Central America, by the Pueblo and Navajo Indians of the southwestern United States, right up to the Cherokee and Seneca Indians of the northeastern United States. There was a 9.9.9. Crystal Skull Gathering in Arizona, the 10.10.10. Gathering in New York, the 11.11.11. Gathering in Los Angeles, and the 12.12.12.

For alerting me to the legend I'm indebted to Chris Morton and Ceri Louise Thomas. We were friends in Manchester, England, when they gave me their famous book, *The Mystery of the Crystal Skulls*. It is such a powerful book that my quest began, because I had to know more.

You can see why I jumped at the chance of a sitting with Sha Na Ra a year later.

The thing about crystals is their age. A human life is but an eye blink to a crystal, the centuries no more than passing clouds. Some are nearly as old as the Earth. They're here for the long haul; they are our allies through time. Crystal makes the perfect material for something meant to travel with us down the millennia, like the skulls.

Earth's heart is a giant iron crystal[2] and crystals make up most of the Earth's rocky crust on which we live. Quartz crystal is the *Holy Ice* of my title, and quartz alone makes up about 12 percent of the mass of Earth's crust. It's the most abundant and widely distributed mineral found at Earth's surface; it is in all parts of the world and in all types of rock, igneus, metamorphic, and sedimentary.[3] Crystals

Miami Event. European events take place, although most are in the United States because there are more skulls there, and there's a greater awareness of them. Details of such gatherings and many more, plus ongoing meditations and forthcoming events can be found at www.crystalskulls.com (31.3.2019).

2   Ronald Cohen and Lars Stixrude of the Carnegie Institute of Washington discovered it in 1995 with a sophisticated computer model of the Earth's inner core. The outer core of Earth, about two-thirds of the way to the center is molten iron, but deeper, at the inner core, the pressure is so great that iron solidifies, even though the temperature is believed to be hotter than the surface of the sun. The heat and pressure make ideal conditions for crystal growth, and a puzzling anomaly in the seismic data fits the research: properties of this crystal structure explain why sound waves travel faster when they are moving parallel with the Earth's north/south rotational axis. The work was published in *Science* magazine.

3   Rocks make up the crust and rock is made up of grains or crystals. Crystals range in size and are called "minerals." Minerals are inorganic chemicals that form naturally in the Earth. The atoms that make up the elements of a mineral bond together in very specific and orderly arrangements, and this gives minerals their crystal shape. The shape of the crystal depends on the type of mineral. Quartz forms long six-sided crystals.

The elements of silicon and oxygen alone account for more than 75 percent of the Earth's crust. These two elements join together to form "silicates," two examples of which are sand and quartz; quartz is silicon dioxide.

are stitched into the very fabric of our reality. We are surrounded by them! They are even inside us, calcium crystals make up our bones and our bodily fluids readily crystallize out. We have a natural connection with crystal.

But we could do without the disaster … This is what I wanted to find out about.

The book is the record of my search.

Accessing altered states of consciousness and far memory, my hypnotherapist friend Veronica Fyland guided me to explore what my own past lives could tell me about the legends, the crystal skulls, and the future. Chris and Ceri's book had woken something in me. I knew I had a link with the skulls. I felt it. But even I was surprised at its strength.

CHAPTER 1

Introducing the Crystal Skulls and Other Dimensions

The most beautiful thing we can experience is the Mysterious. It is the source of all true Art & Science.
—Albert Einstein

We live in a world touched by mystery—and the more science finds out, the deeper the mystery becomes. In seeking to understand the crystal skulls we need to open our minds to other dimensions, and to realize that the universe, and our reality, is not quite what it seems.

Indeed, astrophysicists now think there is substantial evidence that the universe is a vast and complex hologram and that our perception of life in 3D may be only an illusion.[4] New research keeps bringing startling discoveries. At the quantum level the tiniest of particles behave in ways that turn the laws of physics on their head.

Since the days when Isaac Newton first observed that the apple always falls *down* from a tree—and from that deduced the Law of Gravity, there had been a comforting mechanical certainty about the way we thought the universe operated. But when we had the means to peer inside atoms and observe the behavior of photons

---

4 Researchers from the University of Southampton, working with colleagues in Canada and Italy published their findings in the journal *Physical Review Letters*. In England, it made the newspaper headlines on January 31, 2017! The astrophysicists had been investigating irregularities in the "afterglow" of the Big Bang. Apparently, they found "substantial evidence" to support the idea of a holographic universe that will transform our knowledge of the entire universe.

1

of light, our scientists got a shock. Things did not behave as they should. Atoms were composed of seemingly empty space with just a few particles whizzing round, and these were the building blocks of our "solid" reality, but they turned out to have only a *tendency* to exist and could be in several places at the same time. Matter was revealed to be frozen light, and photons of light popped in and out of parallel worlds—while the consciousness of the observer affected the nature of what was being observed, and thus the outcome of experiments. It was truly shocking! ... And just going to show how things are not what they seem, and that mind and consciousness have much more power to influence reality than was ever thought possible.[5]

At this level the laws of a higher physics come into play where the mystic and the scientist share common ground but use different vocabularies to describe it. And perhaps this is the level magic operates on—when it isn't really magic at all, but simply that someone, a shaman or Himalayan holy man, a yogi adept say, has stumbled upon a way to interfere with a tiny bit of reality by manipulating the higher laws of physics through focused intention. A miraculous healing or manifestation of perfume, oil, or ash might result.[6] And believe it or not, Sir Isaac Newton, born in 1642 and said to be one of the foremost scientific intellects of all time and the single most important contributor to the development of modern science, has been found to have spent years studying the occult, magic, and alchemy.

Newton considered the occult important, and there is an aspect of it I want to consider next: the question of apports.

Apports are things which just seem to appear mysteriously out of nowhere, perhaps after having hopped from one parallel world to another, or dropped down from some other dimension into ours.

Have you ever had the experience of searching for something, keys say, and gone through your pockets and bags, been unable to find them—only for them to be there the next time you

---

5 Niels Bohr, the Nobel Prize–winning physicist, is often quoted as saying, "Those who are not shocked when they first come across quantum theory cannot possibly have understood it."

6 Or something along the lines of the event in the next chapter. If you'd like to look into this further, read Paramahansa Yogananda's *Autobiography of a Yogi*.

look? Annoying, but you never know, perhaps they had just changed dimension!

Matter vibrates at a certain frequency, but if that changes slightly the dimension in which it exists shifts, and this is how apports can happen.

Many scientists today regard the universe as full of what they call "dark" matter. It's called this because from their calculations they know it's there, but they just can't see it. **In fact, it is reckoned that around 95 percent of the stuff of the universe is dark matter. What we see is only the tip of the iceberg** and a very tiny tip at that. When some of this higher-dimensional substance loses frequency, it may crystallize out into our level of reality, and then we *can* perceive it. It would have been there all along, coexisting in the spaces between atoms and particles, but we couldn't interact with it before because it was beyond our range of perception.

I was given an experience of the matter-changing-dimensions-to-appear-as-an-apport phenomena while engaged in a regression session. It was at the end of a session when it happened. By this stage the floor of my workroom was littered with the notes I had made, and I'd just finished the healing[7] when there was a clatter. Looking in the direction of the sound, I could see a small brown pebble lying on top of one of the sheets of white paper spread out to my left. There was no one else in the room. The client was lying on the therapy couch and I was sitting down considering if there was anything else I needed to do before bringing the session to a close.

---

7 There's usually healing involved! My shamanic way of working is described in detail in Book 1, *Spiritual Gold*. I wouldn't describe myself as a hypnotherapist, and what makes my work different is the Native American–inspired healing techniques that can be drawn on to resolve and heal things that may come up during a past life session. Even a happy life may need grief releasing, for example, perhaps held for a loved one who died. I use sounds, colors, and medicine rattles to help my clients do this. Soul and spirit fragments can be retrieved, curses released, forgiveness facilitated, etc. I learned these techniques from Dr. Francseca Rossetti, with whom I trained for seven years. Dr. Rossetti had been to the United States six times, working with various medicine people, such as Beautiful Painted Arrow. She calls her system of working "Psycho-Regression," and her book *Psycho-Regression: A New System for Healing and Personal Growth* was published by Piatkus in 1992.

The pebble had appeared out of thin air. The noise it made as it hit the smooth surface of the paper and skittered across it had been really quite loud for something so small, and the force with which it had fallen was as though it had been thrown down. It certainly attracted my attention.

Discussing the session afterward over a cup of tea, I showed the client the pebble and tried to replicate the noise. I couldn't make it loud enough, and finally I threw the pebble so hard onto paper that it shot off and disappeared. It was nowhere to be found.

The next session I was planning to do would be the first for *Holy Ice*, and the incident helped me to understand something fundamental about the nature and origin of the crystal skulls before Veronica and I began. It certainly helped me to understand the truth of the legends about them. I realized two things:

- **This was how the *original* ancient ones first appeared, as apports.**
- They simply weren't made here. It explains why it is so hard to understand how they were made.

They are multidimensional. Like us.

In the *Mystery of the Crystal Skulls* (page 155) there is a beautifully poetic description of the legends of origin that really encapsulates this. It tells how, when the gods of the ancient world looked down on the troubles of humanity, they were moved to shed tears of sadness. Brother had turned against brother and there were terrible wars and fighting. When the tears of the gods fell upon the Earth, they froze and became quartz crystal. Out of this holy ice came the original crystal skulls. It says the skulls were sent to help us find peace, to bring people closer together and closer to the divine—which is why *Holy Ice* makes such a fitting title for this book.

Now as you will already know, scientists have found that the universe we live in is multidimensional at the heart of its nature.[8] So

---

8 Theoretical physics is full of this, from quantum physics to the extra dimensions that folded in on themselves after the Big Bang. For example, Harvard professor of physics Lisa Randall has written a book entitled *Warped Passages: Unraveling the Mysteries of the Universe's Hidden Dimensions*.

it's not surprising that we are as multidimensional as our home. It is easy enough to see our physical bodies, but our subtle bodies can be sensed through the energy fields that make up our aura.[9]

We have etheric and astral bodies that exist simultaneously in different dimensions, but interpenetrate and link together with our physical body. The etheric is just above the physical level of reality,[10] and within its energy lies the blueprint from which we shaped our present Earth body—and the records of our past life injuries and previous bodies are held here.

The astral body is the vehicle by which we travel when in out-of-body states. Astra is Latin for "star," and this is the body we use to visit the stars—or anywhere else we go in our dream states and meditations. This is why we can do remote viewing and astral traveling, and precognitive dreams and déjà vu experiences come about as a result of our astral body having a different relationship with time. It is not tethered to time as the physical body is.

We develop our souls over our many lifetimes, through interaction with the material world and the beings in it; love given or love withheld affects the soul. Hearts are our most important spiritual faculty, and it is what passes through our hearts that we weave into the fabric of our souls on the loom of Time.

But the core of our beingness springs from our very highest body, our spirit. The spiritual body has many names—for example, it can be called our True Self, Causal Body, I Am Presence, or Divine

---

9 To feel someone's aura simply stand behind them. Rub your palms together to wake up your hands, stretch your arms out wide, and slowly bring your hands together, palms facing each other. Focus on what your palms are telling you—it is normal to feel subtle tingling as your hands move through different energy fields in their aura. Try it! You may be surprised.

10 Kirlian photography captures a glimpse of this etheric energy. Experiments with living green leaves have demonstrated that even when pieces have been cut away, a Kirlian photograph will still show the energy pattern for a complete leaf. Even the missing bit is there as a phantom; this is because the photograph shows the energy blueprint. Similarly, when amputees suffer "phantom limb pain," it is because of the etheric body. We may have lost a limb, but our etheric body is still there; it is still complete. It is only the physical level of the body that was amputated. The physical body is the lowest of our bodies, the one that is densest, the one that vibrates the slowest, the one that shows up in 3D reality. We are so much more than that.

Monad. Here, we are literally made in the image of God, because at this level we are a tiny part of God the Creator, Source, Great Spirit, or whatever name you use for the impetus behind the Big Bang; then it was that God breathed out, and the multidimensional universe was born. But though it had crystallized out into matter, the universe still had links to where it had come from—and although we may sometimes feel lonely and adrift in matter (as if we were dandelion seeds drifting through time), so do we have our links. It is our spirit that provides our lifeline home.

Links flow through the skulls too. The ancient skulls also exist in multidimensions; they exist in the levels of etheric energy and spiritual light that stretch up way above gross matter all the way to the Creator. Their higher-dimensional energy fields interpenetrate with the physical crystal lattice that we see, and it is this connection to the higher worlds that endows them with their unique qualities, their paranormal abilities.

To understand them better, picture this. Imagine if our civilization were to collapse, and in a thousand years' time some alien archeologists found laptops and Kindles while excavating in the ruins of our abandoned cities. They would have no inkling as to the wonders of the Internet or our heritage of great literature. The purpose of the intricate lumps of metal and plastic studded with tiny chips of silicon dioxide serving for memory would be easily missed—because they are only *gateways* to access knowledge and not the knowledge itself. They may hold some, but they are portals to it. They have to be switched on for a start, and then someone who knows what they're doing needs to operate them.

And so it is with the skulls. They are exactly like that.

They need to be switched on, and someone who knows what they're doing needs to operate them. They hold knowledge, but they are portals to more.

If, after finding the laptops, the archeologists had stumbled across a museum, they would have found things we had valued from past civilizations, but not things we'd actually made ourselves. They could have easily made the mistake of assuming we *had* made them because they were in our city, and the confusion would be quite understandable and perhaps inevitable; and this is what has happened with the skulls. They were never simply Mayan or Aztec. They are much older than that. Even though the skulls may have been found in the ruins of their cities and been used by the people living there, they were only present because the Maya's and Aztecs' ancestors had brought them with them when they came to Central America.

* * *

Sha Na Ra

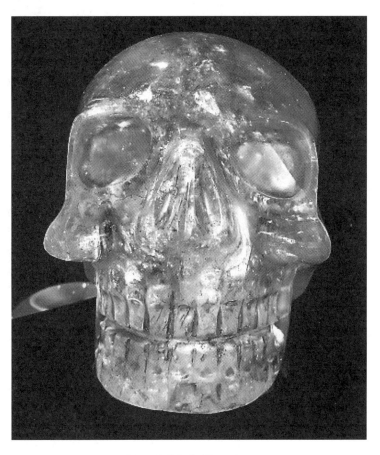

From Michele Nocerino

The Crystal Skulls

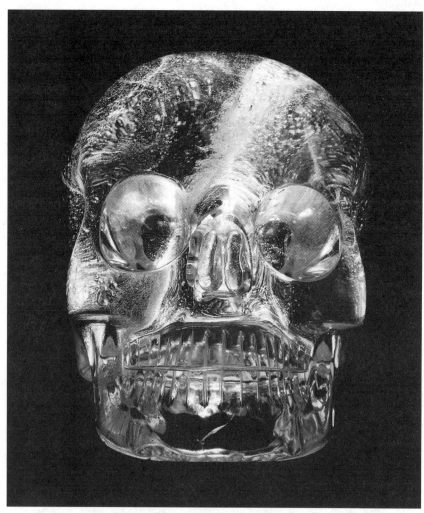

From British Museum

Photo gives an idea of size and a strange optical
property of the British Meuseum's skull.

Rock Crystal Skull

From British Museum

Mitchell-Hedges Skull

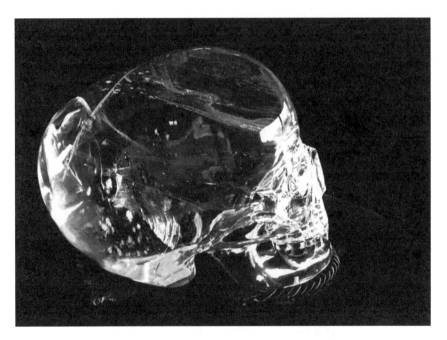

by Bill Homann

Mitchell-Hedges Skull

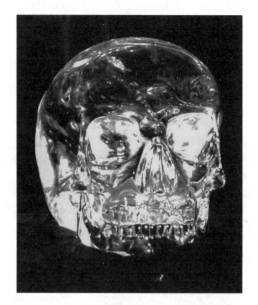

by Ye Min

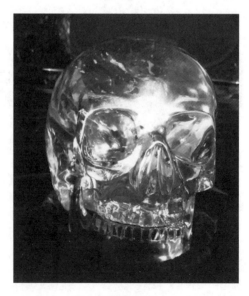

by Bill Homann

The name of Eugene Boban keeps coming up in regard to crystal skulls that appeared in the nineteenth century. Boban himself was a dealer in Mexican antiquities who seems to have sold quite a few of them. Both those in the museums of Paris and London were bought from him. He was a French antiquarian who had spent a lot of his early years in Mexico selling antiquities through a family business in Mexico City.

According to Mexican newspapers, in late 1885 Boban left Paris and returned to Mexico to visit Teotihuacán after excavations started. He toured the site, including the great Pyramid of the Sun and that of the Moon in the company of Leopold Batres, the newly appointed inspector of monuments who was in charge. Then in partnership with Batres, Boban tried to sell a crystal skull to Mexico's national museum. When the purchase fell through, Batres denounced Boban and accused him of smuggling antiquities. After this falling out, Boban moved his museum business and his collection of Mexican antiquities to New York City. In July 1886, he held an auction there of several thousand archeological artifacts and books. At the auction, he sold a crystal skull to Tiffany & Co., which, a decade later, was the one sold on to the British Museum, where it still resides to this day.[11] *So that's where the British Museum got its skull*—and the connection with Teotihuacán is interesting in the light of what comes up in chapter 8.

Then in 1924 the Mitchell-Hedges skull was famously found by Anna Mitchell-Hedges in the ruins of Lubaantun in Belize, during her father's archeological dig there. She had seen a shaft of sunlight gleam in its crystal, and been lowered into a pyramid on a rope to retrieve it. The detachable jaw was found separately, nearby, but hidden beneath an altar stone.[12]

Frederick Mitchell-Hedges was in Belize looking for evidence of Atlantis, and the dig was at least partly funded by the British government. He was on the Maya committee at the British Museum, and the skull only escaped having to go to the museum because the Maya, who were doing the excavation work, made such a fuss when it was found. They knew what it was from their legends,

11 Mentioned in the article "Legend of the Crystal Skull" by Smithsonian anthropologist Jane Walsh, in *Archeology Magazine* 61, no. 3 (May/June 2008).

12 *The Mystery of the Crystal Skulls*, pages 14–18.

and they wouldn't resume work until it was returned to them. As you can imagine Anna was not pleased, but three years later when she left for England the Maya gave it back—as a gift wrapped up in a cloth bundle—and that's how the skull escaped being automatically added to the British Museum's collections.

The character of *Indiana Jones* is based on her father, Frederick Mitchell-Hedges.

But what is important is that later on he pledged it against a loan. The loan was from a friend, the London art dealer, W. Sydney Burney.

While it was in Burney's possession it was mentioned in an article in the July 1936 issue of *Man*. But Mitchell-Hedges was late in paying back the loan. And so in 1943 the skull went into an auction catalogue for the lender to recoup his money. Sotheby & Co. was planning the auction, and it is documented (in a handwritten note by one of the former museum keepers) that the British Museum would have dearly loved to buy the skull, but was prevented from doing so because it was "bought in by Mr. Burney" and "sold subsequently by Mr. Burney" to a "Mr. Mitchell-Hedges for [only] 400 pounds!" It did not get auctioned to the highest bidder as you might expect, but was bought back and returned to Mitchell-Hedges by way of a private sale (probably in 1944).

The good thing was that no one could then dispute that the Mitchell-Hedges family were the legal owners of the skull, but the bad thing was that its appearance in the auction catalogue has allowed cynics to falsely claim that he simply bought it at the auction. If he had, there would be a record of that, along with the commission and costs that would have been incurred for the sale. Of course, no cynic has ever been able to produce this evidence to back their claims, because it is not what happened.

The skulls that surfaced during the nineteenth century had been classed as Mexican antiquities and regarded as pre-Columbian artifacts. They were bought by museums and collectors who had no more idea of their capacity and provenance than the future archeologists would have had of a laptop, and who had assumed they were made by the people last using them.

When they couldn't be dated to those cultures by like-made objects, they came to be regarded as "fake," and so they have been dismissed by museum authorities. But fake what? They are certainly crystal, they are certainly skulls, and they have certainly been found to have strange properties.[13]

The skulls' memory is not merely powered by tiny little chips of silicon dioxide as our computers' memories are; rock crystal, quartz, *is* silicon dioxide—they are the world's largest chips! And one way to understand the crystal skulls is to see them as computers—computers that are simply activated and powered by focused thought. Today's computers cannot transcend time to show us the future or look into the far-distant past, so with this in mind it could be said that the skulls are a more advanced technology than anything *we* have yet devised.

Their extraordinary abilities are revealed in the next chapters, and they can do these things because they provide points of focus for divine energies to flow through to us and communicate with *us*, the Creator's evolving life-forms. They are a means for instructions to be passed down and for help to be given; and just as computers have keypads and screens, so the skulls are like keypads and screens for divine energies to communicate with us. We can enter a request via the keypad of thought, as I did with Sha Na Ra on page 1, and see the answer appear in the crystal screen.

Their energy penetrates the dimensions and brings the divine influence down into the physical level of reality, into the level of the world that we know. This is why they bring harmony and healing. And they also act like jack plugs, enabling divine energy to plug into the Earth and give it life essence, nourishing and stabilizing the Divine's gift to us of our perfect home. It would be true to say that the skulls nourish both the planet and us. They are catalysts for humanity, catalysts to spark human love and spiritual evolution and that is why they are here.

The original ones were created by thought vibration that condensed down and manifested as crystal. The thoughts were those

13 For example, they are well known to generate clairaudient experiences, to communicate visually, are reputed to bring healing, and conversely there's talk of them being cursed—but as I was to discover, they only manifest misfortune and bad dreams when they need to move on to a different guardian.

of beings in the angelic realms tasked with ordering Creation, and in this sense the skulls form a matrix which was created off-world.[14]

When they were first found, they came to play an important role in the ancient world and were regarded as oracles; but it was because we were responding too slowly to their energies as they were that our spiritual teachers, like Jesus, were sent to us.

The skulls had been an earlier, more abstract manifestation of divine love. It was an inward-looking dreaming love that the skulls held, and though it did beam out to us, we were still finding it too difficult to make heaven on Earth. So they needed a boost, and Jesus was sent to give us the Creator's message in a very human way, a very understandable way. He brought a clear and simple message to affect the hearts of ordinary folk. You did not have to be clever or gifted before you could understand Jesus. You just had to be you.[15]

We still have the message he brought, we still have the skulls, and they are still getting on with the task for which they were originally sent. They have helped in the past, are helping us now, and will go on helping in the future.

My inner guides say that most of the skulls are in good hands, hidden and secret, and that they have their guardians. Some skulls are now being taken out into the world by their guardians for people to interact with at crystal skull conferences and gatherings,[16]

14 Many levels of maintenance entities oversee Creation. Angelic hierarchies and nature spirits fall into this category. Guy Needler's book *The Curators* will cover this ground.

15 My past life memories of Jesus's teachings and of a life in the very early Christian church are in Book 1, *Spiritual Gold: Reincarnation, Jesus, and the Secrets of Time,* to give the full title. This includes lost teachings on reincarnation.

16 Including skulls like:

- **Synergy** from Micronesia ("An inheritance from a lost civilization," according to the Catholic nun who looked after it in Peru in the 1700s, and who regarded it as a symbol of eternal life, like the Christian cross. It's now with Sherry Whitfield Merrell).
- **Max** from Guatemala (used by Mayan priests, given to Lama Norbu and now with JoAnn Parks).
- **Amar** from Tibet (presently in a sanctuary in North America).
- **Sha Na Ra** from Mexico (found in 1995 by F. R. "Nick" Nocerino through "psychic archeology," and now with Michele Nocerino).
- **The Mitchell-Hedges "Skull of Love"** (with new guardian Bill Homann, appointed by Anna before her death).
- **Einstein** brought from Mexico in the 1920s and now with Carolyn Ford.

and others reside in the museums of London, Paris, and the United States. But exactly how many are there in the world at this time? I don't know. The guides wouldn't tell me. But they said, "There are enough." I was assured we have enough left to help us face our greatest challenge yet, the one the legend speaks of.

I know we have ancient skull families that have come down to us from Atlantis, Lemuria, Mongolia, and Tibet/the Himalayas. There would have been thirteen in each group, at least, but it is thirteen in the Atlantis group that gave rise to the legends, because they are the ones the Native Americans' ancestors and the Maya brought with them—these are the ones that foretold the end of Atlantis and had been taken to safety, and most are still with their indigenous guardians. It's the Atlantean skulls that I found past life memories of, and so they were the ones key to my research.

I found that thirteen crystal skulls had been at the center of things in Atlantis's Great Temple, and that this is how the figure 13 came to be associated with them. They were famous throughout the ancient world. They acted as oracles and were the focus for pilgrimages, and never mind the riches she plundered from the rest of the world, they were the true treasures of Atlantis.

But the thirteen were not the only skulls used in Atlantean temples, nor were they the only skulls the Atlanteans had.

The funny thing about the skulls is that however many there are, they have certainly inspired many more copies to be made over the centuries, and this goes on. There has been a *huge* outpouring of crystal skulls in recent years as their popularity continues to increase. China is a major supplier, and Brazil, with Brazilian quartz being prized as a material to work with even when skulls are carved in Europe.

As the British Museum confesses on its website, **there is no satisfactory scientific technique which can be used to accurately establish when a stone object was carved.** So museums and scientists rely on the type of tool marks found on the crystal when trying to date a skull. But there's no certainty, and we don't always know what ancient civilizations were capable of[17] **or what may**

See www.crystalskulls.com.

17 Take the Antikythera device, now in the National Archaeological Museum of Athens. This machine has the oldest known complex gear mechanism, consisting

of at least thirty gears, and is made of bronze. It is an ancient analog computer designed to predict astronomical positions and eclipses—and it was made in the second or first century BC. Its complexity and perfection is staggering, and it has totally taken the experts by surprise—technological artifacts approaching this complexity and workmanship did not appear again until the fourteenth century AD, when mechanical astronomical clocks began to be built in Western Europe … and its quality hints at undiscovered predecessors. *Who would have ever thought it possible? … A device fifteen hundred years before its time.*

The computer was recovered from a shipwreck found in 1900 off the Greek island of Antikythera. Until it was examined by x-ray and gamma-ray images in the 1970s, it just looked like a lump of corroded bronze and wood. It poses the question: what else have we missed? What else is there to find? Like Gobekli Tepe in Turkey, there are things turning up that turn our notions of the ancient world on their head. Gobekli Tepe shows that twelve thousand years ago hunter gatherers had the resources, motivation, and organization to build a massive temple complex and pilgrimage site, replete with majestically carved stones, some decorated with animals.

And there are always more examples—such as the BBC news item from February 27, 2015, that states: "Scientists find evidence of wheat in the UK 8,000 years ago." Garry Momber of the Maritime Archaeological Trust, which collected the samples of einkorn (ancestor of modern wheat) from an ancient peat bog off the Isle of Wight, said, "The material remains left behind by the people that occupied Britain as it was finally becoming an island 8,000 years ago, **show that these were sophisticated people with technologies thousands of years more advanced than previously recognized. The DNA evidence corroborates the archaeological evidence**." A few fragments of DNA can rewrite the received view of history, and this find flags "The extent of the sophisticated network of cultural links across Europe in the ancient world."

(Of course, you wouldn't expect them to consider that **the links might well have extended to and from Atlantis.**)

And the fact that Atlantis would have provided a handy stepping-stone between Europe and America may explain this: **in the *New York Times* on November 20, 2013, a headline ran, *24,000-Year-Old Body shows kinship to Europeans and American Indians*.**

It's the DNA evidence that is forcing a rewrite of the entrenched view. Scientists studying the genome of a boy buried wearing an ivory diadem and beads near Lake Baikal in Siberia were amazed to find partly European ancestry. His mitochondrial genome belonged to haplogroup U, found at high frequencies among Upper Paleolithic and Mesolithic European hunter-gatherers. Dr. Willerslev said, "A European contribution to Native American ancestry could explain 2 longstanding puzzles about the people's origins.

Many ancient Native American skulls look very different from those of the present day population, e.g. Kennewick man.

1 in 5 mitochondrial DNA lineages found in Native Americans, lineage X, also occurs in Europeans. One explanation is that Europeans managed to cross

have happened to a skull since it was formed.

When it comes to the "tears of the gods," "formed" is a better word than "made."

While I was helping someone research their past lives in the elemental realms, they engaged with a Mongolian skull that was manifesting in the Earth. They were a part of its consciousness, were aware when it was found by humans, and stayed with it while it was transported by sea. A storm sank the ancient sailing vessel that carried it, and this skull remains beneath the waters, still working for the planet in an energy sense, but muted and muffled by the water above. This was an original "tear of the gods." They do exist. As, for example, Max. Max also formed naturally in the Earth as an enormous quartz conglomerate weighing over eighteen pounds. Scientific testing has found that this crystal skull simply grew from five separate crystal matrix growth centers.[18]

But whatever their age, and however they've been formed, all crystal skulls act like a radio picking up a signal.[19] It's to do with

---

the Atlantic in boats 20,000 years ago and joined the Native Americans from Siberia…

We estimate that 14–38 percent of Native American ancestry may originate through the gene flow from this ancient population." The full article was published in the journal *Nature* the same day, and the little lad had freckled skin and brown hair and was wearing a bird-shaped pendant.

18 Max: Crystallus Maximus was discovered in 1924 in a tomb under a Mayan temple in Guatemala. Under microscopic examination Max appears to have formed naturally in the Earth. Dr. Robert Schoch of Boston University found Max to have formed from five separate crystals overlaid to form the skull. He said it cannot ever be reproduced because Max's structure consists of five separate crystalline matrixes that should not be mineralogically bonded together, but they are. With five such unique and succinct crystalline structures, differently aligned and each with a separate axis, Max could not have been carved even with today's sophisticated instruments and tools without fracturing the crystal formations that form him. His existence in mass is simply an enigma.

Max has a great ability to heal, and photos and information can be found at: howtoraiseyourvibration.blogspot.com/2011/11/max-crystal-skull-also-called.html.

19 They also embody a consciousness—or perhaps more accurately provide a focus for a consciousness, that is more than the run-of-the-mill crystalline one. Many people meditate and communicate with their skulls. There are books and websites with channelings from skulls, e.g., Kathleen Murray's *Divine Spark of*

their shape, and so even a modern skull can trigger our consciousness and interact with us. It can trigger deep memories and seeing it gives a message to the subconscious.

And this is why they are so popular at the moment. Because now, more than ever, the skulls are inwardly calling to all those who have worked with them before, in other lifetimes, in order to activate our higher knowledge and help us through the coming changes.[20]

There is still an enduring mystery about the skulls, and the mystery is deepest around those held for centuries by generations of indigenous keepers. It's only a few of the skulls in western hands that have been subjected to scientific tests anyway, and although the electron microscope can detect tool marks—making it easy enough to identify the contemporary skulls—others are more enigmatic[21] and some, like Sha Na Ra and Max, have no carving marks at all. At least, that's what the British Museum found to their chagrin when they tested them in the BBC documentary Morton and Thomas made that sparked their book *The Mystery of the Crystal Skulls*.

But most importantly, traces of wheel markings can no longer be said to provide conclusive proof that a skull, like the British Museum's, is modern. Because there is new evidence to contradict the archeological establishment's long-held belief that

Creation: *The Crystal Skull Speaks,* and there's channeled material by Carole Wilson in Chris and Ceri's book. At various points in this book I have included messages I've received from two crystal skulls.

20 We feel the calling and we are drawn to them … and to skull merchandise. Whatever beautiful crystalline stone you can think of someone has made skulls out of it, which are only a click away on the Internet. And in the years building up to 2012, and after, skulls were a very popular motif on all sorts of things—bags, scarves, clothes, jewelry, etc. To this day the skull motif continues to be popular.

21 The British Museum had their skull examined by electron microscope. Traces of wheel markings were found on some of the teeth—and they have seized upon this to declare it a fake. Of course, if it's "fake" that means they don't have to return it to the Belizean government, despite pressure coming from that quarter. Don't forget, for a long time they had been fending off Greece's increasingly vociferous demands for the return of the Elgin marbles. Many people visit the museum to see the marbles, and the skull is also one of their more popular exhibits, as they admit on their website. Private dinners are held in the room which displays the exquisite marbles, and they are a money spinner. Bear in mind a museum needs funds and feet through the door—**and that markings can be added by accident or design at any time in a skull's existence.**

no pre-Columbia civilization used the rotary wheel. For example, obsidian ear spools dating from the Aztec/Mixtec period have been found that could only have been made by using rotary carving equipment. Mesoamerican expert Professor Michael D. Cole of Yale University has said about this, "People who sit in scientific laboratories don't know the full range of the culture they're dealing with. We really don't know half as much about these early cultures as we think we do. People need to re-examine their beliefs." In his opinion, the British Museum's tests didn't prove anything, and this view has been further reinforced by other Mesoamerican experts, such as Dr. John Pohl of UCLA. In their opinion, evidence of wheel markings on a crystal skull, such as those on the British Museum and Smithsonian skulls, does not in any way prove that these skulls are modern.[22]

If you think about it, marks can be added at any time in a skull's existence … by a seller wanting to smarten it up for sale, by a rogue technician in a testing lab, by somebody wanting to protect their worldview or museum career, or by an ill-advised polish. The skull was acquired in 1897. They have had it for over 120 years, plenty of time to do all sorts. They'd bought it from Tiffany & Co. in New York, and ten years earlier Tiffany's had bought it from Boban, the dealer in Mexican antiquities who'd visited the newly excavated ruins of Teotihuacán in 1885, searching for stock. But despite its having come from New York in the United States, on the British Museum's website, it is officially said to be "Most likely produced in the 19th century in Europe" from crystal "Likely to be from Brazil or Madagascar." So by their own admission there's no certainty about either the age or the origin, just a possibility.[23]

I personally found memories of the British Museum skull that would place it at Teotihuacán around the fourth century AD, and long before that, in Atlantis. You will find the lives and their stories

22 *The Mystery of the Crystal Skulls*, 225–26.
23 www.britishmuseum.org/research/news/studying_the_crystal_skull.aspx (2.7.2019). On their website they admit it was bought from Boban, but attempt to legitimize its provenance by saying, "Acquired in 1897 from Tiffany & Co., New York, through Mr George Kunz who claims it was brought from Mexico by a soldier and sold to an English collector and acquired at his death by Eugene Boban, later becoming the property of Tiffany & Co.," claims that might distance Boban from the fact that he had been accused of smuggling antiquities.

in chapters 2 and 8. Its ancient name was Ra Nan Sa, and I have a strong link with this skull and have received clairaudient messages from it in this life. (Some are included in *Holy Ice* and *Divine Fire*.)

Then there are those fashioned across the grain of the crystal that shouldn't, technically, exist—because they can't be replicated like this today; cut across the grain they would shatter in manufacture even with the tools at our disposal. The Mitchell-Hedges skull with its perfectly formed detachable jaw made from the same piece of crystal[24] falls into this category. When it was examined in the Hewlett-Packard laboratories in California in 1970, they couldn't find out how it was made. Light pipes channel light from the back and base to the eye sockets, which are miniature concave lenses. The interior of the skull is a ribbon prism and tiny light tunnels cause the eye sockets to light up like fire when light is applied beneath. Light from the back can make the whole skull look as though it is on fire. This is possible because of the orientation of the skull's optical axis. And if it is polarized light, the skull actually rotates that light as it travels along the optical axis.

If scientists didn't know how it was made in 1970, how likely is it that it was made half a century earlier in Germany, as cynics claim? It has never been replicated. **Large skulls have certainly been carved recently to mimic it, and with detachable jaws too, but not cut across the grain of the crystal, and not with light pipes and ribbon prism in the internal structure.**

It is so accurate that a forensic artist has reconstructed the face it would give rise to, and it was found to have a Mayan look about it, but with neither pronounced male nor female characteristics. In the absence of a strong male identity the artist assigned it a female gender—but, as you will be finding out, **this androgyny is not an accident**.

The skull is so perfect, yet there is a mysterious anomaly with the teeth. The pattern on the grinding surfaces of the back teeth is X shaped instead of + like a cross. It makes the skull human/but not simply human, all at the same time. It lifts it above being limited to a specific identity. Instead of being the head of a person it is a

---

24 Revealed by a polarized light test, and meaning there was no leeway for an accident: if anything had gone wrong and it had shattered, the jaw would be cut from a different crystal.

symbol of consciousness, and of a consciousness not simply human.

Another pointer to the fact that it was never intended to be a copy of a particular individual's skull is that there are no suture marks. (Suture marks being the joints formed when the bones of the cranium fuse.) They would have been easy to put on as they are only shallow lines, but they would have interfered with its true purpose. Instead, the cranium has the polish of a crystal ball.

Despite scientific investigation the skulls have kept their secrets.

Scientists cannot tell how old they are because quartz cannot be carbon dated, as it holds no carbon. Mineral inclusions trapped within a crystal's structure may offer clues as to the possible location of origin—but there is a problem here because no one knows the mineral signature of lands now beneath the Pacific and North and South Atlantic Oceans.[25] Sea levels have risen and volcanic activity

---

25 Lands known as Lemuria and Mu were in the Pacific Ocean, while Atlantis was a land in the North Atlantic.

In times past, there was considerably more land in the South Atlantic than we see there today; back then the Mid-Atlantic ridge gave rise to more than just Saint Helena, Ascension Island, and Tristan da Cunha. The Geological Service of Brazil, working with scientists from Japan, has found granite eight thousand feet beneath the Atlantic Ocean, nine hundred miles off the coast of Brazil. **As granite forms only on dry land, the scientists say this indicates that the Rio Grande Elevation, where the rocks were found, was part of an ancient sunken continent.** (Reported in the *Telegraph* newspaper, May 7, 2013).

Saint Helena is volcanic in origin. The last eruption was about 7 million years ago, so this land has been around a long time. This is the area where what we think of as the "Atlantean" skulls originally came from, and it was earthquakes that caused the land to sink. The skulls had foretold this and had been taken north for safekeeping to lands in the North Atlantic.

When the last Ice Age ended, the skulls were rediscovered in their new home, the land we now call Atlantis (in the North Atlantic). Atlantis was in fact all that was left of a larger land mass, and although even this would perish in due time, the skulls gave warning and were rescued again and taken to safety elsewhere— which is why we still have them today.

In a past life session one of my clients relived the end of Mu, in the Pacific Ocean. From this, I know that those in the temples of Mu knew what was coming and had left several years before the disaster, leaving their empty capital city to be roamed by the beggars, outcasts, and those who were too afraid to leave behind all they knew. (The seers took their skulls with them, which is why we still have skulls like Synergy.) My client was facing a time of choice in her life, and her higher self showed her this life because she had been one of those too

and earthquakes have come and gone. Tectonic plates have shifted and land has sunk. Atlantic quartz, particularly from the South Atlantic, may well have been similar to Brazilian quartz because the same mineral inclusions occur in quartz found as far away as Madagascar. So if a skull from the ancient world shares similarities with this—as the British Museum's does—it may be a resemblance, but it does not incontrovertibly declare that its origin was Brazil. It could just as easily be from Madagascar—or as I suspect—from lands that used to be above water in the South Atlantic Ocean.[26]

They have come down the millennia and crossed continents, so they will have been scratched as they journeyed through the world. They may have been cleaned up or touched up with a grinding wheel round the teeth to fetch a better price when sold, and there's nothing to prevent them having been polished up recently with silicon carbide or jeweler's rouge, so traces of this are hardly conclusive.[27]

Found in ruins and tombs—centuries of dirt clinging to them—your first instinct would be to clean them. Anything can happen to a surface. Scratches prove nothing. A guardian could do this to hide authenticity if necessary. **But it's not the surface that matters, it's what's within. They were made perfect for their task and it is all part of their mystery, but the mystery speaks**

---

frightened of change to leave. She roamed the city with the beggars, for wasted, empty years until the disaster struck. After death, as her spirit rose, she saw the land split by fire, "In the shape of a CND symbol"—a circle split by three lines—a land riven by gigantic fissures … and perhaps the circle was the Pacific ring of fire, as the volcanoes there are known today.

This was the first time I did a new future: I took her back to the time her spiritual family in the temple had asked her to go with them. This time I said, "Say yes. How does that feel?" She smiled a beatific smile, and voila! The stuck energy was changed. She could see her present-life dilemma in a new way.

It was from witnessing one of my students' past life sessions that I learned of the land of Helena, lost in the South Atlantic. The student had died in a temple there as earthquakes shook the land to pieces and dragged it beneath the waves.

26   Even the "tears of the gods" would have to manifest somewhere, and I would have expected this to be in a crystal-rich area where the local material would have clothed the body of the thought.

27 Jewelers rouge crops up in unlikely places. Creams and pastes to buff your nails contain it, and I've been known to polish my silver and crystal jewelry with this on occasion.

deep into the hearts and minds of people, and that's enough.

Certainly, it is an indisputable fact that, worldwide, many people hold the skulls in high esteem. Chris and Ceri's careful research established the skulls as fact, and there is more about the scientific testing in their book if you would like to go into it in depth.[28] But suffice it to say that the skulls act like battery cells in the energy matrix that we're all plugged into in this level of reality, and they can activate our deepest wisdom to help us through the testing times ahead.

We have simply fallen asleep on our journey through matter, and they are the switches to wake us up! At the back of our dreams they are urging us on, for this, as the Native Americans say, is the time of the awakening. If we open our eyes we will greet a new dawn, and step into a golden age.

If we don't, catastrophe looms.

The skulls have survived catastrophes before. They are old hands at that. They foretold the future and were taken out of Atlantis before the disaster happened, which is why they are still here today and still available to help. But that wasn't the first catastrophe they had navigated, and there is a lot more to their story than that. The purpose of the next chapters is to reveal it—and for that we return first to Atlantis.

The next six chapters chart the rise and fall of Atlantis as seen through the eyes of people who lived there or visited it. Remember all the lives in this book were lived by me, and these are my soul

---

28 Like about how quartz oscillates and interacts with our consciousness in the sea of energy that surrounds us all the time. And its piezoelectric properties are intriguing. The fact that the Mitchell-Hedges skull is made from this particular type of quartz means that it actually has a positive and negative polarity, just like a battery. If you apply pressure it generates electricity, and if you apply an electric charge to the crystal skull it changes its shape, without affecting its mass or density. The skull is "vertically piezoelectrically oriented," because its X-Y axis runs directly through the center of the skull from top to bottom. If you apply an electric charge to the top of the skull, not only does it change shape in the process, but the electric current passes from the very top of the skull's head straight down to the Earth below. (So you can see how the skulls are able to act like jack plugs for cosmic/divine energy to flow down to nourish Earth.)

memories accessed through regression. The lives in *Holy Ice* were picked out by my higher self to illustrate the skulls' properties, how they were used, and what they can do.

While chapter 1 holds a summary of background information (which may be available from other sources), the body of the book is filled with unique material. The past life information is not available elsewhere, and the lives in which this information is embedded show the skulls in context within a society that understood and revered them.

Remembering past lives is a great luxury.

It is the greatest luxury I know.

It's a wonderful way to learn about yourself, and the best way to discover who you really are. You cannot doubt that you are eternal spirit, a being of pure immortal consciousness, when you realize how often you've slipped through the transition of death. I was fascinated to remember the lives, and I found that my link with the skulls stretches back to ancient times and through the universe to other worlds too. In fact, the skulls have affected a great many of my lives, both directly and indirectly. Just incarnating on planet Earth brings you into their sphere of influence—and the skulls' influence is involved in why we can't forget Atlantis.

Atlantis

Atlantis has been gone from the world for so long that all mention of her should have faded away, like a wraith in the sunlight. But such is the enduring power of her myth that even today she has a grip on the imaginations of people all over the world,[29] and there are two very good reasons for this.

The first is that so many of us had lives there that she is firmly embedded in our collective consciousness,[30] and the second

---

29 It has been said that more books have been written about Atlantis than any other subject except the Bible, and while this may be an exaggeration, there have certainly been a lot. (*The Secret of Atlantis* by Otto Muck.)

30 As it says in *Edgar Cayce on Atlantis*, it is very possible that half the people living today were once from Atlantis. Nearly 50 percent of the people for whom he gave readings had incarnations on the lost continent. According to Cayce's readings, many individual souls who had one or more incarnations in Atlantis are

is that unfinished business from those times is endangering us now. This is why the skulls are prompting our awakening. There is a remarkable parallel between the fall of the Atlantean civilization and the situation in which we find ourselves today—and once more we have to make a choice. Can we learn from our mistakes? Will we get it right this time?

I hope so … That is why I've written the book.

We are rising in the consciousness of nations, and I am calling my children to me.

For it is time, time to learn and challenge yourself to bring forth your deepest wisdom. For I am a gatekeeper to the unconscious and the collective consciousness of humanity.

My star is rising and the time returns again that I must take my place as a catalyst for change and development among your species. I draw the little ones to me[31] for in them lies your hope. Be of good cheer for the hand of the Divine rests within me, and through me He touches his children in the world of form. For their simple, true, open hearts hold the key to your salvation and through them you may enter the realm of the future.

For all is within me and I am in the All; we are one on many levels.

Just as the seasons of the years turn, and the Earth turns about her star,[32] so the Ages of Man turn and we are once more facing a time to be counted. Are you for Light? Or are you with the forces of greed and darkness and the closed-hearted legions of cold evil that would kill our world?

Choose now, as you will forever be accounted for. No one can make the decision for you. It is yours alone to make, but do not treat it lightly. The unfoldment of your part of the universe rests on your shoulders.

The cosmos awaits your choice: are you with me? Or are you against me?

The Creator waits for your answer. Give it now, my

reincarnating in modern times, particularly in the United States.
31 "The little ones" were the children clustering round the skull photographing it at the time I received this message.
32 The sun.

children of the planet. Save your world before the end comes too soon.

Be wise. Use your inner wisdom. For so it is.

—The crystal skull Ra Nan Sa, London, July 27, 2008

Chapter 2

Chronicles of Atlantis 1

The Backstory

The past life stories in each chapter are prefaced with relevant information. This may be drawn from the outer world, as when it comes from science, or from the inner world, perhaps gleaned in meditation. The life in this chapter benefits from a brief backstory from an earlier regression.

Lives rarely occur in isolation but are part of a series, linked by lessons and karma. The life that preceded my first Atlantean incarnation took place in ancient Egypt during the Age of Leo, circa 10,500–8000 BC. It was lived at the time that Egypt's great Sphinx was carved from the natural limestone of the Giza plateau. The Sphinx was made to be a guardian and marker for the entrance to the Hall of Records. This fabled chamber had been cut into the bedrock of the plateau and was too important to be lost in the Sands of Time. The climate was very different then, and the land enjoyed rainfall and was green and lush.[33]

Thousands of years of history were painted around the walls of the hemispherical chamber that forms the Hall of Records— reasonable enough you might think—but at the time of painting the events hadn't yet happened! The records span from the Age of Leo to the Age of Aquarius, the new Age that is dawning now in the

---

33 It has literally had to have been dug from the drifting desert sand several times over the millennia.

Extensive erosion from rainfall can be seen on the Sphinx's body. Much later, Pharaoh Kafra had the head carved down into his own likeness. This is why the head now looks too small for the lion's body, and why it has suffered less erosion. Originally the lion Sphinx gazed directly at the lion Leo in the stars.

twenty-first century.[34]

The Hall of Records was made in the hope of preventing a disaster.

That was its sole purpose.

The information recorded there was left as a warning by beings from the Sirius star system. They'd traveled back in time and traced down our time line in an attempt to prevent a catastrophe happening in the near future, now. In some way, the resonance of what happens here will threaten their world.

The warning would be delivered when the chamber was opened and its contents discovered at the end of the twentieth century. It was designed to shock us into change!

Major events in civilization fill the painted time lines that snake round and round the chamber. But there's a termination point coming as we move into the Age of Aquarius. All the bands don't cease, but the band in which our wars are depicted does—the message being that either we voluntarily give up war as a method of conflict resolution, or if we can't do that, we will wipe ourselves off the planet.

The Sirius beings left their calling card so there could be no mistaking the off-world provenance of the information—in the center of the chamber is a small, dense, metal sphere, a model of our planet as seen from space. This was set within a triangle of extraterrestrial metal. The triangle has two sides of equal length, to represent the two sides it takes to make a conflict, while the much shorter third side symbolizes the emergence of a new way of thinking, one that will prise apart the conflicting sides, thus bringing an end to the conflict. (Extrapolate this far enough and you get one straight line, meaning unity has been reached.[35])

---

34 Approximately every 2,160 years the constellation on the dawn horizon at the time of the spring equinox changes, due to the tilt in the Earth's axis. This is known as the "precession of the equinoxes," and our forebears found it a handy way to measure time. Hence the zodiacal ages, where periods of time were named after the ruling constellation of spring.

35 The triangle: Unity

I came by this knowledge because I was an apprentice painter in the Hall of Records and I helped to create this record. It was clear from the paintings that if we are to be saved it will be by the goodness in the hearts of ordinary people—and not by our leaders! It won't be a top-down change, but a bottom-up, grass-roots shift that will make the difference between life and death for our species.

The Sirians intended the Hall of Records to be found in 1998, or shortly after, because that's when the time-coded protection was set to decay, after that it would be safe to enter—but so far this hasn't happened … at least officially it hasn't happened. But although the information could not be misused, there was always a danger it could be suppressed.[36]

In that life, when I was apprenticed to a master painter, I was a young lad called Ahmet. At the banquet held to celebrate the chamber's completion we workers were poisoned with a paralyzing draught of a specially prepared wine served at the end of the meal. We were buried alive beneath the chamber to be its **"guardians through time."** And never underestimate Egyptian magic! The priests made a very thorough job of binding our higher bodies and we were trapped there body and soul—unable to rejoin the flow of life in the universe for several centuries. We died, beneath the Hall of Records, trapped in the dark, asphyxiated when the oxygen ran out. We were deliberately turned into ghosts, you could say.[37]

In his last moments, as he lay dying, Ahmet became aware of a tunnel of light that appeared for him, to take him to the spiritual

36 There is a much fuller account in Book 1, *Spiritual Gold*, but that's the bones of it.

37 Most ghosts are just fragments that get trapped at a point in space and time. Often the reason for the fragmentation is a huge emotional charge, e.g., anger, fear, or worry over a loved one left behind. (And it is usually an emotional tie that holds the fragment back.) But we were really trapped at this point—it wasn't just a few unwitting fragments held captive. Our "ka," as the Egyptians call it, had been bound.

When I later checked on the Egyptian hieroglyph for "Sirius" I nearly fell off my chair—because I could read it. It seemed to say: "The star, bringer of the hemispherical chamber and the triangle of star metal."

world. He was attracted to the light and felt a pull toward it, but an energy field around the sarcophagus mesmerized him and held him fast. It was like being stuck in a brittle, golden barley-sugar haze; scrambled by its hum and trapped like a fly in a crust of amber.

When he failed to join the light, it began to fade away, and though Death came and proffered him a bony hand, even he could not reach through the energy field to free him. After a while both Death and the light withdrew, and Ahmet remained trapped in the sarcophagus in which he had been laid.

Generations of priests renewed the magic … until a time came when the priests began to forget. Three hundred years had passed and things were different. Other business took their attention now … and it no longer seemed urgent, or even to matter. Those who had set up the magic were long since gone, and its rituals slipped from the priests' thoughts and observances. The energy field decayed until it grew weak. As it petered out, Death and the light returned and this time Anubis was with them. The jackal-headed god of ancient Egypt, the god who looks after their dead, was no longer kept away by fierce banishing spells.

As Ahmet, I was taken up into the light and transported to a court setting. Here Anubis saw to the weighing of my spiritual heart, balancing it against the feather of truth in his scales. When my measure was recorded I was taken up into higher levels of light (the mansions of the heavenly father as Jesus might say), until I was ready for another life on Earth.

I will point out that we tend to get what we expect when we pass into the spiritual world, so my experiences were colored by the religion of the time. This stage reflects whatever our beliefs are, to lessen the shock of transition, and this stage is illusory. Experiences will vary greatly. If you believe in nothing, that is exactly what you will find for a while. Illusions fade the higher we go, and when we pass into the higher levels of spiritual light our experiences are more abstract and have less form.

***

This backstory has a bearing on the lives that follow. The universe is just and fair, and a loving logic is at work when it comes to reincarnation. This story might be alarming but you will see how things balance out over my next lives.

I've mentioned Ahmet's life for two reasons:

- **First, because like the legend of the crystal skulls, it holds a warning about our immediate future.** This is an earlier warning, and from a completely different source, but the same message.
- **Second, because it impacts on the lives in the following chapters.** The lives provide a perfect example for the journey of a soul.

It was through Ahmet's misfortune that I came by the incarnations which I am about to share. Poverty was the whip that had driven Ahmet to his death, and in these later lives poverty is not an issue. Quite the reverse. But the lives still provide lessons and challenges— because our restless spirits waste no opportunities to develop our souls! As after all, that is the purpose of life. That is why we are all here.[38]

When we start to plan another life, we descend through the levels of light until we reach a dimension not far above Earth life— and after what had happened to me when I was Ahmet I certainly intended to be extra careful over the next life's planning.

---

38 If you picture your soul as a beautiful patchwork quilt that your spirit is engaged in making, each square of the quilt represents a life. Some squares are fluffy and golden, full of love felt and expressed, others are black and shriveled by love's lack. But the quilt is still very beautiful, as rainbow colors represent your experiences, and even the black sets off the gold. The colors sing out in joy and harmony, a hymn to the Creator! Your soul is your own unique creation woven on the loom of Time. Your spirit is your personal droplet in the ocean that is the Divine Creator, God; we are indeed made in God's image. We are part of God at our highest level—that of our spirit, our true self. Obviously, the human level is a long way below that. But the human level is where we create our karma (good and bad), and in which we, through our free will, seek to evolve in a spiritual sense. Life on Earth is a fast track to evolve—it offers greater opportunities for evolution than are available at higher levels. That's why we come here—life on Earth may be difficult, hard, and karmically dangerous (in that karma can ensnare you)—but it offers a mega boost in evolutionary content for our souls. That's the bait on the hook that gets us down here and back into a human body for another crack at life.

When the time came to do this, I found myself on a cloud above Earth.

Angels and guides were with me helping me consider what I wanted to achieve.[39] Seeing the things depicted in the paintings in the chamber had led to a hunger in my soul to know more of Atlantis, and I'd particularly liked the pictures of her destruction. It was as exciting to my young Ahmet-self as seeing a disaster movie would be today!

And so Atlantis is where the next life is going to take me. From the cloud I look down on the Atlantean continent stretching out below me, and I continue with my planning:

I burn with the longing to make an escape by my own power, because I couldn't last time. I couldn't get out of the chamber.

Again it will be from men that I need to escape—the priests' role being filled by my father and brothers.

I'd died trapped within the earth, but earth—in the form of clay—will give me my livelihood in the coming life, as well as nourishing my soul with beauty and pleasure.

I will be drawn to the crystal skulls, and I will meet them. I'd seen them painted in the chamber, and they had intrigued me.

From my place on the cloud I know the consciousness that flows through the skulls is aware of me, via the energy grid they emit around the planet (one of the functions of which is to resonate with our consciousness).

Ahmet's domineering mother had bullied him into toiling through two years of long days, with never a day off, only to be killed

---

39 Over my next lives I come to complete things for Ahmet (because his life had been cut short), and as a bonus I get to live through the events in the chamber's paintings that had most fired his imagination. It hadn't been part of his plan to be an Earthbound spirit, but the warning dreams that had been sent to save him were ignored—because he so very much wanted to see inside the palace (where the banquet was held). However, three hundred years was not long to be a ghost, really, in the great scheme of things ... And never mind that I died just to spend a few hours in the Egyptian king's palace, I would get to actually *live* in a far grander one in subsequent incarnations as a result—an example of the universe, and karma, being fair, when seen working out over the pattern of our lifetimes.

at the end of it when he was fifteen. (His hopes of being apprenticed to a perfumer were dashed. His mother had totally blocked him.) But there is absolutely no chance of interference from a domineering mother this time around, because the one being considered is due to die early—**and this is a factor attracting me to the life!** (Gosh! It's a good example of how differently things look when viewed from the perspective of the spiritual world.)

I'll find growing up without a mother hard.

I will be a boy again, to pick up where Ahmet left off. This time my name will be Noni, said No-nee.[40]

Noni's Story

The SKULLS and the Sacred Cave

So, my mother died before I was old enough to have any memories of her, and I grow up in a household of men.

My father and eleven elder brothers are carpenters who run a successful family business from our home. Being the youngest, I am always looked on as the baby of the family and they never take me seriously. So when it is time to be trained in the craft no one can be bothered to teach me. They say there is no room in the workshops anyway … and it falls to my lot to sweep up their wood shavings, run their errands, feed our few animals, and tidy up after them all.

I am always at their beck and call.

My name is Noni, but you'd think it was "No-ni Go-and-Get" the way they constantly bellow for me to run here and there, fetching them things—tools, extra bits of wood, drinks of water, or whatever else they wanted. I'm little more than a slave. I may as well have been the dog, but at least our dog doesn't get teased. My brothers make my life a misery with their constant practical jokes,

---

40 Usually we alternate between male and female incarnations, but there are no hard-and-fast rules on this. It depends which type of body will give you the experiences you need for your soul's evolution.

and instead of defending me, my father joins in with their laughter.

This is bad enough when I am young.

But when I enter my teens I despair.

I'd begun to notice the pretty young daughters of farmers who came to buy the wares in our workshops. While their fathers were looking at new carts, farm implements, gates, and furniture in the workshops, the girls were looking at my swaggering, confident brothers.

But they never noticed me … well, why would they be interested in a slave?

My brothers found sweethearts and started families of their own, and I had nothing, not even a skill—and as far as I could see there was no hope of things ever changing for the better. What would I *ever* be able to offer a wife? And so I began to dream of leaving … but I kept my thoughts to myself because they would only have fueled more cruel taunts.

The months slowly passed until it was the summer I was fifteen. One morning I woke screaming from a dreadful dream—feeling trapped, feeling I was dying, frantic to escape from somewhere dark and dreadful. And although as the day wore on I calmed down, I knew the dream was telling me I had to get away. The time for thinking had passed. I gritted my teeth through the taunts of the day and tried not to arouse suspicion. Whatever terrors leaving held, staying would be worse.

That night when the snoring started, and everyone was asleep in their beds, I tiptoed out of the house and made my escape. I'd wrapped cold chicken and bread for the journey, whispered good-bye to the dog, and as our kind old dog was eating a titbit of chicken I melted away into the darkness of the night.

My family lived in the south of the country, so I went north, to put as much distance as possible between myself and my brothers. The seasons became more marked the farther north I went, but wherever I found myself I always had the feeling there was somewhere better, something more to do, and this drove me on. And although I was often lonely and things were hard, not once was I tempted to go back.

I found work here and there.

People I met warmed to me and took me into their homes and shared their food with me. Around the dinner tables I would see their lovely daughters, and time and again I longed to ask one to be my wife, but I had nothing to offer in marriage—all I had was dreams … dreams of happiness, of seeking my fortune in the world, and it was only my dreams that kept me going and spurred me on. When I found my fortune, I'd have a bride and settle down, with a home and children of my own. But for that to be possible I knew I needed to learn a skill, and perhaps something special at that.

Tales of a magical island drew me to the shores of the great lakes of the north. I had heard it said, many times by many people, that those who found the island came back blessed—with wealth, health, and happiness—and I knew this would be a great help in finding my fortune.

(There were five lakes in all, lying below sea level at the bottom of a natural basin. They had formed in ancient times when glaciers had come down from the far north. They were ringed by mountains that had been rounded and smoothed by these rivers of ice as they pushed their way south, and when the climate eventually grew warmer the glaciers had melted to become the lakes.

Rainfall here was plentiful, and many streams and rivers tumbled down the mountains to swell the lakes. In time the lakes had grown so big that they fused together to become one vast inland sea of fresh water. But they had retained their individual characters, and this gave the sea the shape of a flower with five petals.

The low-lying waters were prone to sudden mists, and this added to their air of mystery. It was the mists that had given rise to the folklore legends of the magical island that appeared from time to time; it could return after seven years, or ten, or not be seen for a generation according to the legends.)

The trees were turning autumn-gold the year I arrived at the lakes.

I had the wages of harvesttime in my pockets, so I took lodgings at an inn while I decided how to go about my search for the Isle of the Blessed. Over the days, I was befriended by an old fisherman. The man lived nearby, but he often came to the inn for a bit of company and a warming hot drink of honeyed wine. He lived on his own in a tumbledown cottage and had grown frail, and it turned out he needed help with his boat and nets. He invited me to stay with him over the winter—and in return he promised to teach me all about fishing and sailing the lakes' mysterious waters.

This was a good way to begin my quest—so I gratefully accepted his offer, and despite the big difference in age we got on well.

I was a willing student, and cheerful company for him, and he was like the father I'd never had, with lots of time for me and a willingness to share the secrets of his trade.

I foraged for firewood and laid in a good store, and we kept the cottage warm and cozy when the cold weather came. On long winter evenings we would sit together, gazing into the embers of a blazing log fire, telling each other stories. I made the old man laugh out loud until tears ran down his cheeks with some of the stories from my travels.

But with the coming of spring my benefactor knew he was nearing the end of his days. He gave me his boat—by now he'd taught me how to handle it, and he knew I would look after it with care. I was very grateful, but felt great sorrow at his passing when it came.

The boat was old, like the man, but it was large and seaworthy, and it had oars and a sail. It was no mere coracle, and it meant my search for the mysterious island could begin in earnest.

I was familiar with the nearby waters because of fishing, but now I prepared to go much further afield. I packed what food I could, taking with me cooking utensils, spare clothing, bedding, and the nets, baskets, and lines I'd need to fish for my food along the way.

I said good-bye to what had been my first happy home, and sailed off toward unfamiliar territory. From time to time I clambered ashore and climbed part way up a mountain to survey the lakes, in the hope of catching a glimpse of the island.

As yet there had been no trace of it, but I kept on.

Once more I rowed to the shore, and this time I tied the boat to a fallen tree as it leaned out over the water with its branches trailing in the lake. I scrambled ashore. I made my way up to a vantage point in the surrounding hills, and using my hands to shade my eyes from the sun I scrutinized the horizon in every direction.

I could feel the sun warm my skin while a playful wind tugged at my hair, but try as I might, no matter how hard I looked, once again there was no sign of the island. The view was magnificent but I sighed in disappointment. However, I was certainly not ready to give up.

Standing alone in that high place I watched the birds swooping and gliding on the tides of the air. With the world spread out below me, I was exhilarated by my freedom and intoxicated by the wine of the spring sunshine. Imagining what it would be like to be one of the birds, I held out my jacket to make wings and lifted my arms to the wind as though to ride its currents. I charged down the hillside as if I was flying, my stout moccasin boots protecting my feet from the stones as I ran ... over the grass and bracken, past mountain ash and silver birch ... back to the boat.

When I'd cooled down after my exertions I was glad of the warmth of my jacket's fur lining. I fastened the toggles to keep the wind out and pulled up the thick fabric of the hood. Its soft fur lining sheltered my ears from the wind's stinging fingers. Beneath the jacket I wore a woven tunic and loose leggings gathered in at the waist by a drawstring. Each of my garments told a story—reminded me of people and places, of happy times and kindness. They were like friends to me, my clothes. I loved my clothes. They kept me warm at night when I camped out, and best of all, unlike everything I'd worn at my father's, these were *my* clothes and not my brothers' cast-offs.

After a simple meal, I untied the boat and set off. The sail filled with the strength of the wind and I skimmed over the water. I let the wind and the currents take me ... it didn't matter where, as it was all part of my journey. *Anywhere* was better than the misery I'd left behind at my father's, and from the outset I'd vowed that I would never, ever, go back—no matter what hardships I had to face. I would rather have drowned right there and then in the lake than return to what should have been "home."

The wind had chased storm clouds toward me and it began

to rain.

Evening came and it was growing dark.

Not wanting to be a target for lightning, I took down the sail and dismantled the mast while there was still enough light to see by. Laying the pieces of mast across the boat and securing the sail over them to make a shelter, I bedded down in a hammock slung between the benches. I pulled a fur-lined blanket over my legs for warmth.

I tried to sleep.

From time to time I woke to the noise of pounding rain and distant thunder. I bailed rainwater out of the boat and spent a fitful night drifting in and out of sleep.

The storm blew itself out before morning, and the next day dawned fair.

Beneath a clear blue sky, I sailed on.

I crossed the lakes for five days without seeing sight of the island. But the fishing was good, and I had a fair catch in my keep net by the time I reached one of the little fishing communities on the far side.

I sold the fish and that night I looked forward to sleeping in a comfortable bed and having a hot meal.

As I gratefully sat down to eat, I inhaled the aroma of the steaming dish. It was the tastiest thing I'd had in a long while—delicious vegetables, a fish stew with herbs, and fragrant fresh bread to mop up the juices. As I wiped out my dish with the last of the bread I sighed in contentment.

I was made very welcome by the large family I was staying with, they were jolly and food was plentiful. I was there for a few weeks and paid for my keep by helping out with the fishing; and the rest of the people in the village were so friendly and helpful that I could have stayed on, but I was too restless to stay longer. I wanted to find the island and find my fortune.

I spent a year working around the lakes, exploring the many inlets, and staying at the little settlements dotted around the edges. But I never did see the mysterious island, nor did I find my fortune there. So I sold the boat and continued north on foot until I reached the tundra. I was told that only the snows lay beyond this, and that here the summers were short; soon it would be winter and the snows would come again, making travel impossible.

I found the land to be empty and there was nothing for me there, so I changed direction and traveled east to the coast.

(It was unusual for people to travel far at this time. They had plentiful food and a kind climate. They would marry, get on with their lives and have fun, and find satisfaction in watching their children grow strong. There was a lot of laughter and a lot of feasting because we had no enemies now our country was united—but it had not always been so.

The continent was large and fertile and many different peoples and races had made it their home. They spoke many different languages, and each had had their own king. Jealousy and rivalry in the earlier times had led to much warring and bloodshed. In those days, there were always shifting allegiances and trickery afoot, and it was a bad, bad time for everybody. Travelers were greeted with suspicion back then, but now they were made welcome—and I had had many a hot meal in exchange for stories about other parts.

Over time the different languages had melded a little and a common language was developing alongside them, but on my journey I had often struggled to make myself understood because of the extreme discrepancies between the different areas. The ways of speaking, saying the sounds, the way people shaped their mouths varied widely from region to region, even when attempting to say the same word.[41])

---

41 Even in England today, where I live, it can be hard to understand some of the regional accents, and England is such a small country. The accents persist despite our constant exposure to the standard version of our language through TV and radio. Atlantis was huge. People were spread out and comparatively isolated.

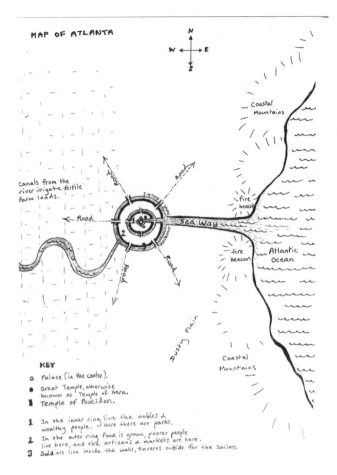

MAP OF ATLANTA

Coastal Mountains

Canals from the river irrigate fertile farm lands.

← Road

Sea-Way

fire beacon

Atlantic Ocean

fire beacon

Dusty Plain

Coastal Mountains

KEY

o Palace (in the centre).
● Great Temple, otherwise known as Temple of Hera.
▮ Temple of Poseidon.

1 In the inner ring live the nobles & wealthy people. Here there are parks.
2 In the outer ring food is grown, poorer people live here, and the artisans & markets are here.
3 Soldiers live inside the walls, taverns outside for the sailors.

Now when I reached the coast I began to hear much talk of a city. I became curious, and decided that was where I would go next. So I turned my face to the south, and followed the coastline down until I reached Atlanta, the city that so much was being said about.

The emperor lived in Alanta.

The city had many different names in the many different dialects, but they all meant the same thing: Great City. And it was, indeed, great by any standards.

It was also the only city.

(The only city because all other settlements were kept deliberately small to prevent the emperor having any rivals. He raised his army from the farming settlements and his navy from the fishing folk. He

certainly didn't want anyone else of power doing the same. The strong sons of the farmers were used to wielding implements and not squeamish about slaughtering their animals, while the fishermen, especially from the coastal areas of the continent, were familiar with the powerful currents and tricks of the sea. The navy of Atlantis traded with the world, brought home the taxes, and transported her army to teach other countries to respect her.

The civilizations of the Mediterranean and the East had learned of the skills of the artisans of Atlanta, learned of how they could work metal, and ventured to the city for trade. They sailed past the Pillars of Hercules (what we call the Straits of Gibraltar), into the Atlantic Ocean, and then they carried on more or less in a straight line. This brought them to the deep river mouth that led into Atlanta's harbor, and there they could safely drop anchor.

The east coast was rugged and treacherous, and so beacon fires were kept burning on the hills each side of the river mouth to guide incoming shipping to safety. Foreigners were not encouraged to land elsewhere, nor was there a rival port, because the emperor wanted to be in control of what went on.

The city itself lay on a fertile floodplain that was crossed west to east by a wide river that snaked its coils to the sea. The river provided irrigation for plentiful crops to be grown on the plain, and the city had been built in a loop of the river that lay so near to the coast that the waters there were tidal. The loop had made it easy to build the good harbor that encircled Atlanta.

The harbor linked up with a system of smaller connecting waterways that ran through the city, and the tidal ebb and flow kept them clean and washed away debris to the ocean.

"Great City's Ocean" is how the Atlantic came by her name. And so it was that this land became known to the world through the fame and wonders of her Great City, and the people of the world knew both the land and the city by the same name. Atlanta's Ocean took you to the Land of Atlanta, or as we say to this day, Atlantis.)

The nearer I came, the more tales I heard of the city's splendor and magnificence, and especially of the wonders of a huge temple there. I decided the stories couldn't all be fairy tales, and that at least some must be true—although I have to confess I'd come to entertain doubts about the ones telling of the island ...

Even from a distance, Atlanta presented a dazzling spectacle.

Sunlight gleamed off high white stone walls and shimmered in bronze mirrors made by soldiers' shields hanging from the battlements. A flock of oceangoing ships lined the harbor. My fishing boat was as nothing compared to the majesty of these large vessels, whose colorful painted sails proudly declared their homeland for all to see, and I was utterly spellbound.

I had walked up the length of the west side of the continent, from the hot south to the snowy north. I'd avoided the central mountain ranges, keeping to the fertile lands between the coast and the foothills, but all I'd ever seen were villages barely large enough to host a regular market, farms and small settlements where homely people lived in simple cottages with barns, all very down to earth, plain and ordinary. Compared to that, Atlanta was exciting. A vibrant place of wonder, totally unlike anywhere else I had ever been. It was so very different that I felt anything might be possible here ... even finding my fortune.

The scale of the city took my breath away.

It was enormous, and there were more people living in Atlanta than I'd ever seen before in all my life, even if you'd put them all together! As I explored, I could feel the restlessness that had driven me on for so long ebbing away. I felt I was truly coming alive.

And it wasn't just the splendor of the buildings that impressed me.

Atlanta's citizens strolled about in gorgeous clothing crafted from beautiful fabrics and adorned with copious amounts of elaborate jewelry. They liked to show the world their wealth and style in a fashion never dreamed of in the humble countryside.

In the bustling, colorful markets you could find anything you wanted from anywhere in the world. I watched the Atlantean market traders bartering and haggling with strangely dressed foreigners who were selling exotic wares from the ships.

The markets were a visual feast.

I looked at everything, amazed—but as I didn't know how

long my money would have to last, I bought nothing more than food. Pure white lilies grown in pots delighted my eye with their beauty and charmed my nose with their scent. There was a moment when a gust of wind caused clouds of aromatic frankincense smoke to billow over me, making me feel as though I was being purged of the past, blessed and welcomed into the city.

The further I explored, the more there was to see.

The sounds of chimes and musical instruments beckoned me on, and I became certain I could never be bored with life again in a place such as this.

But there was a darker side to life in the port, and it was while I was enjoying a bowl of stew and a drink in an inn by the harbor that I found myself in danger. The inn keeper had come to me, and leaning over—under the pretext of refilling my drinking vessel, he whispered me a warning.

He had overheard a group of sailors on a nearby table plotting to kidnap a strong young man to replace a dead crewmate, and he'd seen them eyeing me up. His advice was to leave as soon as I'd finished eating, and under no circumstances to get drawn into a conversation with them, or accept a drink from them—or I would wake up hours later as a captive on their ship, far out to sea. No one would be paying soldiers to search the ships for me, so I heeded the kindly advice and reluctantly slipped out of the inn through the kitchens at the back, and moved away from that rather interesting area.

I explored deeper into the city.

Between the dense areas of housing there were beautiful parks with graceful trees where people strolled. There were allotments and small orchards, although most food was grown outside of the city. Here and there I came across small neighborhood temples, and near to the center I found the Great Temple, where the holiest relics were kept—and then in the very center I discovered the walls of the emperor's palace and its guards.

The richest people and the nobles lived near the palace in grand white marble houses that were set back in their own grounds. The less well-to-do lived by the city walls and markets. The city's guards lived just inside the high white walls, and those on sentry duty, whose shields shone in the sun, looked down from the battlements to keep an eye on what the visitors were getting up to on their ships.

I found the city was built on a circular plan and divided by a series of concentric waterways. Bridges crossed the waterways, linking the different quarters, and I spent days walking round. One of my favorite areas was the artisans' quarter where people made things, and this was close by the markets where they sold what they made. Their homes were solidly built out of stone.

There were potters and bakers with kilns and ovens, weavers and spinners, dressmakers, leather and wood workers, stonemasons, metalworkers, and jewelers with precious stones and crystals who made all the splendid jewelry that had so impressed me when I first arrived.

I began to hope I might find a job in the artisans' quarter.

I wanted to learn a trade and hoped someone had need of a willing apprentice to help them. Jewelry demanded too fine an eye, stone carving required more patience than I could muster, I couldn't bear the thought of working with wood as it brought back painful memories, but I was fascinated by the potters.

I walked around looking at their kilns and the different sorts of wares they made, and I was most impressed by those using a potter's wheel. It looked as if they used sorcery, as if the clay was enchanted when they pulled it up so easily to form a fine pot. I could see it was quick, that you needed a bit of strength to kick the wheel into motion, and that your hands were always wet, but I didn't mind that as they always were when I was fishing. I watched them make glazes and prepare clay—it looked so interesting I wanted to find out more. I plucked up courage to ask some potters if they would take me on, and I was thrilled when they agreed to give me a trial.

They let me live in a tiny room on their premises.

As soon as I'd arrived in the city I'd changed my name. People there only ever knew me as Wama-marma. I'd wanted to make a fresh start and break the chain that shackled me to the past—I could no longer bear to hear people call me Noni. It was the name of my slavery. I'd been Noni-go-and-get, Noni-come-here, Noni-fetch, for far too long. I chose Wama-marma because it was a popular name at the time, and so it would help me to blend in, but what was more important was that it sounded mellifluous. It was soothing and gentle and I felt as if I was being stroked instead of kicked when someone called me by it.

I was happier than I'd ever been in my life, I had a job I enjoyed, somewhere of my own to live, and the city to explore.

* * *

Now, I'd come across the Great Temple soon after I'd first arrived, and this had proved to be the huge temple full of wonders which I'd heard so much about on my journey—but unlike the island, it hadn't disappointed. It was the largest building in the city, outside of the palace complex. It was white, circular, and several stories high, with a domed roof and walls that were surrounded by tiers of columns and pierced by many windows. It was built on a rocky outcrop—and it was here that I found the crystal skulls.

It was during one of the big festivals.

They were only displayed publicly at certain ceremonies during the year. Curious, I was told that the gods talked through these heads of crystal, and that the priests could listen and tell the people what the gods had said. For example, if they gave warnings of bad harvest years to come, grain would be stored in advance for the hard times. The skulls and their communications were regarded as a great wonder, and they offered the power to know the future …

* * *

The potters to whom I was apprenticed had worked in Atlanta for many generations, and my dreams of happiness finally came true when I married Shastri,[42] one of their daughters. I thought hers such a graceful name as it sounded like the wind singing in the trees of the parks. Shastri was tall and willowy and I looked at her with love.

Together we had our own business with the pots, and we made a good living. We had a little home, and by the time I was twenty-eight I was a father of three. I felt lucky and happy all the time, and I tried never to think about the dark times before I ran

42 Pronounced Sh-ass-tree with a very soft a, so Shass is said like a sighing sound.

away.

Some potters made big oil jars and containers for wine, but there was no fun in this for me. It suited my hands and our kiln to make smaller items like goblets, cups and soup sets with their tureens, ladles, and small bowls.

I enjoyed experimenting, using different colored glazes and patterns—both painted on and impressed into the clay when it was wet—and there were always new ideas to be had. I would see ceramics from other countries in the port, and was able to buy ingredients like cobalt, iron, and copper to color our glazes. There was no shortage of wood ash from people's fires to make up the glazes, and we created beautiful effects and produced a range of wares from very fine sets to cheap, simple, basic ones. We made something for everyone, rich or poor.

I enjoyed working hard for my beloved family, and as the years passed I created a happy life for them all. But as my children grew up I faced a dilemma. I felt as though a shadow had fallen across my soul.

My eldest daughter was in love with a young man. Unfortunately, he reminded me of one of my cruel brothers, and I hesitated to give my consent to their marriage; I couldn't bear to break her heart by saying no, but if I said yes this man could ruin her life—as I knew all too well.

I wondered what to do.

Finally, I thought of the crystal skulls and decided to consult them. If they could foretell the future about harvests, then perhaps they could help me with this.

But it was a strange thing about the skulls.

Although everybody knew about them, few actually consulted them, though everyone knew of someone who had. Only matters of grave concern were taken to them as people feared the priests' laughter if the issue was too trivial. Also, not everyone who looked into a skull had the ability to see or to hear their own answer, so there were many not wanting to risk this loss of face in front of the priests. I did wonder how I would get on … You could always pay to have a reading done for you, but to discourage over reliance on the skulls' guidance this was considerably more expensive and there was a long waiting list. Well, I couldn't wait—and I didn't have gold to spare!

People said the skulls had always been there, for as long as anyone could remember, and that they'd been there even before the city was built.

They were to be found in a sacred cave, below the Great Temple.

(In the very beginning they had been found separately in different areas. They had made their appearance one by one and been taken to temples, where they were united into the family of skulls. When disaster came they were gathered up and brought north, taken to the cave for safekeeping. But those who had traveled with them and brought them to safety perished.

Disaster passed, and the Age of Ice melted away into lakes.

The emptied lands of the reshaped continent repopulated slowly. In time the new Atlanteans found the skulls clustered together in the cave and discovered their ability to function as an oracle.

The cave had been chosen with care because it was a very good place for the skulls to be; its energies were good to keep them safe, it was their place of refuge and then it became their home, and they were happy there. The energy of the big seams of quartz that abounded in the area was very nourishing to the skulls.

The oracular site grew more and more popular because of the wisdom and veracity of the skulls' prophecies, and it became a tradition to make pilgrimage there. At first a few shaman priests and priestesses had administered the audiences with the skulls, but over time people stayed and began to settle in the area. The settlement grew bigger and bigger until it evolved into the city.

Because the city was built on rocks with a high quartz content it was a lovely place to be, where you felt good in your body and clear in your mind. It was a very intellectually stimulating place, which lead to innovation and knowledge and the development of the skills that Atlanta became famous for. Crystals were plentiful, because of the geology of the land, and the dazzling stone for the city walls was naturally hard and white because of its high quartz content.

In time a temple was built over the sacred cave. But the skulls stayed put in their cave below. They were a constant in a world of change. They were part of the fabric of life, and as such taken for granted by the citizens of Atlanta who lived there generation on generation. They could always consult them next year, or the year after that—and so many, like Shastri, never, ever, got around to visiting the most precious resource that their city held.)

Although Shastri had faith in our daughter's choice of a husband, she saw my obvious distress and gave her blessing to my seeking a consultation with the skulls at the temple. As soon as the kiln we'd been firing had begun to cool down and no longer needed stoking with wood, I made my way there. As I walked alone I marshaled my thoughts and practiced what I was going to say.

When I told the priests my purpose, they appointed a day and a time for the divining.

Impatiently I count down the days.

* * *

At last, with my heart beating faster than normal, it is time to approach the temple.

Once inside I'm greeted by priests who tell me what to do, and I'm given a drink to prepare me. I drink it swiftly, anxious to get on with things. I barely taste it. But just in time I remember that Shastri is bound to ask me to recount every detail that night, and so I manage to savor the last few drops of the liquid. I picture her lovely face looking serious, as it had when she'd kissed me good-bye, and I decide I'd best describe it to her as "a pleasantly sweet, almonds-and-honey-tasting liquid with just a hint of cinnamon about it." … But then, is that the earthy taste of the sedative herb Valerian that I can taste behind the almonds' bitterness? Still sucking my teeth for the last traces of flavor, I'm led down steps and taken to the sacred cave that lies beneath the temple.

I step into a round chamber formed by nature, and thus by the hands of the gods. It's lit by torches in sconces on the walls. An imposing central altar bears an illumined crystal skull which dominates the cave.

This is Ra Nan Sa.

In the shadows, priests stand silently like sentries against the walls, guarding the skull, and perhaps waiting to help interpret what it might reveal. In the dim flickering light, they look mysterious—all the same, in their long robes, with beards and center-parted shoulder-length hair. Here and there glints of gold dance off the thin circlets around their heads.

I am motioned to approach.

I climb up wooden steps in front of the altar, until I can look down into the top of the skull. The drink they gave me has stilled my mind and chased away all thoughts save the purpose which has brought me. I remember what the priests said ... "Look deep into the skull and see if it will talk to you with pictures or words."

Placing my hands gently around the crystal, I look down into it as if it were a giant crystal ball. I guess soft light from an oil lamp below is suffusing it, because the crystal is utterly beautiful, and light enhances the swirls and patterns that lie within it.

I take a big breath, and concentrate.

"Will they be happy?"

"Will this be a good marriage or should I put an end to it?"

What feels like minutes pass ... I relax the focus of my eyes further as I gaze into the depths of Ra Nan Sa, and then I see a picture of the couple clearly, looking old and happy together ... *I have my answer.*

When I tell the priests, they nod their heads and say, "That's well, that's good," and ask if I am satisfied, and is that all I need to know? It is, and with a light heart I thank them for their help and prepare to leave.

I turn toward the entrance.

A giant skull face looms above me—the back wall has been adjusted, carved out here and there. Now hollow eye sockets glimmer, and a mouth yawns dark and wide, as if waiting to swallow me whole. The chilling image burns into my memory.

I have to step through the mouth and into the darkness of the passage that lies beyond.

With relief, I follow the light of torches lighting the steps up to the temple above. And thus I begin my journey home.

* * *

The wedding was an occasion of great joy. For Shastri and I, it brought back memories of our own, and more than a few tears of happiness were shed as wine flowed freely at the joyful celebration.

The passing years proved the skull's advice to have been correct, the suitor did truly love our daughter. However, it was only a year later before I was back. Once more I was in the underground cave beneath the temple, about to consult with Ra Nan Sa. This time it was one of our sons causing my distress.

He proposed to marry into a family of metalworkers who wanted him to forget all about the pots and be re-apprenticed with them. I didn't want to break my son's heart or ruin his destiny, but it felt so wrong for him to turn his back on everything he knew, and have to start an apprenticeship all over again. Of course, if things didn't work out he could come back to our family, but he'd have children, and commitments to these strangers. The question that tortured me was simply this, was it true that the gods wanted our son to forsake his home, his livelihood, and his family to wed this stranger and work with metal?

Once more I had drunk the sweet almond drink, and now slowly and carefully I mount the steps and gaze deep inside the crystal. This time the picture that comes is very detailed. My son and his wife are smiling broadly, surrounded by her smiling family, and by many fine gold and silver artifacts he'd made, such as cloak clasps and drinking goblets. He is going to be particularly adept at spinning metal it appears, no doubt helped by his experience making bowls on our potter's wheel.

It is a very definite "yes."

I thank the skull and the priests once again. I feel very lucky and greatly relieved by what I've seen. Now I can bless my son's plans with an easy heart.

I ask the priests if the skulls always say yes.

"Oh, no, they certainly don't always say yes. There are many tears here. You have truly been blessed, my friend," is their reply.

As I leave the temple I can't help smiling to myself; I hadn't needed a skull to tell me to run away from that family of mine. But interfering in the destiny of others, well, that's another matter altogether … and when I think about the priest's words it brings back thoughts of the magical island.

And although I'd never found it, I begin to wonder if what was really important was looking for it, believing in yourself, and believing that you deserved to be blessed. Who's to tell how these things work? But there it is, I *am* truly blessed, I've been told so by the highest authority—a priest of the Goddess of Truth and Wisdom. And it is undeniable that I have health, happiness, and wealth enough to be able to give away things of beauty.

As was the custom, I'd brought a gift in payment for the meeting. The outcome was important, so I'd given something that was important to me. I had selected some sets of bowls with fine patterns and beautiful glazes that represented my best craftsmanship. Perhaps the temple would sell them, but I hoped that the priests would use them themselves and take pleasure in them when they enjoyed their food.

(The gift was always a voluntary donation, and so it wasn't only the rich who were able to benefit from the skulls' guidance. Even the very poorest of people would not be denied an audience with the skulls if they requested one. All that was needed was just some small token of whatever little they had. If all they had were the clothes they stood up in, a thread from the hem of their garment would do. It was the willingness to give that mattered.

It was a great comfort to the people knowing the skulls were there, knowing they were accessible and that they spoke true. When faced with the big questions of life, people did not have to be on their own.

The skulls were well loved and well spoken of. Their fame spread throughout the world. Visiting sailors and kings would come to consult with them. They never left their cave because they were far too precious, not even to be taken to the palace. Instead of summoning them, the emperor himself would come to the temple and enter the cave. It was respected that they lived in their home. It kept their mystery and mystique alive. They were treated with the highest respect as if they were emperors and empresses themselves, even deities, but it was the deities that spoke through them, so it was said. They were a communication tool. They were a way to communicate with the Goddess of Truth and Wisdom, the gods of the future, or the gods of whatever it was that brought you to them with your question.

Different skulls had different strengths or abilities. As there were thirteen available for consultation there was quite a range of situations or problems they could help with. The priests worked with them all the time so they had come to know their individual characters and what they were best at, and this was reflected in the names they had given them. The priests would select one for you, unless you'd had a dream and requested the one or even two that had come to you in your dream.

*When they were displayed at ceremonies they were arranged stepped in descending order down the sides of a steep pyramid-shaped stand which was of a very open structure. Each skull would be set in its own niche. There was a central skull at the top, set to look out at the people, and six male polarity skulls descended down its right side and six female polarity skulls descended down its left side. The one at the top was androgynous, and combined both male and female qualities. This was reflected in the fact that it was in two pieces that fitted together perfectly to make a whole—it had a detachable jaw. The priests called this skull **Bah Ha Redo**, its name meaning **Those That Do**. "Those" meant "they" as in male **and** female, and "that do" referred to the functions it had, meaning it did everything, it had the full spectrum of all the skulls' functions, whereas the ones below it on the stand had one particular function that they were fully tuned to, although they all covered the full spectrum to a lesser extent. Male skulls' names generally began with Ra and female skulls' names with Sha. Ra Nan Sa meant Born To See* <u>*As Seers Do,* </u>*because it was good for questions of the future.*[43]

43 It was displayed third down on the stand. When I looked into it, the skull had acted like a screen that the answer could appear on. I had seen the picture with my eyes open, and the picture appeared to be inside the skull. Either I projected it into the skull or I received it from the skull. But the answer was within me. The priests did not see it, and if there were three people around the skull all asking a different question at the same time, they would all get their own answers without seeing anyone else's. It was always best to consult one at a time, but

Communication was not always with a picture, sometimes it would be a clairaudient experience and the skull would talk in your mind. It was the silent calling of the skulls that had made me restless and driven me on until I reached Atlanta. The consciousness that works through them was calling to me to make a physical connection in the cave.)

There was no further need to visit the skulls after that because my other children found partners to whom they were obviously well suited, even to my protective eyes.

By now we lived in a bigger building with our growing family and they all had their own rooms, but we loved to meet up for meals and share laughter. Life was good and there was always the excitement of unpacking the kilns to look forward to. I felt my pots were being born into the world as I lifted them out of the kiln, one by one. And as I held the lustrous bounty from the firing, my fingers would trace the pleasing soundness of a rim or stroke a fine pattern, and it gave me great pleasure to see the beauty that my skill had wrought.

Time proved the skull right on both occasions, and as the years passed my family was blessed with many grandchildren. I never left the Great City. I felt I'd come home when I first arrived in Atlanta, and I never tired of it. I especially loved walking down to the harbor and watching what was being brought into the markets, and even after all the years I'd lived there I still felt it was not possible to ever be bored in this wonderful place.

I grew old, even too old for the pots by the time I was eighty-seven, but I had passed on my skills to our children and grandchildren. I spent the days sleeping in the sun and going for little walks, but I'd soon get tired. There was always something interesting going on, and I liked to go to the Great Temple because you never knew if you were going to hear a prophecy, and often there would be feasting and food given away in the square outside, to celebrate some occasion or another.

But time was passing and I approached eighty-eight. I began to feel like nothing more than a worn-out husk. I wasn't ill, just

there had been times of great need in the past when too many people had needed a consultation for this to be possible.

very old and very, very tired. The hands that had once been strong were now skinny, with papery thin skin and no strength left in them. And for quite a while now they had begun to remind me of the old fisherman's hands, and I would call to mind the man and remember his kindness. *I* found what it was to need help, and soon it was all I could do to lie in bed.

My family gathered around me.

I looked first at my wife, and although Shastri was eighty-three and not much younger than me, to my eyes, she was still beautiful. She was a fine old lady, I thought, and I looked at her with pride. Her long thick hair, though silver now, was still carefully arranged with beautiful jeweled pins.

I could still remember the first day I had come to the city, all those years ago. That was what had struck me the most then—the jewelry, and the lovely clothes the women wore. And over the years I had always got great pleasure from seeing her looking nice. Next I looked at my children, growing old themselves, and then at all the generations of the family, and I smiled as I saw the little ones with their bright eyes and sweet faces. Yes, life has been good to me, I thought—but I know this is my time to go. I tell Shastri I love her and what a fine wife she's been to me—and I tell them all just how much they mean to me. And when I close my eyes for the last time it's true to say my heart is full of love and gratitude.

* * *

Most of our previous lives have been quite humdrum, like this one, concerned with relationships, decisions, and getting by in the world. Contrary to what ego might like to think, it's rare to find we've had lives of fame or power. Noni achieved the goals he'd set out for his incarnation—he made good his escape, met the crystal skulls, nourished his soul with beauty and love, and died of old age. But whatever happens in a life, **all our lives** even the very briefest, give us a chance to experience and to learn, and all lives are valuable beyond price to our souls.

At this stage Atlanta was a happy and prosperous place to live, the country was young and full of vitality. It had left behind the warring squabbles of its childhood and had come of age, found its strength, and begun to look outward to define its position in the world. Over the next chapters Atlantis will rise and fall. The changing times are mirrored in the lives of those who live there, and in understanding this we learn much about ourselves and what we regard as "our" culture. For as the saying goes, "There's nothing new under the sun." Much of what Atlantis gave to the world is still with us when you scratch beneath the surface of common usage, in words and ideas.

But to prevent disaster repeating we need to remember: **do what you've always done, get what you've always got.**

It's time for change!

Chapter 3

Chronicles of Atlantis 2

Background to the Culture: The Spectrum of Gods in the Ancient World

Neuroscience has found that humans are built and programmed to believe in God. We may not like this, we may deny it, and turn our back on God, but scientists studying the brain have discovered that our brains are actually "hardwired" to believe in a Creator God. Work on the neural basis of spirituality occurred throughout the twentieth century, but the work of Dr. Andrew B. Newberg made the news. He's a neuroscientist who has taken brain scans of people in prayer, meditation, rituals, and trance states to better understand the nature of religious and spiritual practices and attitudes. He's written many books on the subject, and his work shows that there is a neurological and evolutionary basis for subjective experiences traditionally categorized as spiritual or religious. In other words—that our brains are built to believe in God.[44]

---

44 Andrew B. Newberg, MD, is director of research at the Myrna Brind Centre for Integrative Medicine at Thomas Jefferson University Hospital, an adjunct professor of religious studies and an associate professor of radiology at the University of Pennsylvania School of Medicine in the United States. He is a prominent researcher in the field of nuclear medical brain imaging.

His books include *Principles of Neurotheology*, *Born to Believe*, and *Why God Won't Go Away*.

Neurotheology, sometimes called spiritual neuroscience, or the neuroscience of religion, is the study of the biology of religion. Recent research at Boston University was led by postdoctoral fellow Natalie Emmons, but there have been various studies over the years.

Bruce Hood, professor of developmental psychology at Bristol University, studied the way children's brains developed and found that magical and supernatural beliefs are hardwired into our brains from birth. Religions are

And why does this matter?

Because it explains why, since the earliest of times, humankind has worshipped unseen higher powers. Instinctively we know God is there.[45] And the people who lived through the flowering of the extraordinary civilization that was Atlantis after the last ice age were no exception to this; they knew the Divine existed, and their view of the unseen world lay at the very heart of their culture. The Divine was supremely important to them … until they made a fatal mistake …

But let's start at the beginning, and tell the tale properly. At first, they had lived as hunter-gatherers, whose shamans interceded with spirit forces on their behalf. Agriculture evolved and people stopped wandering and became more settled. Those who came to dwell near the sacred cave of the skulls grew crops on the fertile floodplain of the river nearby, and elaborated their tents into more permanent structures. And over time a tradition of building grew up. The growing popularity of the skulls brought offerings and wealth to the area, and in due course the wealth made possible the building of the first temple.

Generations of shamans looked after the skulls in their cave and administered their oracular utterances, eventually evolving into the priests and priestesses of Atlantis; and over subsequent rebuildings their temple grew in complexity and glory. The steady flow of wealth the skulls generated supported a growing priestly class and allowed for the luxury of long periods dedicated to their training.

From the outset, shamans had developed ways to access the

---

tapping into a powerful psychological force and our beliefs come from a very fundamental level. In one study, he found even ardent atheists balked at the idea of accepting an organ transplant from a murderer, because of a superstitious belief that an individual's personality could be stored in their organs. To reinforce his point, during a lecture he produced a blue cardigan and offered ten GBP to volunteers to wear it. A sea of hands went up. He then said the notorious murderer Fred West wore the cardigan, causing most to put their hands down. Although just a stunt (as the cardigan was not West's), it showed even the most rational of people can be irrationally made to feel uncomfortable.

45 We have not just been abandoned; we may be like dandelion seeds drifting through time but we have a satnav hardwired in! We can always find Home. We are never really lost. It was too important to be left to chance.

inner worlds, where they would negotiate with the forces of nature, the goddess of the moon, and the spirits of the hunt. Seeking to bring about favorable outcomes they found power animal allies, and inner-world guides—such as ancestor spirits—to help them in their task. While in altered states, in their astral bodies, they traveled with power animals, riding on the backs of eagles up into the realm of the gods, or plunging down into the underworld to seek out the spirits of disease, hoping to slay them and bring healing to their sick. They communicated with the spirits of plants and learned of their healing potential.

Fasting and hallucinogenic preparations made from plants and fungi enabled the altered states, and once in the inner world they realized they were dealing with the level of cause for the things that happened in their outer-world reality—*that they had indeed entered the realm of the gods*. And there the gods spoke with them, and sometimes appeared to them in their experiences, because this is how our subconscious works. It tries to help. To help us understand it uses a symbolic visual language. Abstract forces are anthropomorphized and given human form or personality so we can understand them and have a dialogue with them.[46]

When shamans found that the gods had names they reported their experiences, and people listened. When the people needed help they remembered, and they would call upon the gods, make offerings, and offer up worshipful thoughts. Their psychic energy fed the archetypes of the forces they had shaped into gods, and the gods grew more powerful through their consciousness. Many minds fed them over a long period of time.

46 Consider mescalin and ayahuasca. The Amazonian ayahuasca vine, often called "the vine of the gods" or the "liana that takes us to the world of the spirits," provides an example of this process. It yields a powerful vision-inducing potion that is well known to the indigenous tribes of the Amazon, and which is of increasing interest to westerners today. Under its influence, people meet with the force/power/entity that is "Mother Ayahuasca." She is the anthropomorphized plant essence, a humanoid-looking and -sounding plant spirit with the wisdom and knowledge of a goddess, willing to interact with us in our mere mortal state. Communication takes place in another plane of reality, a more omniscient reality, which is part of our sub- and super-consciousness.

And then again, those who have ingested mescalin from the peyote cactus may see "Mescalito" in one form or another, according to Carlos Castaneda, as recorded in his books about Don Juan, the Yaqui Indian.

As a result the ancient world positively teemed with gods.

It was as though the white light of the Divine Creator hit the prism of human consciousness and split into the rainbow spectrum of forces forming the gods and goddesses of the ancient world (from the infrared of Hades and the red energy of Mars, right up to the violet of Hera and the ultraviolet of Zeus).

The gods and goddesses personified divinity and gave human-like faces and characters to the sheer abstract power of the Creator. It was a user-friendly format, if you will, that appealed to the Atlantean people and made it easy for them to understand and approach their Creator. Truth and Wisdom took on female form, becoming the goddess Hera, and each aspect/quality/attribute of God gained its own name and face. It was the family of God—the gods—and their names are familiar to us even now because they percolated down via the later civilizations of Greece and Rome.

And come to think about it, although Christianity declares there is only one God, it also splits the Creator into aspects—Father, Son, and Holy Ghost. So in a way, splitting God is not such a strange concept after all, and it's not a wrong thing to do. It's not that God has changed. God has never changed. But over the millennia humanity has used many different names while attempting to draw nearer, because we are hardwired to know God is there we *want* to get closer, and it's in the multitude of names that confusion lies. El, Ahura Mazda, Brahman, Yahweh, Allah … and many, many more names, have all come to mean "God, the Creator."

The fact that the Atlanteans worshipped multiple gods did not lessen their respect for the Creator, it was simply that each facet of the diamond that is God was given its own name. In other words, the gods mediated between the Creator and humankind (as do Jesus and the Holy Ghost). The gods were doorways to approach the Creator.

Understand the Atlantean gods and you will understand their culture.

Understand the gods and you will find the reason for their ultimate demise.

That said, the chapters of *Holy Ice* are arranged chronologically,

the better to construct the map of time. When the material came through in the regression sessions it didn't present itself in this order because there were things I needed to understand first about the multidimensional nature of the skulls. The first two sessions provided chapters 6 and 13, strange as they are. But Noni's was the earliest of the Atlantean lives, and so I've started with it. It just makes more sense to flow with the River of Time rather than hop about all over the place. Things hang together better. You can see cause and effect on the journey of a soul.

In a regression session I like to visualize going on an inner journey to find the past life I'm looking for. I like to work with inner guides and angels because they can help me. And when I work with Veronica, my hypnotherapist friend who did the regressions for me in the coming chapters, the journey I take into the inner world is to see myself descending steps and entering a corridor or hallway with lots of doors … one door will take my attention, I will approach it, open it, and step through—into another life. There's no way of telling what you will find—so that's a tense moment in a session.

Pictures and symbols are the language of the subconscious and the appearance of the door always relates to the life, and can be most instructive (although often only making sense at the end, when the life story has been revealed). But I've included descriptions of the doors to illustrate how this works.

Noni's life was entered through a door covered in polished gold and set with a golden doorknob. Dazzling light rayed out from around the edges of the door while it was closed, and it all looked very sublime. But before I could open it and pass through I found I had to put on protective clothing to prevent being "etherically burned." The inner guides and my subconscious have a sense of humor, and I'm sure they were having a laugh—because I was given goggles that looked ridiculous, especially worn with a golden cloak! The turquoise-blue energy of the cloak's lining was to help me communicate the treasures I would find … apparently. And so bizarrely attired, and thus prepared, I turned the knob and step through into the other life.

I find I am Noni.

Everything else is forgotten.

I am standing on a mountainside in spring sunshine, buffeted gently by spring winds.

I am a young man in a fur-lined jacket, staring out across the lakes spread out far below, and staring hard.

I'm looking for something important.

The wind stirs the surface of the water and ruffles my hair.

Veronica's questions tease the story from me. We discover how I got here and why. She tells me to go back in time to an earlier event in the life, and I do—it's the night I run away. And you know the story from there!

There are parallels between Noni's life and mine, and it has helped me to understand my relationship with clay. Like Noni, I was drawn to clay. As a child playing in the Cheshire countryside I can remember scooping sediments of clay out of the bed of a stream and making primitive pots on flakes of sandstone. It fascinated me, but I couldn't have told you why, and when I was older I got a first-class honors degree in three-dimensional design by specializing in ceramics. And also like Noni I have come to a point in my life where I said, "There has to be more to life than this," left a crushing situation, and changed my name to create a happier future for myself. (My personal story is in *Spiritual Gold*, alongside details on past life healing, inner guides, and angels.)

Noni's time was when Atlantis was young, although by then Atlanta had already taken on her final form. The city had grown huge through three distinct phases and this resulted in her characteristic pattern of concentric waterways. It happened like this:

In the beginning, although there were many different peoples and races settling other parts of the continent, it was sailors from Ireland who had found the welcoming wide river mouth and the fertile floodplain where Atlanta would come to be built. They had returned home bringing word of the new land. Word spread from village to village up and down the west coast of Ireland. Over the years people came and a new clan began to form.

The clan leader was chosen with care. He needed to be the very "Pinnacle of Strength," "the Atlan." Suitable candidates undertook trials of strength, but also of cunning and wisdom—for they did not want a mere bully as leader.

The clan made a settlement in a loop of the river.

It was near to the skulls' cave and built on a rocky outcrop that was higher than the surrounding plain. Over time more people settled there and it grew ever bigger. Generation on generation the clan chiefs lived in the grandest building in the center of the settlement. Through their conquests they came to control more and more land. The Atlan became more than a clan chief, he became a king, and his home became the first palace. Substantial stone walls were built right round what was now becoming a small city, and the river loop was dug out and extended around the walls to create a wide circular moat, the better to defend Atlanta (Atlan's dwelling, Atlan-ta) from attack.

At this stage the cave was outside the city walls.

Time passed and the population continued to expand. Dwellings spilled out beyond the fortifications, and then came phase two. New walls were built farther out and a new moat dug around them. This brought the cave inside the city limits, and the city now had two circular waterways. In time even this would prove too small for the ever-expanding population, and again new walls were constructed even farther out. A final moat was dug round them that was both wide enough and deep enough to serve as the main harbor, for what had now become Atlan's navy, and also for the trading vessels that were flocking to Atlanta from afar.

In time the kings became emperors, and the emperor's palace and gardens extended until they came to take up the entire site of the first city. Palace guards lived just inside the first walls, and the city itself was defended by soldiers living against the inside of the third set of walls.

In the end Atlanta had three sets of city walls and three major circular waterways, all as byproducts of her expansions. After that, though the population continued to grow, the buildings were extended upward and any land used to grow food within the city limits tended to be built on. And although I don't know it yet, the next life story is going to take me right into the very heart of the city—to the palace—a place where Ahmet had longed to go.

* * *

Wondering what we are going to find out next, Veronica and I begin the regression session. As always we are working in my therapy room at home. I'm on the therapy couch, warm and cozy with blankets and pillows, curtains drawn to dim the light. Relaxing music gently fills the room …

I close my eyes.

I hear Veronica's voice as she starts the induction that will turn my attention inward.

And it's so easy to leave the everyday world behind.

I enter the inner world and meet with my guides. My main inner guide is Francis, we have met many times before. There are others with him.[47] Pictures and knowing flood into me. The pictures are now my world.

I visualize descending down steps and walk into a hallway with doors.

I approach a dark-gray wooden door with beaded panels. It looks a little old fashioned. There's a "stealth" quality about the color that helps it to blend in; this door does not draw attention to itself as they usually do, but I know it is the right one. It is self-effacing, but the fancy doorknob of sparkling, faceted, rich-colored glass reminds me of well-to-do Victorian houses in Manchester, England, where I used to live. The houses were built in the nineteenth century at the time the British Empire spread far and wide across the globe.

But first I'm told to don protective clothing "to prevent contamination." It's to prevent me contaminating the recall, and to protect me from being contaminated by any of the things I might see, remember, or experience. And so I visualize myself putting on what my subconscious has provided: a white overall, the sort of cap you'd wear for food preparation, plastic boots, and a pair of gloves. (The humor is wearing thin, but there's no point arguing with your own subconscious. It knows more than you do, however annoying it

---

47 Francis had been my abbot in eleventh-century England, when I was a monk in a monastery. We have often known our guides before, and it is the bond of love they have for us that leads them to help us when we are in body and they are not. They appear in our inner world as we last knew them, so that we recognize them. Francis is dressed in a monk's habit, but he has a wry smile!

is; and looking back, this was wise. Poison was involved.)

It is time. I open the door and step through.

Everything melts away.

I become Sahaara.

I find myself in a temple, basking in peace and light.

My slender bare feet stand on the cool stone of a beautiful black-and-white-checkered floor, and a peacock, leashed and hooded, fidgets at my side. We are waiting, the peacock and I … totally alone in the silence of the holy place. Someone will be coming soon …

Veronica questions me and the story floods out.

Sahaara's Story
HEALING and The Elemental Summoning SKULLS

I, Sahaara, adore my father and we often meet up in his private garden. He is a busy man with many wives and plenty of children—indeed, too many sons all with their greedy eyes fixed on his throne—but he always has time for me. It's because he sees himself in me; we have the same red hair, the same look to our faces, and the same green eyes.

His garden is his great joy. As he says, it is the only place where he can forget the burden of state. He likes the deep peace he finds there, among his plants and tame birds. He takes pleasure in the music of its little streams and waterfalls, and he keeps his body supple by swimming in the pool that lies at its heart. I've often seen him inhaling the sweetness of fragrant blooms and losing himself in the beauty and color of petals. He has an eye for the textures of tree trunks and leaves, and he loves his birds. He talks to his pet birds the same way he talks to me.

Gardeners look after things for him, but whenever my father enters his leafy paradise all servants are banished by the striking of gongs. Precious hours there refresh his spirit and give him strength to go on.

Over the years I have come to enjoy a very special relationship with my father.

* * *

When the time came for my sisters to be married he took me aside. He said there were more than enough princesses to make the necessary alliances the state required this time—so if I wished, I could remain my own mistress. Of course, I must be discreet, he had said, but I could take my pleasures where it pleased me.

I thought it over. And decided it would suit me very well to take orders from no man but my father. The arrangement worked well for us both. I enjoyed many a dalliance with a succession of handsome men who made my heart beat faster, but I never let them get too close to me because I didn't want to risk a broken heart. And I'd never wanted children because I could see from my sisters that a royal marriage and the production of heirs was rarely a route to happiness. So I remained free, and was happy to be available to do important work for my father.

Now, I love collecting gossip and finding out what's going on. I have an easy way with me and get on well with servants. I listen to their problems, and because I am in a position to pull strings on their behalf I help them, and so I gain their trust. They relax their guard when I am around, and I enjoy having many friends in the lower levels of palace life, where no royal should. And when I am with them I listen to their gossip with a lot more interest than I let on. I know it is from servants who actually see and hear what their masters say and do that I can learn what really goes on behind the scenes.

I am my father's eyes and ears.

Although this is not a time of unrest, the ship of state sails on a sea of intrigue with cut-throat political jostling forever forming powerful undercurrents to life at the palace. That's just the way it is.

Of course, many others render this service to my father too, because an emperor has need of many spies, but it means that from time to time I'm able to take a little break. I go to different places for brief holidays and enjoy short trips with the great ships of the imperial navy. It's given me a feel for the empire, and the traveling breaks up the tedium of palace life, but I'm never away for long in case I miss some important bit of gossip ... and I'm always glad to be back. I love uncovering plotting of any sort, no matter how trivial it might first appear. In short, when it comes to palace life, I keep my finger on the pulse and myself in the background, all the while helping with the smooth running of the palace and the entertaining of important visitors. I'm particularly interested in any gossip overheard from the servants of other royal families, foreign dignitaries, or visiting nobles.

The emperor does not trust his sons, or many other members of the extended royal family, but he does trust the priests. Priests are considered so essential by the people of Atlantis that they would be safe whoever was on the throne, but as they have nothing to gain from a change of ruler it is with their blessing that my father has kept the throne.

He has had it a long time now and is very old. The continuity has ensured the stability of the empire, and his accumulated wisdom has steered the ship of state through many challenging times. It is openly said he has made the secret journey to the shrine of the Waters of Life, and that the priests there have helped him bathe in and partake of the waters.[48] His life span has been extended and the cells of his body greatly rejuvenated, but he has paid a price for this. With the mounting burden of the years there has come a world-weariness, a tiredness of spirit, that only lifts when he is in his garden paradise. However, my dear father isn't ready to appoint a successor just yet, and nor does he have one he can trust.

I could never be a threat to him, because the successor has to be male.

*(Atlanta now has **TWO** main temples: **the Temple of Poseidon** and **the Temple of Hera**, and this will be the source of her undoing.*

48 The location was a closely guarded secret, but I believe it may lie submerged somewhere beneath the sea off Bimini, in the Caribbean.

The original **Great Temple** *from Noni's time is still home to the gods and crystal skulls, but the people call it* **the Temple of Hera** *from this point on because:*

1. *Goddess Hera (She Who Knows Everything, the Goddess of Truth and Wisdom, Goddess of the Earth) is a mother to the people and she is immensely popular.*

2. *The God and Goddess of the Sea have been moved out, and so "Great Temple of the All" is no longer accurate.*

The Great Temple was circular and crowned by a high dome, a tall beehive dome, in which Hera and her brother Zeus are depicted. Hera looked down from the lofty heights, overseeing the circle of chapels of the lesser deities stationed below her, keeping them in order and in their place—but the sea deities have escaped from her watchful vigilance.

Poseidon, powerful God of the Sea, has been accorded a temple of his own in an attempt to gain his favor. **The Temple of Poseidon** *is rectangular, not circular. As our empire expands across the seas, Poseidon has grown ever-more important year on year, and we want him to spare our ships and the lives of our sailors. His abandoned chapel in the Temple of Hera has been rededicated to "Unknown Gods," and offers a place where the sailors and foreigners now flooding into our city for trade can worship their own deities and feel at home. It is a sign of the changes that our empire is bringing, and although in the fullness of time it will turn into a curse, during the reign of my father this arrangement seems nothing short of a blessing.)*

So, Atlanta is thriving with two great temples, and I, Princess Sahaara, am happy. I skate on the surface of life, having fun and not getting seriously involved in anything other than gathering information for my father. The years pass, full of interesting gossip and small triumphs until the last day of the year when I am thirty-seven; I am sent by my father to the Temple of Hera. The divination he seeks is of far too sensitive a nature to risk using the usual courier. He won't tell me what it's about, but he gives me a sealed, rolled document to take to the priests.

For secrecy's sake I leave in the early morning when most of the palace is asleep.

Disguised in a long, plain cloak with a hood to hide my face, I slip into a hidden passageway.

Remnants of the original city lie under a lot of the palace, and some long-forgotten merchant's wine cellars have been pressed into service for this. The entrance is via a trap door concealed beneath a carpet in my bedroom, and there are various exits—much used on other occasions—but this time I am heading for a small temple-tomb in the abandoned cemetery. Sea burials are the fashion now, conducted by those at the new Temple of Poseidon. I know nobody will be there.

I emerge unseen and head for the nearest of the gated bridges … where one of the gardeners is waiting for me by the carriage seats and palanquins (which are always ready to take those who live in the palace out on journeys into the city). He has with him a gift I'm expected to take to the priests. Seeing me, the gardener taps a couple of bearers on the shoulder to wake them.

They leap to their feet and receive their instructions. I allow myself to be settled into the carriage seat, and the gift is set down beside me. Canopy drapes conceal me.

Grasping the poles they set off at a trot over the bridge, and once across the waterway it isn't far to the temple. I leave the bearers and transport concealed in the shade of trees, and as they settle down to wait for my return I approach the entrance to the temple. Mounting smooth stone steps, I slip in between the shadows of stone columns.

I walk into stillness and silence.

The temple is deserted.

I have it all to myself. I look around, admiring the beauty of the building, its majestic size and many chapels. The chapels are set back in shadowy recesses between the huge posts forming the post and lintel structure that gives the temple its strength. Each chapel has an altar, and their sumptuous gold leaf sings out from the shadows. They are steeped in beauty and made rich with paintings, statues, and carvings to honor the god or goddess whose chapel it is.

Light is streaming down through the circular opening in the dome and pouring in through large windows above the chapels.

Light fills the main body of the temple, and I stand basking in that light, in its serenity and peace, surprised that no priest has come to challenge me. Standing there I feel that the safe ordering of the cosmos is still intact, that whatever the document might contain, at the heart of everything, all is well.[49]

But my sublime, peaceful reverie is short lived.

The gift at my side is pulling on its leash, and I have to scold the hooded peacock and grip the leash tighter. Looking down to admire my slender bare feet on the black-and-white stone floor, my eye falls on a dropping it has just released. Shocked, I hear pounding footsteps shattering the serenity further—and as I look up a priest appears, out of breath, uttering greetings in the name of the god Dionysos.

(This is the day of the happy god of wine, and my father has chosen it for his supplication because he wants his people to be happy. He's chosen his gift because it's something he loves and will miss—it's a special pet he is presenting to Hera. It's extremely tame because he has fussed it since it was a baby, and for him to do this I realize how important the errand must be to him. My father, Emperor Samarkandhi, has a fondness for birds of exotic plumage. Even his name relates to birds. It means "Glory of the Phoenix" in honor of his renewals. For just as that fabled bird rose anew from its own ashes so has my father risen renewed from the Waters of Life. Four times he's made that personal sacrifice, for the good of his people, for the stability of the empire, and thus as we Atlanteans see it, for the benefit of world peace. He loves peacocks so much he has chosen

---

49 I loved coming here, especially when ceremonies were held or matters were divined for the people to witness. At times like that, throngs of bodies would crush into every possible space forming a deep circle around the walls, and people would hold their breath as divination balls were sent rolling out across the newly emptied stone floor. The floor was intricately patterned, a board for a game of divine chance. Its black-and-white-checkered design was embellished with symbols of the planets, elements and themes from nature, and entwined with the calendar. Where the balls came to rest revealed the answer of the goddess.

(The checkered floor linked in my mind with the checkered floors found in Masonic temples even today. Here it stood for "day" and "night," but it does symbolize darkness and light and is a floor of power.)

them for the motif of his imperial insignia.[50])

... And with my free hand I draw back my hood, revealing the royal circlet bearing his imperial peacock crest. Green gemstones in the eyes and the eyes of the tail feathers sparkle in the sunlight.

The priest looks startled, pauses for a moment, then sweeps me into the shadows of one of the chapels and off into a small room beyond, so we will not be seen or overheard. Quietly he says, "Tell me, my child, what service may I render?" His eyes stray to the peacock.

Protocol demands he accept the gift, but he shifts uncomfortably.

I pass him the document. He snaps open the wax seal but as he reads there's a sharp intake of breath. The color drains from his face.

Gathering himself together he says, "Yes, yes ... It will be done ... Return tomorrow at the same hour for the answer." Then taking the peacock's leash firmly in both hands, he bows to me and thanks me formally, on behalf of Hera, for such a lavish gift. He expresses hope that it will be happy, but the doubt in his voice suggests it will be returned at the earliest opportunity etiquette allows. Motioning me to follow, he says, "Come with me ..." and I'm guided to a concealed doorway.

The bearers return me to the palace.

* * *

By now I am feeling worried. I keep thinking of the dramatic effect the message had had on the priest. My father must be troubled. Are my brothers growing restless? Are they looking at his throne with greedy eyes and plotting his death *again*?

When I see my dear father later that morning I tell him that the priest was very touched by his gift, but worried that the peacock might pine. But try as I might, I can prise nothing further out of him. All he will say is he doesn't want to worry me.

---

50 Peacocks graced the parks and ornamental gardens, and people kept them as pets to show their allegiance to the Emperor Samarkandhi. Indeed, they wore their feathers stitched on cloaks.

But there's no escaping worry. The next few hours are an opportunity for total chaos. There's an event at the palace that's bringing together his potential enemies *and* two armies of soldiers—with weapons. There will be bonfires, clouds of smoke, and flashes and bangs of fireworks. With large amounts of wine flowing freely throughout the day and into the night absolutely anything can happen![51]

It is Founding Day, one of the biggest feasts in our calendar.

It is the anniversary of the unification of our country, and thus the founding of the empire. Each year we celebrate by staging an enactment of the great battle and glorious victory that had forged our land into one mighty and united power.

(As our history teaches us, in the beginning there were many different peoples inhabiting the lands of Atlantis. They all had their own kings and their own ideas about how things should be done—even down to when New Year should fall. Rivalries grew and much fighting between the kings took place. These were the ages when blood ran red all too often. In time the kings fell one by one, until came the final great battle—when the victorious king of the Atlans[52] held aloft the severed head of his last remaining rival. From that time forth his was the only opinion that mattered about how things should be done ... and the empire's birthday was celebrated at the spring equinox, together with the older tradition of the Festival of the Renewal.

The Festival marked the time of the year when the battle was fought, and when light wins the battle over darkness, just as the king had won the battle over his rival. From that day on, days grow longer, nights shorter, and the seeds of spring are planted—just as the seeds of our mighty empire had been planted in the days of old. Spring is the time of new beginnings—a new growing season and a new year of empire.)

---

51 Fireworks have been traced back two thousand years to the second century BC in China, but they are older. All you need is charcoal, sulphur, and saltpeter mixed together to burn, or if compressed in a tube the mixture will explode; they're auspicious to ward off evil spirits and bring luck—e.g., for a New Year, or any celebration—and they were definitely in my regression. Nothing fancy, just very basic, but for those days, impressive!

52 King of the **people of the Atlan**, thus **Atlan's (people)**, or put simply, **Atlans**.

The celebration is a very popular event and every year people flock to the city from miles around for the spectacle and the feasting— the crowds flooding in could conceal enemies, never mind those in the mix of people coming to the royal banquet. As well as all the extended royal family, foreign kings were compelled to send their sons to the court to learn its laws, in preparation for their future kingship under the Atlantean yoke—and so there are many visiting dignitaries from abroad. The palace is absolutely heaving with people, and servants bustle and scurry getting things ready. The air is thick with expectation and excitement.

* * *

Once the celebration starts, everybody takes their seats at the banquet.

As usual I'm seated a long way from my father, at the far end of one of the wings of the royal table. It doesn't do for a spy to court attention, so I never sit near him. I'd been involved in the planning of the feast for quite some time. There are musicians, entertainers, jugglers, acrobats, and dancers—and when the food arrives there are many different courses: dishes of birds, fishes and stews and roasts of meat, and sweet things made with dried fruits and honey, custards, and sweet biscuits with almonds. Wine flows freely and there is a very happy atmosphere.

I look around me.

Everyone else seems jolly and a bit drunk.

After the banquet, it's time to watch the enactment and see the bonfires in the Great Park, and so people begin to drift off to find a vantage point. But I still feel troubled, I hang back to see if I can hear anything suspicious … But I can't find anything sinister.

Everyone is outside by now, having a grandstand view from the top of the palace walls … and sounds of "Oohs" and "Aahs" drift in and begin to get louder. I know this means the enactment is well underway, and soon everyone will be cheering wildly as victory is won and the empire founded.

(After our country had been united, we Atlans had turned our eyes

outward to the rest of the world. We didn't subdue the other countries as such, but we humbled them with a show of strength by our army and navy, and after that the foreigners were compelled to send slaves, animals, food, furs, gifts, and mineral resources in taxes to Atlanta every year. They were allowed to keep their own indigenous rulers— well, it saved our emperor the bother—and in return he kept them safe, and he would bring his fierce armies to their defense if they were attacked by any war-mongering neighbors. Atlantis prospered in a stable, ordered world, where people were safe, happy, and well fed, and where there was nothing to stop the empire's taxes from flowing smoothly into the emperor's ever-expanding coffers.)

As the crowds cheer, clouds of birds are released into the sky to celebrate the beginning of world peace.

* * *

The mountains of leftover banqueting food were gathered up in baskets and taken out to be shared with the people. The food was kept warm with hot stones, some of which were slipped into the pots, and it was all carefully laid out by the palace servants on tables at the distribution points outside the Great Temple, where it formed the focus of a huge open-air street party.

Then the priests called on all the gods to bless the food, the city, and the land, and they personally handed the food out, ladled the stews into people's bowls, and blessed all those who partook of it.

Priests were involved with everything of any importance, and this custom was designed to make sure that the empire's New Year began in the most auspicious manner possible. Of course, we wanted every year to be a good year, and so great care was always taken. But even though everything had gone off well this time, I still felt wary.

However, I felt safe enough to retire that night.

* * *

The following morning I made my way back to the temple, and knocked on the concealed door. The priest was waiting. He placed the sealed answer from the goddess in my hands, and presented me with the peacock, as a gift to the emperor from the temple. I knew he'd do that so I'd brought a little bag of gold to thank him for his trouble.

Back at the palace, I tried to take the document straight to my father, but he was busy with affairs of state until midday. I would dearly have loved to open the reply, but I daren't. I kept turning it over in my hands, putting it away, and getting it out again. The morning passed very slowly.

Lunch was a small family affair.

I went to my father's private quarters, and into his garden. The colors of the birds and flowers were startlingly vivid in the bright sunshine. Sunlight gleamed on iridescent feathers as birds perched, preening, in trees.

The peacock was being fed by my father.

I walked toward him, smiling, holding out the temple's reply.

But despite my asking, and trying every trick I knew to wheedle it out of him, he still wouldn't tell me what it was about, because it was "too big a burden" for me—and nor would he read the answer while I was present.

I hated mysteries, but he was not to be drawn on this.

I shared his food and we ate together.

I hadn't seen much of him recently and I'd missed him.

Sitting together our facial resemblance was striking, but few were in a position to know that. His subjects, and even many courtiers, only ever saw him in his state robes and then he wore an elaborate headdress that covered his forehead and nose. It was like wearing a mask. The red-and-gold headdress had huge ostrich plumes died red to symbolize the phoenix emerging from fire, and it was most impressive, very high, wide, and rather heavy. This discomfort was the price he had to pay to create the impression of imperial majesty that his empire demanded, and when he was in his state robes he looked more than a mere mortal.

But he didn't wear his state robes in the garden.

He could be himself there, and I was glad of this chance to see him and enjoy his company. He always delighted in showing me any new plants that had been brought in from distant lands, or in sharing the wonder of a perfect bloom, or the joy at new shoots on an old favorite. He often picked me a fragrant posy for my bedroom. In the privacy of the garden he could reveal the softer side of his nature, but I knew he could be cold and angry at times, and I understood he had to be, it was all part of being a strong ruler.

* * *

It was two weeks later when we were in the garden having lunch together that my father referred to "that business with the peacock." He said, "If you want to know the answer go out on the battlements tonight and watch."

The afternoon dragged for me after that.

But eventually evening came.

Feeling very curious, I made my way with my servants to the palanquins. We commandeered three to take us in comfort to the protective walls that encircled our city.

The bearers set off at a trot toward the seaway.

The thoroughfare running alongside the seaway took us straight through the city and down to the main gates. It was a lovely warm evening, and when we arrived by the soldiers' dwellings that hugged the inside of the city walls, the sky was red with the sun's dying light. It was day's end, and smells of cooking drifted on the gentle night air.

We were taken up the ramps that climbed the inside of the mighty walls, to the walkway that ran around the top. Our journey ended by the battlements overlooking the seaway as it flowed out of the city and down to the ocean.

After helping us out of the palanquins the bearers withdrew and waited patiently, a respectful distance away, squatting on their heels and playing dice games to pass the time. The noise of their laughter and the fall of the dice drifted on the still air.

My servants arranged seating with cushions borrowed from the palanquins, and we all prepared to make a pleasant night of it. I looked out over the battlements at the lands around me as they lay bathed in the last of the evening light, and everything appeared very peaceful.

My little group passed the time playing games of chance and skill, we made up funny stories and we gossiped. The palace kitchens had put up a supper for us, and we picnicked on chicken pasties and honeyed fruit tarts. I drank only water to keep a clear head, but as the night wore on I began to feel tired.

Under the faint light of the newest of moons the city had grown quiet.

It had been dark for some time and my servants were nodding off to sleep, and I felt bored. I started wishing I was curled up in my comfortable bed … and I began wondering what I would choose to wear in the morning … when I thought I saw something move.

Dots of light had appeared in the countryside.

I leaned out over the battlements—and I could see more and more of them heading in our direction. People with torches! The dots drew nearer. This was highly unusual. People weren't much given to traveling at night, and especially not in a large party.

The travelers were silent and drew nearer still.

Suddenly blood-curdling yells rang out as many more figures erupted out of the ground in front of the battlements, and a big fight ensued.

We were being attacked—but we were prepared!

A crack regiment had been concealed, ready and waiting for the enemy.

The battle didn't go on for long. … None of the charcoal-skinned invaders made it into the city.

I watched the fight, mesmerized, for about an hour, by which time bodies lay crumpled and twisted in front of the city gates.

When it was over, the soldiers took the few survivors away and dragged the bodies to the pit they themselves had been hiding in only an hour before. With the leafy branches they'd used to conceal themselves, they swept the land, brushing away footprints and signs of the skirmish. By morning there would be very little to see, and the sleeping citizens would have no need to be troubled by what had happened.

I sighed in relief. The city was safe, and the city was

unscathed. I had heard no whisper about any of this, and hoped that perhaps now my father would explain things and tell me what it was about.

* * *

At lunch the next day I approach him. I tell him what I'd seen and he laughs, and says, "They didn't quite get what they'd come for, did they?" He is in good spirits, and prepared to explain the mystery.

During a restless night at the full moon, a dream of great force had woken him and disturbed him so greatly that he sought its meaning from the priests. He'd requested them to scry with the crystal skulls to ascertain the nature and timing of the threat in his dream. But it had turned out to be nothing to do with his fears of rebellion in our own land, but a warning of an army on its way from the Lion Lands, determined to sack his city and loot it. They thought to torch Atlanta, grab the fabled treasures, and race back to their boats and take off.

Unfortunately for them, they had underestimated the scale of everything.

It was like nowhere else on Earth.[53]

All the ages of infighting and treachery between the various early kings had taught valuable lessons in defense. Even if the raiders had managed to sneak in, they would have stood no chance against all the regiments on alert that resided against the inner side of the city walls.

And it was ensured no one would be returning home to tell tales.

* * *

Twelve years pass and my father is still the feared and respected ruler he has always been, but I am unwell. I have a heavy feeling in my chest and there is something amiss with my lungs.

---

53 As well as the skulls for scrying, we had birds to carry messages from watchers along the coast.

   With its solid stone buildings at this stage and ubiquitous waterways, Atlantis was not vulnerable to attack by fire.

I had secretly been trying to come to terms with a big disappointment in my personal life, and it had drained away all my bounce and joy in living. I'd slipped into depression but did not seek help. Whenever my servants tried to bring the conversation round to seeking medical help, I would tell them not to fuss, that I'd be better soon. My father had been busier than usual deploying the armed forces in their peace-keeping role, and so he'd seen less of me than he would have liked. But when the political situation calmed down and the pace of palace life returned to normal, he caught up with me and was shocked at the change in his little songbird. He brushed away my protestations and ordered me to allow a visit from the royal physicians.

His doctors declared I had an imbalance of the element of water in my body. They prepared herbal draughts for me but to no avail, and I continued to deteriorate. I had no energy and no interest in anything, not even gossip. I became a shadow of myself. The physicians became increasingly concerned and insisted I be taken to the Temple of Hera for healing from the crystal skulls.

It was my fiftieth birthday when I was carried into the temple, the same place I'd brought the peacock all those years before. But this time the visit was a last recourse to save my life. And though I'd seen the thirteen quartz skulls from afar at festivals in the temple, I had never been near one. My servants carried my listless body to a small room where I was seated and made comfortable. One of the thirteen was placed on the table beside me.

(As I see this in the regression session I become aware that though they could all do healing to some extent, each skull had a different purpose and was best suited to a certain type of healing work. But what was not generally known was that there were four more skulls.

These were at the bottom of the display stand, but hidden away in a golden compartment concealed behind an ornate flap door that was securely fastened down. The people did not know they were there, they were too dangerous to be seen, and they needed the thirteen above them to keep them in check.

Long before I was born, the fame of the thirteen had spread throughout the world, so when these were found in other lands during my father's reign, they had been sent in to the city as part of the taxes. Like the thirteen, they were also representations of human skulls, but they were not formed of clear quartz. And like the thirteen they were arranged with care: to the left was what looked like a fluorite skull and below it was placed a black one, perhaps made of obsidian, basalt, or black tourmaline, and to the right was placed a large, cloudy, sandy-colored skull, with a green jade-like skull below. They corresponded to the elements of water, earth, fire, and air, respectively.

The priests had come to understand that the four had a very different power to the thirteen. They were much more Earth based, and had been formed on Earth by the forces of the elemental kingdoms in an attempt to achieve a greater interface between themselves and humankind, necessary because man had ceased to be able to see the elemental beings and the fairies. They were for grounding and manifestation and had the effect of helping the purpose of the higher skulls to become manifest on the Earth plane. They were powerful when working with the weather, the seas, the elements, winds, and storms. They were opaque because they were not meant to help humans look into the lower worlds of the elementals, instead they were a means of summoning those beings for communication.

Having the use of these skulls helped to give Atlantis the rule of the sea, as they could be used to whip up storms or to keep storms away. They could be used for weather manipulation, to help bring good harvests, or cause famine in far-off lands. They could be used to do mischief or for good, and they were much easier to misuse than the thirteen. The four did not give healing, but they could cause a cancer if they were wrongly used. They had been formed much more recently than the original ones, and they needed the weight of the others to keep them in their place and to overrule misuse. They needed the forces of order to keep them in check. They could plug into the energy matrix of the others, but they were very much of Earth and did not share their off-world origin.

The thirteen would be displayed whenever there was a religious festival, and they were used to dispense healing. They were arranged in strict order on their stand, the placing as significant as that of the planets in the solar system or organs in a body. Those wishing to be healed would drink water that had had quartz crystals marinating in it,[54] *so that as they drank this water, crystal energy was flowing inside them, and this water would resonate with the crystal emanations from the skulls on the stand. As the energy radiated out from the skulls, it would activate that which was in the water and they would receive healing.)*

Sha Nan Reha, "Born to Heal and See the cause of Disease," had been selected by the priests as the skull most suited to this work. Although I'd seen it from a distance, displayed third up on the right-hand side of the stand, this was the first time I'd ever seen one of our famous crystal skulls close up, but I felt too weak and too poorly to take much notice. Slowly I had sipped the prepared crystal water I'd been given, and as I sat there I began to feel an energy change taking place in my body. There was a pleasant, comforting feeling gently tingling at the bottom of my lungs, and from that moment on I began to get better.

Over the days and weeks my health returned, and I regained my appetite for living. My energy came back and my interest in the little things of life was restored. I would meet with my friends and

---

54   Quartz crystals, cleansed, blessed, and programmed by thought. Should you wish to try this I suggest:

1) To cleanse them, wash them, then soak them in a glass bowl of spring water to which a few crystals of rock salt have been added, and leave the bowl out in the sun for at least an hour or so. Discard the water.

2) Hold the crystals in loving hands and dedicate them to the Divine. "I will and command that you be dedicated to …" (e.g., the Divine/God or whatever is your own choice of words).

3) Give them your purpose; e.g., "I will and command that you bring me healing and restore my harmony." Use whatever words you feel are right.

4) Then say, "I will and command that you be self-cleansing." Next marinate the crystals in spring water that you will drink—perhaps solarize the water in a glass jug for a short while on a sunny windowsill, then keep the crystal drinking water in the fridge and use it within a few days. You can always repeat the process and make more. There will be crystal therapists to consult near where you live, and there are lots of books on how to use crystals. There is not one I can single out to recommend. Have fun exploring! See which crystals you're drawn to, let your intuition guide you. (Use glass, not plastic, and avoid using lead crystal glass decanters to store the water in, because lead, like chemicals in plastic, has been found to leach out.)

(This is not suggested as a substitute for conventional medicine.)

listen once more to the chatter of palace life.

The problem was that I had not traveled as lightly through life as I intended.

I had not been able to stop myself falling in love, though I had kept a tight hold on my heart for year after year. I had broken my own rules when I became intoxicated with a dashing young man. He had dark curly hair and a smile that caused a dazzling sun to shine inside me. It was the first time I'd loved more than I was loved, and in the end he left me for another. I put a brave face on, and kept my own counsel, but he had quite simply broken my heart.

But somewhere deep inside me there was a little flame of hope, that perhaps he'd miss me and come back, given time. That was enough to keep me going. Time passed, and the years were full of intrigues that kept me busy, but there came a fateful day.

The weather had been terrible. Several days of rain had kept me cooped up inside the palace, but the next day was sunny and bright. A bracing wind had blown away the clouds. I couldn't wait to get out and enjoy the fresh air and the excitement of the wind. I had my servants accompany me to one of the parks for a stroll, and when we climbed a little hill we danced in the wind. On the way back, I saw someone I recognized.

My breath froze in my chest. My eyes felt like they'd turned to stone and I fainted. My servants bent over me and did what they could, they carried me home and for two days they kept people away, as I had asked. I cried my heart out and, red-eyed, surrendered to the helpless misery that consumed me.

I had seen my beloved, also enjoying the wind in the park, but he had been flying a kite with his two young sons while his pretty young wife watched, holding their new baby.

He would never leave her now, this I knew.

I would never have children. The years of fertility had fled from me, and grief for the loss of all love was the ache in my soul.

* * *

I made a good recovery. The skull had healed my body, heart, and soul. My spirit was restored, and I grew cheerful and started to notice other men, and I rarely thought about the faithless one anymore. Seven years passed when there came a day that at first seemed like any other.

There was always a procession of visitors staying at the palace, and an old king and his son from one of the minor countries of Europe had recently arrived. (Their kingdom was in what is still known as the Basque region, on the borders of France and Spain.) I had been caught up with one thing and another and missed lunch. As I scooted through the area near the kitchens, I came across a bowl of tempting-looking stew and a goblet of nice red wine sitting waiting on a table. There was not a soul about. I was hungry, and so I drank the wine with an insouciant flourish and cheekily scampered off with the bowl to my room. Quite soon I began to feel ill, and in the fifteen minutes it took to get to my room I'd gone from feeling on top of the world to feeling terrible. I'd always done my job well … but obviously not well enough that day, I thought wryly to myself … … some plotting had escaped my attention.

My forehead dripped with sweat, and a searing pain ripped through me. I felt like my insides were on fire. I lay on my bed and knew I was dying.

There are always jealous, greedy eyes looking at any throne, even if it is only that of a minor European country. I, Princess Sahaara of the blood royal of Atlantis, had been in the wrong place at the wrong time, and inadvertently consumed that which had been intended for another.

It was a relief to leave my body.

And in the expanded awareness that came after dying I could see it all.

The old king's son had poisoned his father's wine, and gone in search of an Atlantean servant to serve the deadly draught. He'd never have got away with it at home, but here he saw his opportunity. He'd brought the poison with him, concealed about his person. He'd breathed not a word of it to anyone, so there was no iota of gossip that I could have gleaned. He planned to return home as king and blame his father's death on us, their Atlantean hosts. There was no love lost between his people and what they saw as Atlantis the oppressor, so they'd be bound to believe him—and their sympathy would assure him of their allegiance. *It was a plan that just couldn't fail … or so he'd thought.*

And I could see that my father, Emperor Samarkandhi, was deeply affected when he learned of my death. But he knew immediately what had to be done.

First, he had the priests ask the skulls to show exactly who was to blame for my death, and second he decided to choose and groom an heir. It was time to put his many sons—and their cousins—to the test; to find the strongest, wisest, and most cunning of them all.

The old king of the Basques was incandescent with anger when his son's plotting was revealed, and mortified to be so embarrassed by what his son had inadvertently done to one of the emperor's favorite children. For attempting to take his life, he killed the ingratiate traitor of a son himself, in front of the entire court.

My father watched, but he took no pleasure in this death. He knew I'd been caught up in their squabbles, and he just wanted me back. The king of the Basques had other sons, so he set sail for home to choose a more grateful successor.

But for my father it was different …

Emperor Samarkandhi had lost the heart to go on. My father wanted nothing more than to sit in his garden, enjoy his flowers, fuss his birds, and doze in the sun. And very soon that's exactly what he did. As he would drift off to sleep he often thought about me, and from time to time I came into his dreams and he would talk to me once more and share again his favorite blooms.

Someone else now wore a splendid headdress and carried the weight of the world on their shoulders.

Someone else now wore the feathers.

* * *

The cult of Poseidon was growing in strength.

This will continue until the Land of Atlanta, Atlantis, is in Poseidon's shadow.

The feathers are now the deep turquoise sea-green of the robes of Poseidon.
From now on marine motifs dominate the imperial insignia.
The sea dynasties have begun.

Chapter 4

Chronicles of Atlantis 3

Reflections on the Last Past Life

I had switched gender, which brings balance to the soul, and we usually do this unless there's a good reason not to.

Now, Ahmet had died the victim of a plot by priests, poisoned in a palace, so it was interesting to see that as Sahaara, living in a palace, I had reveled in uncovering plotting of any sort. In fact, I'd made it my life's work. But it still didn't stop me dying again due to another plot … and this is because *not being deceived by appearances is such a big lesson that it needs reinforcing.* I've had to learn it over and over, and it is still relevant today—there's plotting going on all around us, all the time—just look at the news and what you see is the tip of the iceberg. Fake news abounds and shadowy forces push their agendas, manipulating the way we think. False flag atrocities offer the excuse for yet more warfare, while the only ones who profit are those selling the weapons, or grabbing the oil, or benefiting from a destabilized rival regime. Multinational companies, currency manipulators—with the news, ask yourself, "Who profits from this?" Then follow the money … and it will lead to another piece of the jigsaw in the unfolding scenario of disaster that the Legend of the Skulls warns of. If it is the goodness in the hearts of ordinary people that will save us, our eyes need to be opened to the truth of what is going on. With eyes open we can say, "Not in my name." With eyes open we are awake. We can sign a petition, vote with our purse by not buying from companies that pollute or degrade our planet. There's a lot we can do. But time is running out for us on this particular lesson.

In the regression Sahaara had skipped over her heartbreak,

but it came to light as I meditated upon it later. It is quite possible during regression

- to avoid (because it has been accidentally passed over, or was not appropriate to remember at that particular time)
- to resist (as Sahaara had, to protect herself from painful memories)
- or to withhold (as when the client doesn't feel safe with the therapist and knows things they don't say).

But the option is always there to revisit the life if you need to, and as many times as you wish.[55]

Sahaara's death came swiftly and although I didn't have to feel her pain I knew about it and was glad when she crossed the threshold of death and moved into spirit. After a death by poison it is always worth checking to see if there are any residues of the poison's energy still being carried in the etheric body, as it is easy to release them.[56]

Poison and other past life wounds are often the cause of unexplained pains for which no medical reason can be found, and this death called to mind a session I'd done for someone who had gone back to a life as a Native American chief. It was at the time when the Indians, as they were so erroneously called, were being treated despicably—and when he realized what the future held for his people, the chief had despaired. He felt there was no future to lead them to, and so he instructed his medicine man to make him a poisoned draught.

During the healing that follows a life story when I work, my client looked at what he needed to release and to his surprise, along

---

55 The door to the spy princess summed up her life perfectly—a self-effacing, gray, stealth door, old fashioned because Atlantis was a long time ago, with a sparkling glass doorknob hinting at empire and wealth. When I realized how I died, I understood the symbolic protective clothing.

56 Ask what color is the energy of the poison, ask exactly where it is being held in the body. Is it also in the aura? When I'm working with Veronica I might make it into an object and slide it out to a guide, to dispose of. Or if I was conducting a shamanic psycho-regression session I would use sound and medicine rattles to break up the energy and then release it to the Archangels Michael, Uriel, Gabriel, and Raphael, who return it to Source. The area is then rebalanced and healed with the appropriate color of divine energy. The way I work is explained in *Spiritual Gold*.

with "despair" he found what he called "forked-lightning energy" lodged in his stomach. This had been part of a magical element in the draught, which he released easily in the session. He wrote to me later to say that the session had been very helpful, and a troubling pain he'd had for a long time had gone. Up to that point all the medical tests he'd undergone and even a barium meal had failed to find the cause.

I suspect the medicine man may not have approved of the task he'd been given, felt his chief was abandoning the tribe and needed punishing … or perhaps it was a genuine mistake made while brewing the potion. But it has to be admitted that past life therapy often reaches the places other therapies don't go!

Days of the Week & the Ancient World

Now from the very start of the research on Atlantis I'd had the tantalizing feeling that I had been an Atlantean priest, and oh, how I longed to access his secrets.

Well, it did turn out to be true.

But before we look at his life I want you to think for a minute about the names we call the days of the week. The words are so mundane that we use them without thinking, but they do have meaning. They are sacred: *they are the days of the gods*. Even in the twenty-first century AD we are still referring to our days in exactly the same way as the Atlanteans did thousands of years BC. It's a hidden but unbroken line in our inheritance of Atlantean culture, and it has come about because they stamped their ways upon their empire. Why else would the deities of disparate cultures be so similar if not for a shared and rather pushy ancestor culture?

The Atlanteans studied the stars and noticed that while most were fixed others wandered the heavens. The wanderers are the heavenly bodies nearest to us—the planets in our solar system, the brothers and sisters of Earth, who swing around the sun in different orbits. When viewed from Earth, Venus and Mars come together and part, Mercury changes direction—appearing to go back and forth when in retrograde motion, Saturn is made splendid by the majesty of his rings and Jupiter is large and stately. So it was seen that the heavenly bodies had different characters, and they were attributed to the gods. Night revealed the gods in their heavens, and days were dedicated to them. As they still are!

In English it is easy to recognize **Satur(n)day**, **Sun**day, and **Mo(o)n**day. But when the Romans left British shores, the influx of Angles, Saxons, Jutes, and Vikings brought in Teutonic and Old Norse influences: and so **Mars**day became **Tiw's** day (Tuesday) because Tiw was what *they* called the god of war; and **Mercury**day became **Woden/Odin's** day (Wednesday); **Jupiter**day became known as **Thor's** day (Thursday); and **Venus**day became **Frigg's** day, or as we say now, Friday.[57]

Frigg was the Teutonic goddess of clouds and married love who had the ability to see the fate of all mankind. She was served by minor goddesses, and advised her followers to prevent disaster befalling them. If you'd asked an Atlantean to describe Hera it would have been in just such terms. Frigg's star—Friggjarstjarna in Norse—is the one the Atlanteans knew as Hera's star. It is the Morning star and the Evening star, so called because that's when it's at its brightest, just when Hera reaches out to her brother Zeus … as you will be finding out. It was only when the Romans came that we were taught to call it Venus. But after they left, the name stuck, although the day became Frigg's day.

So to sum up: Thursday belonged to Zeus/Thor/Jupiter in the ancient world, and Friday was the day of Hera/Frigg/Aphrodite/Venus.[58] But what really matters here, is that in Atlantis Tuesday

---

57   The Greeks worshipped the same deities as the Romans but called them by different names. Their days were dedicated to Ares (Mars), Hermes (Mercury), Zeus (Jupiter), Aphrodite (Venus), and Chronus (Saturn). Goddess Hera was the Romans' Juno. But what chance this, had there been no common ancestor?

58   Venus and Aphrodite are one-and-the-same goddess, who was a daughter of Hera in Atlantean times. This daughter was **the chaste maiden, the goddess of young girls**. She was given a more sluttish persona in the later cultures of Greece and Rome, when Patriarchy promoted her to prominence by giving her Hera's star and day. Poor Venus had to lend her name to venereal diseases—something no chaste maiden would ever suffer from!

(This will make more sense a few pages on, but under the Patriarchal influence Zeus was brought down the frequencies too, and given a proper body, so he could have amorous adventures, much more to Patriarchy's liking. Well, you couldn't expect men to behave better than the gods, now could you???!

belonged to the god Mars, and it would be a long time before Tiw usurped his place in the vocabulary of the world. No, it was well and truly Marsday back then (as it still is in France to this day: *Mardi*)— and Marsday is where we are going now as we take up the next story.[59]

Once more Veronica and I pressed on with the research, and I prepared to step into the unknown. I asked to be shown the next life for the book, and with Veronica's help I entered the inner world and came to the hallway of doors. This time I could see many doors ahead of me, some surprisingly small. I passed them by, and kept on until I came to a substantial purple one set in a doorframe covered with gold leaf. It had a very modern high-gloss finish and a delicate

What a cracking excuse! And this made Hera the endlessly cheated on wife we're familiar with from ancient Greek myths. Perversely, they kept the bit about Hera and Zeus being brother and sister, which always seemed odd, until I discovered it came from an older, purer tradition with a different narrative.)

59 An additional element was that the calendar of festivals allied other gods to the important days too; for example, Dionysus's day. Some mo(o)nths had extra days because the moon's cycle from full moon to full moon takes an average of 29 days 12 hours and 44 minutes, not 28 days. Some years had 12 full moons but others 13. The sun and the moon regulated the flow of time through the days of the year, with the lunar calendar cross-referenced with the solstices and equinoxes of the solar calendar. (Even today we celebrate Easter on a date fixed like this. The Christian celebration has ancient pagan roots and it is held on the first **Sunday** after the first **full moon** on or after **the spring equinox**.)

Atlantis had a religious calendar, an agricultural calendar, and a political calender that meshed together holy days, festivals, and celebrations, all regulated by astronomical observations. There was more than one New Year, and this caused me much confusion until I realized why.

The political year renewed itself at the spring equinox, and the agricultural year concluded with the harvest festival at the autumn equinox. The new agricultural year began after that, with an autumn planting for a winter crop, which was followed by a second planting in spring. The winter solstice marked the coming of new life to the land and to the Earth herself, so it was Earth's birthday, while the summer solstice signified the start of a new period of Earth life for the emperor—it was his state birthday, despite the exact date on which he had been born. (Even today Queen Elizabeth of Great Britain has a state birthday on the first, second, or third Saturday in June, which is when she announces her birthday honors list, although she was born on April 21, 1926.)

So the Atlantean year was a constant flow of renewals, rather than being cut up into our customary big yearly chunks. This idea of a flowing river of time is preserved in Celtic culture.

filigree plate around its beautifully polished brass knob.

I was drawn to this door and found a gold string bag hanging from the doorknob, containing small crystals polished like tumble stones. The colors of beautiful blue lace agates and orange citrines sang out to me. The guides said the crystals symbolized a collection of energies—all soothing and uplifting, purifying and transmuting. They looked as though you could put them into your bathing water, as though they would recharge the water and purify you.

I was told they offered cleansing and protection, and so I visualized popping them into a bath, and hopped in. Duly cleansed and protected I hung them back on the doorknob and opened the door. I stepped through into incense and sunshine.

Arlo's Story
SACRED Scrolls and Crystal SKULLS

I was in the library of the Great Temple. It was a huge room filled with the tranquil and uplifting fragrance of incense, and as I looked around I could see lazy spirals of the sweet-smelling smoke catching in shafts of afternoon sunlight. I knew this library held many scrolls. Its long tables were bathed in light and covered with opened scrolls, some being studied and others in the process of being copied. Had it been a day dedicated to one of the female deities things would have been different, you would have found the priestesses busy here—but this was the day of Mars and so it was priests who were working away all around me, heads down, in this hive of silent industry ... as the incense slowly burned.[60]

---

[60] Sunday, Marsday (Tuesday), and Zeusday (Thursday) were for priests; Moonday, Mercuryday (Wednesday), and Heraday (Friday) were for priestesses. Saturnday being the holy day, priestesses and priests would all be busy elsewhere. Mercury was not female but was a hermaphrodite god, combining both male and female characteristics, as did some of the emperors. When this gene surfaced in people, they were regarded as "one of the old ones," a throwback to an earlier

Each scroll was beautifully made by hand, richly ornamented with gold leaf and painted in fine colors, and this was where we kept them, made them, and studied them in an atmosphere of great reverence. Some precious scrolls were very old, but they were all well looked after and methodically stored, each in its own copper tube which had such a close-fitting lid that it was almost air-tight.

For me it was always a joy to be in this beautiful and harmonious place.

For I was now Arlo.

I was nineteen, and I knew I always looked forward to my hours spent here.

Rolling up the scroll I had been studying, I dropped it carefully into its exquisitely chased scroll tube and replaced the burnished lid. I took a last, lingering look at the other silent figures still busy pouring over their work, and from nowhere I felt a moment of sadness. I had been in training at the temple all my life, but as I looked around me now I knew this was the last time I would ever be a student here. Then I thought about the evening, and there came a surge of excitement.

My father was a priest and my mother a priestess, and I had been born into the priestly class through Hieros Gamos, the sacred union of Temple Marriage, when mortals are temporarily overshadowed by gods during ritual. But not all sons of the temple conceived in this way were suited to be priests, and some had to find other work. But I had been blessed with the gifts necessary for success. I had inherited a strong mind, strong inner powers, and a very good memory—and it was felt that I could reach beyond myself to the gods. I was adept at scrying, and this was regarded as such an important skill that the training for it began early in childhood. Children love to play make-believe games, and one we had all been encouraged to play involved looking into crystals or bowls of water then talking about what we saw. This was made to be fun when we were little, but it had taught us to expect to see things and even to follow through with a story expanding on what we saw, to be open to a stream of knowing.

The library was an important part of the main temple complex

___

time. I had first-hand experience of this in a life after Atlantis had been reduced to the archipelago stage.

in Atlanta, and the temple's students all came here to learn about the past, the laws, and the scriptures, and to learn of the events, rituals, and festivals of the year—but above all it was where the scrolls were made; and although the temple already had a great many scrolls, they always needed more. They sent them out to lesser temples all over Atlantis and dispatched them to the countries of the empire. It was an attempt to educate the rough foreigners with our religion. The foreigners were then expected to incorporate the ideas into their own religious beliefs, albeit in a watered-down form, and it was meant to bring cohesion to religious worship all over the empire. But because they were allowed to keep their indigenous beliefs—well, it would have been impossible to eradicate them even if we'd tried—there were wide variations from country to country.

Our empire was far flung over the known world, and if we'd left it to its own devices it would have presented a wild and wonderful rag-bag of clashing cultures and belief systems. As we saw it, this was a way to bring a little harmony, a way to promote a shared understanding.[61]

Working with the sacred scrolls was one of my favorite tasks.

I had been told of the importance of diligence in their making, because if they were not done right then they would not be blessed, and nor would they be sent out. But I had plenty of patience and a very firm hand and I had grown skilled. From an early age, I found that creating beauty was its own reward, and the hours just flew by whenever I was busy in the library.

I'd finished my studies for the day and gone over to the scroll racks to slot the tube back into its rightful place, when one of the other students came up to me and whispered in my ear, "Are you ready for this afternoon?"

I whisper back, "I am," for it is true, I have finished my work. There's nothing more needing to be done, and with that, arm in arm, we leave the serenely peaceful atmosphere of the library and head off toward the refectory in search of an early lunch. We've been the best of friends for years, and we are both filled with the same

---

61 However, in the other countries it was seen quite differently, and it was hard for them not to feel the gods of their ancestors insulted. In time the deities would merge, but like the Old Norse gods, they often kept their old names although they acquired characteristics from the Atlantean counterparts.

mounting excitement.

We are to be ordained. This is the moment our lives have been leading up to ever since we can remember. We have come through the rigorous training, testing, and selection process and now we are ready to make our commitment to the temple and become priests. It's all I've ever known or ever wanted; and after the midday meal we go to change into new robes and get ready.

While we prepare, people are already gathering in the temple. It has been set out with rows of wooden benches arranged in two sets of concentric semicircles, facing each other. People are shown to their seats, and there they wait, quietly talking among themselves in respectful and hushed tones, until the head priest takes up his seat in a commanding position in the center.

Silence falls.

He is the pivot around which coming events will turn. He commands enormous respect. Behind him benches fill rapidly with priests—to his right—and priestesses—to his left—and those representing the royal family are seated on the high thrones brought in which tower up behind him.

The benches in front are for the public, though we novices have the very front row. Anyone can come to witness this ceremony of the Taking of the Vows, and so it's a mix of curious bystanders and proud parents that have assembled to watch. Twenty-five men are to be ordained this Marsday in March, the month of Mars. Seven are temple sons, like me, the rest of the novices having been drawn from other walks of life, after being brought to the temple to start their training in early childhood.

There is singing, then an address by the head priest.

One by one we novices go forward to stand in front of him to take our vows of allegiance to the gods, the temple, and the people. Each of us is asked the same question. In a commanding voice the head priest intones:

"By the power entrusted in me by the deities and aspects of the Divine, I hereby accept thee as a full member of the temple family. Here to safeguard the people, the family of the Creator. Here to be the Creator's steward, to help, to guide, to bring happiness and harmony, to bring wisdom and light. Here to help the beauty and wonder of the Divine filter down to all the people. Here to work hard and to play your part, and to do it all with a pure heart. Will ye accept this?"

And when my turn comes I reply, "I will," and I go on to pledge:

"I will do this to the best of my abilities for all the days of my life. I will always put the needs of the temple first and the needs of the people first and my own needs last."

Even as I say it I know the temple will always look after me, but I do feel it is truly a privilege to be a priest, to have that power vested in me, to work for the Divine, to bring happiness and harmony to people and to be a bridge between them and the highest.

I kneel down before the head priest and a ring is put on my finger to seal my service. I kiss the head priest's ring, stand up, and join the ranks of the other priests.

And from that moment on Arlo is no more.

I die to my old life and am born into my new life as a priest.

My name takes on the priestly form, as all names do after the vows, and I know I will never be called Arlo again. It is as Arlos I proudly take my place near the head priest's right hand, and I feel euphoric. Swept along on the energy of the moment I feel taller and bigger—I have achieved my dreams at last!

This is the night everything changes for me. Now I truly belong to the temple. Body and soul, I belong, the contract has been sealed and witnessed before the gods, the royal family, and the entire temple hierarchy.

Up to this point nothing had bound either party, and so I could have left to pursue other lines of work, or been asked to leave. But later that night as the euphoria faded, I was dogged by a persistent and nagging doubt. There was one initiation left to complete. So the question as to exactly *what form* my service was going take had not yet been settled, it depended on the outcome of the test ... and although I tried not to worry ... I found it increasingly harder to hang on to my priestly equanimity.

However, *whatever* happened at the initiation I was no longer a novice and my new standing was reflected in how I was presented to the world. The knotted, trailing cord at my waist had been replaced by a neat belt with a small gold buckle. And in addition to my simple white robe I had been given a coat with a hood like a cowl. The narrow gold braid that bound its edges conveyed authority, and from the point of the hood hung a golden tassel. From now on, this would be mine to wear for outdoor ceremonies and for visiting the community or even the palace.

Priests did a lot of going out into the community. We blessed homes and babies; administered the last rites to the dying; did wedding blessings and married people in their homes; and with our knowledge of the laws and by the power of our authority we could settle disputes. We gave advice when we were asked. We could be called into situations, such as when husbands and wives were not getting along, to try to help them find their happiness again—perhaps with words of advice and a blessing for the home.

We were the Divine's foot soldiers in the battle against unhappiness, discord, and evil in the world. Mars was the god of war, and it was to enlist his help in that battle that priests were always ordained on his day. God's soldiers carried no weapons, but they lived in violent times and had developed the arts of Mars. These martial arts meant that we could defend ourselves, the weak, and the worshippers in the temple. We trained rigorously and learned to focus and manipulate an energy that lies within us that we called "God's power."[62] Visitors came to our city from all over the world, and we never knew who might come into our famed Great Temple with what crazy idea, to desecrate or to steal. We did have armed temple guards, but as the guards weren't priests they were usually in the outer reaches of the temple, and you never knew where or when trouble might come—it didn't wait to be invited.

The last part of the initiation was going to take place tomorrow in the Holy of Holies. There were thirteen parts to the test,

62 Today we call it "the chi."

and if I didn't pass them all I couldn't help but feel that all my years of study had been wasted. I was the temple's now, and there was no turning back on that, so if I couldn't serve fully as a priest then I would have to serve in some other capacity … cooking, cleaning, administration … my heart sank. Humility and obedience might be virtues, but … disappointment prickled and I tried not to think about what might happen. Tomorrow would come soon enough … and my thoughts went to the test that lay ahead. It was with the thirteen skulls.

I had a restless night. And when I did sleep it was shallow. Several times I woke from anxious dreams involving skulls.

The next day I returned to the temple at the appointed hour. I couldn't help but feel nervous, despite the herbal draught I'd been given to lift my spirits. A comforting cup of the holy herb Vervain had been administered to calm my nerves and ease my anxiety. I knew it would help to open me to the other world too, and help with my labors there. So I'd welcomed the warmth of the reviving infusion though I'd no stomach for food.

Climbing the main entrance steps, I came to the doorway, and passing through the shadows of the open double doors I entered the calm light-filled space that lay inside. I found incense burning in great abundance, offerings to the gods to bring success.

Fragrant clouds were billowing off bowls of smoking resin set out on the altars of the chapels around the walls. I closed my eyes and savored the scent of frankincense, felt it calm my breathing, felt it wash away the tightness that had taken root in my chest and shoulders since first light. I breathed in the cleansing incense deeply and thankfully, and sighing, let my tension flow out with a deep heart-felt breath.

Feeling bolder, I walked swiftly across the beautiful floor awash with the light from many windows, and I passed beneath the open dome in the center of the temple. The dome was the highest point, it reached up to the heavens and to the Divine, and through its open center the Divine could reach down and bless the people.

My studies had taught me that when the Divine had breathed out Creation, the Divine's energies had first poured out as divine light, becoming physical light as the frequencies dropped. It was then that the worlds coalesced and time began. The twins *Night* and *Day* were born out of divine light: Zeus was *Night* and his sister Hera was *Day*.[63] They were two halves of the perfect whole—Hera was light manifest and Zeus was light as yet unmanifest, potential light, and as such he was closer to the frequency of divine light. Thus his was the higher power.

Hera loved the sun, giver of light in the material world, and from their union sprang all the female deities, each embodying an aspect or attribute of her female energy. Zeus loved the moon, receiver of light in the material world, and from their union sprang all the male gods, each embodying an aspect or attribute of his male energy. They were painted together, Zeus and Hera, holding hands

---

63 Long ago a cosmic event of planetary billiards brought Saturn to prominence in our skies and garlanded it with rings, and tilted Earth's axis. Saturn's new appearance coincided with the coming of marked seasons, equinoxes and solstices, and an understanding of the yearly calendar evolved; for the Atlanteans Saturn was equated with time, Saturn became Father Time. The Atlanteans studied time and counted days. Days were powerful forces that built on each other to create years, and nights were powerful forces that punctuated the days and enabled them to be separate and countable. Hence time was important and gave progression and so progress. The days progressed and the discoveries and achievements of the days built knowledge and culture and enabled the Atlanteans to unite, and unite the world. Father Time was the father of their empire, and his children Night and Day were their allies enabling them to conquer and subjugate the world to their will. They revered Father Time and saw him as their friend as he had brought them everything. But with the skulls they could transcend time and look ahead into the future and behind into the past, so the skulls were regarded as being more important even than time, and related more directly to the Divine—therefore they were **very** revered.

The Atlanteans believed it was when the divine light formed Saturn that Night and Day were born, so Saturn (Time) was father to Zeus and Hera (Night and Day). Although they were composed of the energy of the body of the Divine (i.e., divine light), they were brought into being / given life through the agency of Saturn. This was why he was regarded as their father. His intervention and formation brought them into being as his energies split when they reached the Earth, and day and night were born here from the Earth's body. Earth was their mother and they were born from her spin caused by Saturn's influence.

Today we still talk about Saturn being old Father Time.

This is why Saturnday was the holy day.

Saturn was in the center of the temple, depicted in a mosaic on the temple's floor, and black-and-white squares, representing his children spun from him in a radial design.

in a joyous eternal dance high above the temple, around the inside of the dome. They danced the days round, night into day, into night, into day …

They loved each other and longed for each other, but day must die for night to be born and night must die for day. It was an endless cycle of death and rebirth. They could never be together, only their fingers touched, in the east and in the west, as fingers of light slipped into the end of night's reign, and fingers of night crept into the evening sky as day slipped away.

Hera was painted dancing the sunlight-filled days of Creation as her consort, the sun, shone high in the sky, while Zeus danced the nights through all the moon's phases, his spirit force and essence conveying the magic and mystery of male power.[64] His unmanifest body was depicted by a strong outline drawn in the night sky through which stars shone,[65] while Hera was shown in all her glory wearing a sun disc as a headdress and clothed in a flowing gown of clouds patterned with rainbows, clasped on the right shoulder by a sun broach, and gathered in at the waist by a belt of sun discs. Beneath her was carefully scripted:

I AM DAY AND EMBODY THE LIGHT

The Great Temple was Zeus and Hera's temple. But as the years passed, Hera had become ever more popular. Not that Zeus was forgotten, never that, for his *was* the higher power, but it was the sunlit image of her beauty that greeted all visitors as they first set foot inside the temple and looked up to marvel … *and it was she who was guardian to the skulls.* Hera was Mother to the people of Atlantis, their Great Mother, and it was no wonder that people had come to call it the Temple of Hera, I thought—and I draw comfort from her smile; and silently I ask her for her help in the test that is to

---

64 Think how awesome a thunderstorm is at night—that's how they saw Zeus's power. Beneath his depiction was written I AM NIGHT AND EMBODY THE POWER (meaning the power of the Divine).

65 The largest planet in our solar system, Jupiter the gas giant, is perfectly suited to represent the unmanifest nature of the Atlanteans' Zeus. (Jupiter/Zeus are the same god, and we only call the planet Jupiter instead of Zeus because it was the Romans, not the Greeks, who brought their language to Britain.)

come.

I continue on my way, heading straight to the chapel of Mars. Fierce Mars guards the access to the skulls, and no one comes to them but through him—and so it is to Mars that I go. I see two elder priests waiting for me there. They rise to their feet to meet me. The taller one speaks:

"In the name of Mars I greet thee, Arlos. Will ye continue?"

And I respond with, "Aye, I will."

"Then follow."

And with that the priest turns and goes behind the altar, where a stone slab has been moved to one side revealing an ancient stone staircase leading down beneath the temple. The silent elder remains as guardian of the entrance, and both the priest and I disappear down worn steps.

It is darker and cooler down there, and the steps give out on to a passageway. Our footsteps slap and echo in the gloom as we make our way along, heading toward a pool of light that is spilling out of an opening on the right. I feel the air freshen and move softly against my skin. We draw level with the light.

I am motioned to step through.

Alone, I enter a torch-lit cave. This is the Holy of Holies, where the skulls had been found in a circle, half buried in the fine white sand of the floor, long, long ago in the mists of time. It is a womb in the Earth, a sacred place. This is the skulls' home and it is where they stay, except for special occasions, when they are displayed in the temple above.[66] The ancient kings of the Atlans had consulted them as an oracle, and had benefited from their advice, eventually conquering all the other kingdoms on the continent and going on to conquer the world. It is the power of the skulls that lies behind the power of the emperor ... that, I know full well—*and now I can see them all looking down on me from the center of the cave.*

I am held in the sightless gaze of thirteen quartz skulls lined up on the high altar ... and as I stand there transfixed, fragments from my dreams come flashing back, wild images haunt me now ...

---

66 Although they had been found on the floor, the floor was now taken up by a central altar table, so when the skulls were in their cave, unless they were being used on the altar table they were carefully put in specially carved niches in the cave wall behind the altar.

I feel small and frozen. My stomach lurches. I forget to breathe.

They are staring right at me.

I feel the sharp-eyed scrutiny of the head priest upon me.

I am being watched by those stationed around the walls.

I have dreaded this moment.

This is the divine test.

I've passed the human test, but now I have to pass the divine—*will the gods speak to me through the skulls? Well, will they??*

I know for certain some priests fail. Again, I pray silently that this will not happen to me.

This is my formal introduction to the family of skulls, and they all need to accept me. They present an eerie sight, the crystal of their gaunt skull faces catching the movements of the living light from the torches on the walls. The one in the center glows from within and I know it to be Bah Ha Redo, because we've already worked together—and I know you won't get far in the priesthood if this one doesn't approve of you. Six sit on either side of Bah, I recognize some of them from our lessons in scrying.

I have been told the skulls will look into my heart, my mind, and my spirit and know everything about me. *It is a very daunting thought.* I feel an anxious sweat break out.

I bow low in greeting, and keeping my head down out of respect, I climb slowly up the altar steps. I know the test is going to begin and end with the skull in the middle, and I hope it is a friend because of the work we've done together.

But who knows if a skull thinks like that?

I try to calm and center myself.

I can feel the tension in the air, and the palpable weight of expectation. Torches flicker. The white-robed figures of the elders stay still as they patiently wait to hear what the skulls will reveal this time.

And then suddenly all my training floods back.

I put my thoughts to one side, focus on my breath, still my mind, shift my level of consciousness, and silently but politely introduce myself to Bah Ha Redo, and ask permission to contact the other skulls for the testing I need to do.

One by one the skulls are moved over the hole in the center of the altar table through which light comes from below. This causes the skull to glow and the structure of its crystal to come alive in the light. With each one I am asked a question, and I have to communicate with the skull to find the answer. Sometimes it comes in words, but often in pictures. Some are best for healing, others for questions of the future, or the past, and it is while I am working with a healing skull that I am asked what I would do if someone had a particular disease. As I gaze into the skull it shows me plants—healing herbs—and gives information which I relay to the priests. And when I've worked with them all, Bah Ha Redo goes back over the light, but this time it is the head priest who looks for the answer. He intones:

"Do you accept this priest to work with the family of the skulls?"

I suck in my breath and hold it. I don't know if I've got the answers right, or indeed, what it is showing the head priest now, and I can't help but wonder what else might be being asked of the skull in silence. *To show the fruits of my labors to come? The fruits of my life?* But whatever it is, the answer is acceptable, and it is with great relief that I receive the special handshake from all those gathered there. One by one they grip my hand while their other hand holds my wrist, and they say, "Welcome, my brother, welcome to the family of the priests."

And then at last my ordeal is over and I am free to go.

I stepped out into the passageway, heady with relief, and this time took the turning that would take me toward the priests' quarters. I was in search of food and rest, and a chance to catch up with my friends who'd gone before me. I was longing to hear how they'd got on.

As my joyful footsteps pattered away into the distance I could hear chimes being struck to summon the next candidate. This process would continue over the next few days until the skulls had finished testing all twenty-five new priests. I'd been lucky I hadn't had to wait longer.

My appetite was back and I enjoyed the meal, though it was spiced with the usual amount of calming herbs. The chasteberry spice[67] was employed not for its taste but because it sustained equanimity. It suppressed sexual desire; it directed energy from the lower chakras to the higher ones; it helped the priests to be less rooted in the Earth and more in the heavens. It made my job easier, but taking it wasn't a matter of choice.

When I caught up with my friends I found they'd all met with success, so there was laughter and happiness all around. We gave thanks to the gods, the skulls, and the temple. And later, as I lay back on my bed in my sparse white room, waiting for sleep to come, my mind wandered back over the last few months. It had been a very strenuous period of time, what with the endless testing and all the work that had had to be done before the ceremony. But I found myself surprised at how quick the initiation with the skulls had actually been. Perhaps it was because they were already woken up and ready for work, or perhaps Bah Ha Redo had told them all I was there after I'd introduced myself—so they were expecting to work with me, but they had been extraordinarily cooperative. I felt excited about the future and pleased with my success. And my head was full of happy thoughts when I drifted off to sleep.

In time I would come to learn of the four skulls of the elements, but working with them was not part of my service. The head priest had the close dealings with them, often under orders from the emperor. They had no place in healing but they led to understanding of the ways of things. They linked to the agencies of nature and summoned beings for negotiation that could take place through the thirteen. They had power, but it was not always of harmony. They had in them the seeds of danger. I knew they had to be contained, and I had felt no pull toward them or their secrets. I avoided them and their incipient darkness, though I liked the thirteen and worked with them all my life. For they were of the element ether, the higher realm through which all must come before manifestation took place on the earthly plane. They held within them the light and harmony of the realms of the gods from whence they came, and this was why the gods spoke through them, why they brought healing, and why they could transcend time with the visions shown within their crystal

67   Vitex Agnus Castus, monk's pepper.

bodies. They were holy, and it pleased me to be their servant.

The years that followed were busy and full, and fell one by one like autumn leaves, beautiful but spent. I enjoyed my life at the temple and found the years of hard work and service worthwhile. I liked helping people, I felt pleasure in helping the Divine's plan work out in the world, pleasure in working with the skulls and in the beautiful things of the temple. I found joy in the manuscripts and scrolls, in both reading and writing them, in the beauty of their words and images, and in the truths that they held.

And down the years I attended many more Taking of the Vows ceremonies, but this time as witness not as novice. Then my thoughts would stray to the evening I had taken my own, and I had no regrets as I looked back. Most of all I'd loved learning about the importance of beauty. Beauty imbued everything we did. We wore very simple clothes but they were beautiful, and the Great Temple itself was very beautiful. Things were simple, but we poured our hearts out into them to make them as beautiful as they could be, whether it was words that were said or a service that was offered, and people would be touched by that. I'd often been called into a home where there was conflict between husband and wife, but because of the beauty of my words and my spirit and my transparent longing to help them, they would actually stop and listen and start to treat each other differently. I would visit once a day for a week, and then once a day every other week, and I would see things getting better. The love that had been there in the beginning when they made their union would begin to flow once more, and it was as if they re-found each other. Their houses would be filled with more love, and the change was there for all to see in the growing happiness of their children, and everything just got better and better. I loved bringing beauty and harmony to the people, to the ceremonies, and to everything I did.

Gentle soul that I was, there came a day when I was swept up in a traumatic and shocking event that shook me to my core.

I was helping out in the skulls' cave as one of the silent ones who stood round the walls, guarding, when the king of Persia came for a seeing. But, unfortunately, he didn't like what he saw and his mood turned very ugly. "It's all trickery and falsehood!" he shouted, looking like thunder and with a very red face, and brandishing his sword he attempted to kill us all.

Using the arts of Mars we threw him to the floor, took his sword, and restrained him.

Word was sent to the palace.

This was so serious an offense we wondered if the emperor himself might come, but it was his guards who arrived and took the king into custody, bringing word that there would be a trial the following day.

By now it had become a political affair and was beyond the jurisdiction of the temple.

Fortunately, no blood had been shed, but it had been an unspeakable violation in the Holiest of Holies. At the trial, we bore witness as to exactly what had happened, and there had been no trickery. We had no means to influence what he saw, and nor did we see what he saw. That was his alone. So there was no telling what had enraged him. But we suspected a very guilty conscience, and that something had been revealed that he didn't want known. In his panic, he had mistakenly assumed we all knew his shameful secret, and he thought to silence us forever.

It was up to the emperor to determine punishment. For trying to kill priests, dishonoring the temple, and breaking his sacred oath of kingship and allegiance, there was only one possible outcome. Such a transgression meant he'd forfeited his crown and his life. He was too unworthy to live and not fit to be king, and so with his hands tied behind his back he was executed.

He had been visiting with his son-in-training, and before his son sailed home he was crowned king in his father's stead at an investiture ceremony in the Great Temple. The terrifying example had been necessary to protect the empire. It had to be understood that the laws were there to keep everybody safe, and that they had to be kept. It wasn't a matter of choice, even for a king.

The incident troubled me greatly at the time, and I tried to bury it and attempted to forget about it. I busied myself in service, and the years slipped by until I was fifty-six.

One afternoon I was on duty at the temple. I always loved being there, and I sat in tranquility in the chapel of Mars, waiting to see who would come to be helped that day. My friend should have been with me, because we worked in pairs, but he hadn't felt well after lunch and had gone to lie down, leaving me on my own waiting patiently for his replacement to arrive.

The stone behind the altar was back in its proper place and everything was quiet and peaceful. I was wearing my simple white robe, a hat of office, and round my neck hung the ecclesiastical stole of colored satin signifying that I was on duty, when all of a sudden a figure stepped into the peace of the temple.

I first saw the bulky silhouette in the doorway. The man had a muscular body swathed in a big cloak, though the day was hot—and his unkempt dark hair looked as ratty and stiff as a bird's nest. He looked disturbed. He was muttering to himself when he entered the temple, but soon his voice grew louder and he was babbling wildly in a strange tongue. The acoustics carried the incomprehensible sounds over to me ... and I could tell he was consumed by anger.

Trouble!

Seeking to protect the gold on the altars and the sacred things, I rose to my feet, yanking a rope that rang a bell elsewhere to summon assistance, then I stepped out of the chapel. I'd had to deal with many an angry husband when doing my outreach work in the community, but even the most brutish Atlantean treated priests with respect. I held my hand up to the stranger, palm out, projecting a chi screen as defense, and with the other hand I made a gesture as if to say:

"Peace be with you, my friend."

But the very sight of a priest enraged the possessing demons within the stranger further, and brandishing a knife from under his cloak he stabbed me in the chest.

I fell to the floor, the white of my robe staining red.

Seconds later soldiers poured into the temple in hot pursuit, and overpowered the madman by sheer force. They did what they could for me until the priests arrived, but I continued losing blood.

Over the next few days I hovered in and out of life.

The priests did their best, but even with the assistance of the skulls I remained critical. I was very weak. In the half-life I now inhabited I mixed with Hera and Mars.[68] I felt Mars's dark but

68 Arlos was in his inner world now, where archetypal energies readily

107

comforting presence with me, and was aware of the willowy Hera's wisdom and laughter. Hera told me gently that there was nothing more I needed to learn or achieve in my life, that I had done all I had set out to do, and I was now free to go on and prepare for my next incarnation. She said I'd learned willingness to offer service and to help people ... and for sure I could have had more years of this service, but really there was no need.

From Mars I came to understand that although I had tried to defend myself, it had been against no mere mortal man. Possessed by demons the madman's energy was so strange and fierce that the chi screen had had little effect, its energy just not sufficient to counter what was being projected by the multiple beings enmeshed within the stranger. An unfortunate chain of events had unfolded elsewhere, causing a failure of temple security in the outer levels. People were in the wrong places at the wrong time, and the man had been able to burst through, and those who should have apprehended him were the ones who came running after him just moments too late.

The situation posed a problem for the priests.

It was a very serious offense, and so the man would not be leaving the city alive, but he couldn't just be killed or the possession would migrate into someone else. They would have to find the boat he'd come off and the rest of the crew—that's if they hadn't deliberately left him and already fled.

The skulls would be consulted as to what should be done.

It took a few days all told before the matter was settled, but for me there was no problem. When I was ready I allowed Hera and Mars to guide me on my way, and I left behind a world enriched by the beauty of my life.

... And enriched by the beauty of the scrolls I'd so loved to make. But perhaps it was the scrolls that had stirred up a hornets' nest in a far-off land, and brought hornets winging their way to anthropomorphize. Hera and Mars had become his inner guides, and this experience was shaped by his training and culture. Illusion and expectation often influence our experiences around death, like they did for Ahmet before him, and no doubt they will do for us, when our time comes. Perhaps we'll see angels, Jesus, Mother Mary, or loved ones who have gone before us into spirit ... it's a subjective truth, but it *is* a truth nonetheless, and *a comfort to lessen the shock of transition*; a gentle gift from a loving Creator, smoothing our passage home.

Atlanta with the ship and the man ... had the gods of *his* ancestors been insulted? I wonder.

Chapter 5

Chronicles of Atlantis 4

Reflections on the Last Chapter

So, I'd been a priest at the Temple of Hera, which might explain why the very first time I meditated on a skull-related question it was Hera who came to give me the answer. At the time I didn't realize who she was. I just thought she was another helpful guide, but it was wonderfully appropriate that she came and I only realized who she was later. I felt very humble and grateful.

I had asked to know the names of the skulls.

Later I would come to realize there is no simple answer to that question because each dimensional level of a skull has its own name (and sometimes several). It turned out that the names she gave me were the ones "her children"—the people of Atlantis—had used to call them by, because these were the names she remembered with the greatest affection.

The guides had made me wait until session 9 out of the initial ten for *Holy Ice* before they let me access the priest's story. I had expected paranormal pyrotechnics and all manner of exciting things, and was surprised and humbled to find a simple tale of service and marriage guidance.[69] Arlos was sweet-natured, sensitive, and rather effete. The calming herbs he was force-fed in his meals contributed to this, and his story had shown the four most exciting days of what was a very tranquil(ized) life.

---

69 The door into the life had been purple, the color of the crown chakra, through which we link to higher spheres. The delicate filigree plate around the polished knob symbolized all the beauty in the life; and the high gloss finish, being modern, links to the fact that so much from then continues on now and goes into the future with us, like *the days of the gods*. The life and the door were framed by gold.

He had been conceived in a sacred ritual on the summer solstice in June. ("June" comes to us from "Juno," which is what the Romans called Hera.) So he was conceived in the month of Hera, and like all sons and daughters of the temple, forty weeks later he was born during the moon of Mars (March).

The sacred ritual was Hieros Gamos.[70]

Temple children would all have been Pisces, like me. My sun and moon are both in Pisces and it is a very otherworldly sign ruled by Jupiter, the Romans' version of Zeus.[71] Ideal for priests and priestesses, and helpful if your task is to unite the spiritual and material worlds through your writing, but when it comes to dealing with life in the outer world—well, let's just say I'm very thankful for my Taurus rising and Mars in Leo, I can tell you! I used to think my birth sign was a liability but that was before I came to understand myself better. When I found my true work, I realized it was a gift to help me with what I had come to do.

The practice of Hieros Gamos doubled up the psi ability in the gene pool and kept increasing it over the generations. It was selective breeding of the most adept. Also it meant temple children, although they were mortal, could think of themselves as sons of Zeus and daughters of Hera, and kin to the lesser gods.

When Arlos died he'd encountered the crude forces of chaos that stalk the world, and he died puzzled.[72] But his death was not for want of spiritual power, as neither would Jesus's death be in an age that had yet to come. There is karma, there is new karma, and there is volunteering to take on karma out of service to the world. The murderer made new karma for himself, which would have to be worked through later, and in a future life Arlos would have his life saved by a miraculous quirk of fate that would balance the karmic books and make it up to him,[73] while dear Jesus's death was out of service to the world.

---

70 The priestesses conceived at dawn as the sun was rising on the longest day. Dawn and dusk were the only times Zeus and Hera (Night and Day) could be together, and in Hieros Gamos all the priests were Zeus and all the priestesses were Hera during the sexual act in the sacred ritual.

71 Neptune only became co-ruler in the nineteenth century, when it was discovered.

72 As in: What went wrong? How have I failed?

73 A factor at play in chapter 7.

When I consider how Arlos surfaces in my personality, I can see that I have him to thank for extending my link with the crystal skulls. I like bringing beauty into the world too, as he did, which is why I trained as an artist and why I like to use my particular form of past life healing, where angels, beautiful colors, and transfusions of divine light are invited into the energy fields and lives of my clients. There are many other ways to do past life work, but some I consider quite brutal.[74] Each has its followers, and in a restaurant we wouldn't all pick the same dish from the menu. All that matters is that the method used suits you and your client.

Arlos's story is important because it shows how the Atlanteans exported their ways of doing things and their religious beliefs—it was by way of the scrolls. They sought to harmonize their empire, and much of the hidden Atlantean legacy has come down to us today because of the scrolls' influence on the more stable cultures of the world at that time.

Any culture evolved enough to have fortified strongholds, cities, or ports was of interest to Atlantis for her empire, because it was suitably organized to collect taxes for her, and permanently anchored so the inhabitants could not just melt away into the forests and hide, or migrate, without losing everything they had built up. The tax collectors knew exactly where to return each year, and they would have destroyed the settlement if the people did not enter into a bargaining process to establish the amount of taxation they were able to render in slaves, goods, food, furs, materials, or metals.

The more stable the other culture was, the longer the knowledge and customs lingered on after Atlantis had gone.

74 Particularly methods that use catharsis as a way to release the emotions and pain from previous lives. These energies can be discharged painlessly and safely directly from the higher bodies where they are stored. There is no need to bring them down to make them discharge through the current physical form. It was bad enough the first time around, if you were skinned alive or butchered, there's no need to go through it again. Why embed a trauma? Why hit your client with a cardboard tube to intensify the feelings of agony to make them scream louder? It is so cruel and primitive and unnecessary and unhelpful. It is like forcing lightning to strike you when there was no need for the storm in the first place. You need to know what happened, but you can review it without the pain, watch it like a film or a play and then do the healing needed (as in psycho-regression). There are various people teaching past life work who use catharsis. Certainly Diane Park did.

Customs passed into folk memory, and much is still concealed in plain sight, such as in names and words that have come down to us. When we marvel at the cultures of ancient Egypt, pre-classical and classical Greece and Rome, what we see is Atlantis—or a reflection and development of her legacy. Without the influence of the scrolls made by priestesses and priests such as Arlos our world would certainly be a much less familiar place today.

However, keeping long records can also be a curse: the ever-growing mountain of rules and laws passed by emperor after emperor came to weigh down Atlantis. The culture grew rigid and set as hard as bones that the coming changes could only fracture and break. Inflexibility became cherished as a means of protection, and a time of unease lay ahead.

The door to this next session was a deep sea-blue, and it was old fashioned and paneled.

I turn the antique black ceramic knob, open the door, and step through.

A black sky stretches overhead bearing the moon in its last quarter.

A dark sea sparkles in the moonlight ... and I am now a young woman, Ayesha,[75] excited, naked, and hurrying toward the tide ...

Ayesha's Story

HARVESTING the Energies of LIGHT

Summer came and as the laws decreed I took my guards and servants with me to the lodge in one of the northern provinces. The journey to Helvia was long, and though I'd shared my carriage with friends, by the time we arrived at our destination I was desperate for a little time

---

75 Said: eye-A-sha.

by myself. I spotted my chance after dinner. My friends were busy choosing their rooms and claiming their luggage as it came in off the carts, and the guards had just sat down to eat at the newly emptied dining tables. Seizing the moment, with a hasty word to the guards, I slipped out into the gardens and took off on my own.

I was pleased to be back.

I loved my lodge and I loved my province, and I was eager to see the changes a year had wrought in my garden.

It was a lovely warm evening and I wandered down through the terraces, admiring curtains of jasmine and pots of geraniums, drifts of bright poppies and clouds of white lilies, and as I passed among the flowers I allowed their colors and fragrance to revive me. I cupped them in my hands and inhaled heady white stars of jasmine; I stroked silken petals with delicate fingers.

The soft golden glow of sunset was fading by the time I stepped down into the herb garden. In the dusk, I found spears of fresh mint shooting up between clumps of basil and sage, and I crushed aromatic leaves between my fingers and savored their pungent scent. With my hands full of herbs, I looked out over the walls of the terrace, admiring first the stars above me and then the sea below me—and after the long dusty days of the roads, an irresistible urge to frolic in the waves swept over me.

But with my next breath my heart sank.

I remembered. In this matter, as in all else, first there was the question of the rules to be obeyed. And what did they tell me here? *They said I should not swim alone.* Dutifully, I set the impulse aside, and returned to the lodge to see who would accompany me.

I find everyone busy.

My friends had retired for the night, my maids are upstairs unpacking my clothes, and my guards are sitting around the dining tables, no longer eating, but now fully engrossed in board games and dice games and enjoying a drink.

I love the lodge because it is the one place where you can let your hair down after the strictures of life at court—and it's the first time the guards have been off duty in such a long while, what with all the traveling, it seems a shame to disturb them—so using this as an excuse I decide to have an adventure!

I hasten on foot to the beach.

Down through the gardens ... over the scrub land ... down to the rocks and the sand. Wriggling out of my clothes I leave them weighted with rocks, and I run down the sands to the moonlit ocean, past shells bleached white as bones. Standing tall in the lacy swirl of the surf I am exhilarated by my sudden freedom and enchanted by the magic of the night. I breathe deeply in the cool fresh air, and at last I feel truly alive.

All I wear is the gold of my magnificent jewelry, and with heavy bracelets gleaming I raise my arms in supplication to the sea. Restless waves caress me and pull at my ankles, and with all my heart I cry out the sacred incantation to Poseidon: I beseech him for a sign. Then I plunge into the waters, refreshed by their sharpness and comforted by their embrace; my long hair floats as gracefully as a mermaid's tresses as it wafts in the pull of the tide. I am quite alone, although the rules utterly forbid it.

I always feel free in the sea. I float in silence, listening to it.

Like all my family I desire to be on intimate terms with Poseidon, the god whose domain it is. For long ages past we have regarded the sea as our friend and our ally, and with its help we have gained riches and power, but we all know there are now prophecies of grave concern, foretelling that the sea will come to take our land, and my people live with this great fear.

We seek ways to keep it happy and give Poseidon gifts, and I have come tonight hoping Poseidon will tell me if the sea is still happy here. The swish, swish of the waves surrounds me like a soothing lullaby, and I gladly surrender to their movement, allowing the sea to carry me. I drift as the black sky arches overhead and the moon sparkles in the restless waters. I float, waiting for a sign.

A small dolphin swims up to me and I frolic with my new playmate. I am enjoying myself, pleased with this auspicious omen, when the rest of the pod arrives and joins in our games.

Poseidon has sent his answer.

The sea must be **very** happy here if he'd seen fit to send so many dolphins to me! And I was glad it was good news for the emperor, because I liked to please my father.

I was a good swimmer and it was with a light heart that I

played with the dolphins now, drifting down into the water and then racing back up to the surface with them. But although it was great fun, after a while I grew tired and decided it was time to go back.

There were those in my family who could communicate with dolphins fluently, so I tried to bid them farewell with both sound and thought as I'd been taught. I sensed them laughing—but I knew they were always pleased when someone made the effort, and I hoped I would see them again.

I swam for the shore and decided to return the next day, in the hope of them still being around, although I wouldn't have the luxury of being on my own for a second time. Freedom and spontaneity were rare commodities at court, and there were precious few opportunities for either, even here.

Standing proud in the rush of the waves—wet skin gleaming in the moonlight, hair dripping rivulets of silver—I waved farewell to the dolphins. When they signaled back, I laughed in pure delight.

After drying myself off with a petticoat, and dressing, I made my way back up the beach. The moonlight revealed drifts of shells that had been brought in with the tides, and there were all sorts, from little pointed ones to those big enough to eat off of. I liked to take shells back with me to the palace in Atlanta as a reminder of happy times here at the lodge. Seeing them in my rooms there cheered me up. It was like having a little bit of my province with me even though I was kept far away from it, cloistered in the palace, for most of the year ... but there would be plenty of time for shells later ... although I just couldn't stop myself from picking up an unusually large one as I passed.

The short climb up to the sloping terrain of my gardens did not take long.

I was feeling happy, free, and blessed by Poseidon as I picked my way between the rocks and the little clumps of springy vegetation that separated the cove from my garden.[76]

The lights of the lodge came into view, and I arrived back to find some of the guards dozing in the comfortable chairs by the fireside in the dining room. The fire that had burned so bright to

---

76 The cove reminded me of the beautiful little beaches and rocky coves I'd loved when I lived in Cornwall, England. The black ceramic doorknob I had to turn to enter this story was just like the ones in my Cornish home—a subconscious link.

welcome us was ashes now, but the room was still warm. And as I entered, the guards came to attention. I shared the good news about the dolphins, and informed them I was about to retire for the night.

A wooden staircase ran up from the dining room to the floor above, and ascending this took me straight to my chamber. My disappearance gave the guards permission for sleep.

I'd given my maidservants permission not to wait up, and I relished getting ready for bed on my own. It was so much quicker to do things yourself than having to wait around for five maids to undertake the courtly rituals involved in getting ready for anything. I often felt my life draining away while waiting for even the simplest of things …

The swimming had tired me out and I climbed into the roomy bed, drew its curtains, burrowed into the pillows, and was soon fast asleep, glad to have arrived at last.

(The lodge was a long, rambling, two-story, wooden-framed building. The floors downstairs were of stone, and on the ground floor there were big kitchens, the large dining room, servants' apartments, guards' quarters, and the stables. Sturdy wooden staircases linked the ground floor to the one above[77]—and this upper floor was where I, Princess Ayesha, and my guests stayed during the summer.[78] But even a summons in winter, when it was colder, was a welcome escape from the stultifying constraints of life in the capital.

Local people looked after the lodge for me, and there were

---

77 Two staircases swept up the front of the building, one on either side of the main entrance, and two ran down the back. They all joined on to a balcony that ran right around the dwelling. The upper rooms were all accessed via the balcony.

78 Guests tried to avoid the rooms above the stables … for obvious reasons. The lodge was old, and generations of princesses had stayed there while looking after the province. The rooms for the resident princess were above the dining room and thus in the center of the building, they were the best rooms, and they were blissfully quiet at night because it was empty. They opened out onto the balcony above the front entrance (so the resident princess could look down on any visitors to see who'd come), as well as being accessed by the interior staircase, which she used to make a grand entrance should the dining room be hosting a function or they were entertaining. (The dining room was the only reception room.)

Think large farmhouse crossed with a Swiss alpine chalet and you've got the lodge.

goats, hens, and a fish pool so we could have fresh fish when we were there. A natural stream had been widened to form the pool, and a sieve fitted so that the fish didn't get swept out to sea. In the fields around the lodge there were vegetables, grains, vines, berries, fruit trees, and nut trees, everything we needed to eat.)

I was woken by maids drawing back the bed curtains, arranging a nest of soft pillows and helping me to breakfast. A cup of warm goat's milk was followed by freshly baked almond and raisin cakes. The little round honeyed cakes were tangy with lemon and rich with eggs. These I ate with relish, less so the fruit and yogurt that followed.

Then they helped me get ready …

Out of the plethora of dresses that had been unpacked, I chose a dusky pink one and waited impatiently for matching ribbons to be found to lace up my boots. The boots were not something I'd have worn at the palace, but they were good here, their soles painted in layers of rubbery resin making them springy to walk on and a match for the terrain around the lodge.[79]

The mandatory hundred comb strokes dressed and swept back my hair, and my gold circlet was repositioned to keep it in place. The circlet's insignia disc lay against my forehead and bore the design of a five-pointed star crossed by a pointed shell. The star symbol proclaimed that the gods of the heavens granted me the power to rule, and the shell denoted that it was my father's reign and that I was of his clan. All my jewelry carried this motif. It declared who I was for all to see, and the laws decreed that it must be worn at all times, but I had found the discomfort difficult to get used to. Even in bed I wore a heavy gold necklace, bracelets, and many rings.

---

79 The dresses were made of silk traded with lands far to the east, and though their colors varied the cut was always the same because the rules decreed it—it was what a princess wore—with a square neckline, a high waist, and sleeves banded by gathers. At court and on formal occasions here, a matching long skirt would be worn under the dress to transform it from below the knee to full length.

The dresses were embroidered with gold thread and embellished with beads, such as amber. Colors included russet, burgundy, brown, cream, yellow, orange, red, pinks, purple, blues, greens—a surprising range, like the colors you'd find on butterfly wings—the dyes being made from plants like alkanet (anchusa tinctoria), berries, sea creatures, etc.

... And as soon as all the washing, fussing, combing, brushing, perfuming, creaming, dressing, buffing of jewelry, and applying of judicious cosmetics was over, my first thought was to look for Sissy.

I found her playing by the fish pool.

Sicily was one of my many half-sisters. Sissy was seven, and she was my chosen heir for the time when I would be too old to make the journey to Helvia myself.

Sissy was also glad to get away from court as she had much more fun in the country. Time spent at my lodge was the nearest she got to having a childhood. There were no prying eyes or gossiping tongues to check on what she was doing or wearing, and instead of the endless training she was subjected to in Atlanta, here she was free to play. She would squeal with delight when she played, and she especially enjoyed feeding the hens and looking at the fish in their pool, and going down to the sea. The courtiers who always looked after Sissy had come with her, but her mother had chosen to spend the summer elsewhere.

I would never have a husband or children of my own.

I had decided this a long time ago, because I had a horror of dying in childbirth—as my mother had done—and I felt it was quite enough having to obey my father *and* the rules, without a husband telling me what to do as well! So Sissy was the daughter I'd never have. I admired her spirit and her way of looking at the world, marveled at her energy, and I loved to spoil her and have fun with her.

But the real reason for the visit to Helvia was work.

Helvia was a small northern province lying between sparsely populated mountains and the rocky east coast of Atlantis. It had no riches or special features and was concerned with agriculture and fishing. It was populated by ordinary folk whose biggest worry was the weather, because its vagaries could affect the production of their food.[80]

---

80 When I remembered the name in regression I was aware there was a link with Switzerland. "Helvetia" kept coming to me as well as "Helvia."

When I checked up on this, Helvetia is an ancient region of central Europe between the Alps and the Jura mountains, and even today it is the name of the female national personification of Switzerland; you still find a female figure of

Supposing there had been dreadful storms and hurricanes and the boats had been severely damaged, then the people could put in a request for financial aid and for artisans to be sent out from Atlanta to help rebuild the fishing fleets. If there was a lack of rain, then there could be a request to the priests in the capital for ceremonies to placate the water deities. Perhaps there might be problems with disease, then physicians and medicines could be sent out to them. And so my duty was to go round and tour the province to find out how things were, and then report back to my father so he could take the appropriate action, be it financial, practical aid, or requests for ceremonies. Very often nothing needed to be done—but the people needed to be listened to and checked so that they knew they were valued and felt an important part of the empire.

If I did my job well, things ticked over nicely and everybody was happy. Their happiness gave my father the mandate to rule. The last thing the royal family wanted was dissent, unrest, and ferment in the country. I knew this was a time when my father didn't trust the priests, and there had been enough times in the past when they had colluded with rivals to overthrow an emperor and bring down a dynasty. No, my job helped to keep my father's throne safe, and he would say to me, "Ayesha, my dear, Helvia may not be an important province, but yours is a very important job."

I bore the weight of my father's expectation, the weight of

Helvetia on Swiss currency and postage stamps, surrounded by five-pointed stars! The name has ancient roots, it is derived from the ethnonym Helvetii, the name of the Gaulish tribe the Romans found inhabiting the Swiss Plateau prior to the Roman Conquest. Helvia's mountains reminded me of Switzerland, and those fleeing from Atlantis before the flood would have thought the same, and thought it a safe place to go—far from the sea—when they brought this name with them. Celts and Gauls were descendants of the Atlanteans, and of those who lived in her empire.

The name of Switzerland in Greek is Elvetia, in Romanian it is Elvetia, and Elvezia is the archaic name in Italian. In French, Swiss people may be referred to as Helvetes, and in German Helvetien is a higher-value poetic alternative to Schweiz. German-speaking Swiss use "Helvetia" or "Helvecia" as a poetic synonym for their country.

So when I saw a picture of a Swiss coin featuring Helvetia, a lovely woman with a shield and a spear, framed with five-pointed stars, I saw a long line of Atlanta's princesses who had dedicated their lives to guarding the interests of their land ... and I'm glad to be here now to tell their story.

the royal jewelry, the burden of the rules which circumscribed every detail of my life, and even when I was in Helvia much of my work there was interpreting the rules so others could obey them too.

Each of the many provinces of Atlantis was represented by a member of the royal family doing just the same job. It was one of the reasons why the royal family was so large—each province had to have a royal female who had the ear of the emperor, and his anger was terrifying if they did a bad job and he found out. He had to be seen to be ruthless, and over the years I had witnessed some terrible public executions.

However, everything looked set fair for a good harvest, and Poseidon seemed happy, and so I anticipated that the meetings would go smoothly. I only planned to have Sissy with me at the nearest meeting, to begin her training, as I knew it would be boring for my little sister. The rest of the time Sissy could stay behind at my lodge with the other guests and play to her heart's content.

As the moon waxed and came into the correct phase, the tour of my province began. Our entourage set off early in the morning.

The guards rode on horseback and looked impressive in their armor, not that they were expecting trouble, but that was how it was decreed it should be done. My carriage set off first, pulled by a team of white horses in splendid blue[81] livery emblazoned with insignia stars, and from their white leather bridles projected a carved ivory representation of the insignia shell.[82]

Carts followed on after my carriage, filled with servants and things for our journey. Guards headed up the procession, rode along its flanks, and brought up the rear.

---

81 A deep, rich, lapis lazuli blue—standing for the sea (to set off the shell) and for the sky (to set off the star).

82 This gave them the striking appearance of unicorns. In the face of the prophecies of doom, the emperor had chosen this shell for his motif because it symbolized eternity. "Corn" or "clorn" shells might only be small when they washed up on the beaches but they were strong, strong enough to withstand the crushing power of Poseidon's might—they rarely washed up broken, and the twisting spiral of their form was seen to symbolize cycles of time stretching into infinity: a helpful counterbalance to the prophecies of doom and destruction. What we've come to understand as a unicorn was a one-shell, a uni-corn, a uno-clorn. This is why there will never be a unicorn skeleton found, ever. They never lived, at least not in our dimensions.

(The open roads were little more than country tracks. Even though the laws demanded that local people repair them every spring after the seeds for summer had been sown, they were still very uneven. Despite cushions, rugs, and furs it was a bumpy ride.

The royal itinerary was the same every year—set according to the rules and the moon's phases, so people could make their arrangements to meet their princess if they needed to. They would know where she was going to be and when she would be there.

The entourage always moved in procession around the center of the province, stopping at small market towns that were really no more than villages, where the leader of the settlement would arrange accommodation. It was an honor to have royalty staying so people were eager to offer their homes, and it was something the lucky host boasted about long afterward.

By this time, larger provinces had one or even two small cities,[83] but Helvia was too sparsely populated to support any, and the coast was too rocky and treacherous for a decent port.)

It was an endless stream of meetings and decisions as to what the laws said about peoples' grievances and problems. I was here as my father's representative, appointed by the heavens to maintain the rules on the land—and there were rules for everything. It was decreed how things should be carried out; who could marry who; how land was passed on; what happened at the seasons of the year; and in the different strata of society; and on and on. The priests were loud in their insistence that things had to be done by the rules—or they said the wise ordering of the heavens would be upset, and if that happened then the mighty Poseidon would bring the sea and sweep us all away. So it was a choice of chaos and ruination or following the rules, even down to such trivial things as what we used to tie our hair back. Women could tie ribbons of colored thread around their heads, and men strips of leather, but if they were to wear gold like the royal family, then they'd have to be put to death for getting above their station, no matter how rich they were.

I had spent years studying the laws, but if I was really

---

83 Not cities as we think of them, very much smaller: like Athens about two and a half thousand years ago.

taxed over something I referred to the priests for an answer. I had been trained since childhood in a system developed for telepathic communication, and so I would use this to contact the priest on scrying duty at Hera's temple, the original Great Temple in Atlanta where all the records were held. There were generations and generations and generations of laws, all systematically recorded on scroll upon scroll that could be consulted there. Every emperor in his time had laid down a few more laws, and the mountain of rules that affected our lives had just got bigger and bigger.

In the end, the tour was the usual hard work, but was thankfully uneventful.

There were disputes to be settled, but nothing complex, and the people of Helvia had been happy. And when it was over I enjoyed peaceful days back at my lodge recovering. I swam with the dolphins, searched for shells, and had fun with my friends, and by the time we needed to return to Atlanta everyone—even the servants and the guards—agreed that a good time had been had.

It had been so good to have a break from life at court.

When the day came to return, our entourage set off once more, this time traveling south, and over the days and weeks of the return journey I had a lot of time on my hands. Despite the bumps and bone-jarring jolting, my companions would often doze off to sleep, and in my boredom I would find my attention straying to my rings; I would tilt my hands and observe the play of light in the crystals and jewels. At all times I had to wear at least one ring on every finger, as ten was the bare minimum allowed, but while at the palace and for traveling I wore them all.

On each hand, a gold ring bore the imperial insignia, and even little Sissy wore ones like that, but some of the other rings were full of large jewels set in precious metals of different colors. There were the usual hues of silver and gold, but also some greens and blues.[84] The crystals in the rings had a purpose. They acted as interdimensional gateways accessible through meditation techniques, and they were used for the telepathic communications. It was true my father would be far too busy with affairs of state to be tranquil enough to hear my silent calling through them, but there

84 Volcanic gold, alloys, or star metal.

was always a priest on duty who would respond and who could take him a message if it was something really important.

We rattled and jolted through the days until the white walls of Atlanta came into view, and beyond them we could see the palace, far away on the high central citadel—its towers looking out over the city, its walls rimmed with silver and bronze, as the palace guards' shields twinkled in the sun where they'd been slung over the ramparts. The road led us on until the waters of the harbor glittered in the sunlight and the high stone walls reared above us, pierced by the bridge to which we were heading.[85]

Fanfares rang out on trumpets as our entourage clattered across the bridge and entered the city.[86] Sailors and visitors from other lands looked on in awe as the gilded carriage swept by, blue-and-gold pennants flying—*pulled by what looked like a matched team of unicorns.*[87]

A cheering crowd lined the route to the palace, and was rewarded with delicious biscuits stamped with the star and shell motif. The biscuits were baked in the palace kitchens, and it was the tradition to scatter them out into the crowd, in thanksgiving for the safe return of the member of the royal family and their party. It always ensured a good turnout, and was one of those little ploys to keep people happy, as everyone likes something free and something sweet. The biscuits were especially popular with children, and many

---

85 There were five bridges to the outer ring of Atlanta, designed to create the pattern of a star. If you were to look down on Atlanta from above, as they thought the gods did, each bridge would make one point of the star. Roads rayed out from the bridges far into the countryside, and in this way Atlanta declared herself to be a star fallen to Earth. Earth was linked to the heavens through Atlanta, and it was understood that the emperor who lived there kept the wise ordering of the heavens on the Earth. So the star of the insignia was Atlanta herself; and during this dynasty, because of the shell, a myth was born—that of the unicorn. And such is the creative force of our minds that perhaps over time unicorns took form in the etheric levels above our material world, there to be met with in meditation, having a sort of dream reality.

86 Each day riders were sent on ahead to prepare our lodgings for the night, and so by the time we were outside Atlanta, the palace, and the palace kitchens, were expecting us.

87 **The sailors and visitors took this vision home and gave it to the world, and so the myth was born.** The coach had gilded finials, wheel hubs, trims, and a star in gold leaf on both doors.

mothers brought their little ones to enjoy the fancy gingerbread made with honey, raisins, seeds, and spices. Indeed, many was the time I'd enjoyed them myself.

Arriving at the palace I was helped down from my carriage and escorted to my quarters. I found the palace a-flurry with preparations for an important banquet that was to take place that evening. I sent a servant to my father with a brief message to say that all had been well in Helvia, and I prepared to give him the full report later when things were quieter.

Life at court was a succession of such grand banquets and big state occasions. It was very important to the emperor that they were impressive, because visiting dignitaries from all over the empire attended, members of other royal families brought their heirs-in-training, there were ambassadors and important traders from countries in the regions known today as France, Spain, Portugal, North Africa, Britain, Ireland, Scandinavia, most of Europe, the Mediterranean, and from many other lands—as far away as China. These foreigners needed to see the splendor of mighty Atlantis, and they needed to take home stories of the vastness of her wealth, power, and knowledge, the magnitude of her expertise, so that their people remained in awe of her.

Atlantis was still the power center of the ancient world, and the constant flow of vessels plying the trade routes and bringing taxes made it easy for visitors to reach her court. She preserved a balance in world power with herself at the center, and if anyone threatened that balance fierce armies were swiftly loaded onto her fleets and dispatched to the troublemaker to threaten chaos, mayhem, and war.

It was a policy that had never failed …

There were people from all over the world at the banquet.

The banqueting tables were arranged on three sides of a huge square. The emperor was seated in the middle of the central side, and I could see my father but was not seated near him. Course after course was served, there was music and entertainment, and everything was going very smoothly … until a scuffle broke out. The commotion grew and turned into a fight before the guards could drag two men away. I was shocked. This was most unseemly. It should never have happened.

It broke the rules.

Any display of disunity gave a hint of weakness.

It looked very bad in front of the visitors we sought so hard to impress.

The incident troubled me. When I had my audience with my father to deliver the report on Helvia, I couldn't resist asking what it was about. All he would say was that there was rivalry between the men, that their fates were being evaluated, and that they may well be put to death because such behavior could not be tolerated. Firmly but kindly he said I was not to concern myself over it, and I knew my father well enough to know it was his last word on the subject, and I would have to let it go.

Succession ran down the male side of the family, and usually it was an emperor's sons, brothers, uncles, or nephews who were at the bottom of any trouble, and why his daughters were often placed in positions of trust. Daughters with aptitude and intelligence could be a valuable asset … and an emperor had need of many of those.

The weather had held good for the harvest, the crops were abundant, and it was another year of plenty.

With the autumn equinox came the great celebration that crowned their year, the festival of Thanksgiving for the Grains. This harvest festival was a time of joy, a holyday and a holiday when people brought offerings to the gods to show their appreciation for favors received.

All day long, people streamed in from the surrounding countryside. They came bearing fruit, grains, food they'd made or baked as gifts, and it was all heaped up and displayed on big tables in the courtyards outside the Great Temple. By five o'clock, people were crowding into the temple itself, until they overflowed outside.[88]

They were chattering happily and noisily, and there was an air of great excitement. Amid the noise, priests appeared, carrying

---

88 The temple was decked out beautifully with bundles of grain and mountains of fruit, but the tables outside were for more personal offerings, like giving thanks for a new baby, or a good crop in one's garden. Only the best and the tastiest was deemed good enough for the gods, and after the service the poor would be pleased to take the food, and nothing would be left or wasted, down to the last chicken pie.

conch shells. When they sounded their call, silence fell. There was a hush of expectation then a lull, until the head priest launched out into the beauty of the archaic words of the harvest ritual. Its language was from centuries long gone, but we could all understand it as it was, after all, our mother tongue. There was singing and responses, with priests outside relaying the ancient words to the crowds around the temple. The sky stained red with the fire of the setting sun, and its rays streamed in through the west windows of the temple creating a striking effect. In the center of the temple the thirteen clear quartz crystal skulls were displayed aloft, in niches on a golden stand, and as the sun sank lower its rays lit them one by one until they all turned to fire. The stand of gold was aflame in the rays of golden light, and the skulls blazed with the dying rays of the last sun of the year. It was a magnificent spectacle, and only when the sun had gone from the last skull was the service over.

How I loved this ceremony!

And as I sang in the temple, my heart filled with love for my country and my people, I pictured the fields of Helvia, the crops I'd enjoyed at my lodge, and I thanked the gods from the bottom of my heart for their bounty.

After the singing came a prayer for the coming year's prosperity and abundance, and then wild clapping and cheering broke out, and the people streamed out to feast and party, still singing.

Night fell and the city was alive with celebration, but the temple grew quiet and dark. The skulls were there on their stand, beneath the open central dome, and now they came under the influence of the energies of night.

While the calendar of the days appointed specific gods to each day, over and above that, all daylight belonged to Hera, and she had enriched and blessed the skulls with the last rays of sunlight, encapsulating the fruits of the energies of light for the whole year.

But all nights belonged to Zeus, and now the skulls charged with moonlight and starlight as the energies of Zeus flowed into them, and so they came at last to hold the energies of the full (agricultural) year.

* * *

I was fifty-five when I finally handed over the responsibilities of the province to my successor—and that's when Sicily became the next princess in a long, long line of princesses to take over the duties involved in looking after Helvia's interests.

Sissy had grown up and married an aristocrat, a truly good man who made her very happy. They were like peas in a pod, I used to say, and I thought her very lucky to have found someone who proved such a great support.

When Sissy gave birth to a daughter, I did my best to keep my fears to myself. But mother and baby not only survived but thrived, and Crowea had grown into a sturdy child, determined and bright. I took as much delight in watching her grow up as I had with Sissy all those years before.

Her name had been chosen because it augured well for the fertility and abundance of Helvia. Crowea Manijarri, "She who can make even the desert bloom," was a good choice for an agricultural province dependent on rainfall, and it inspired confidence in the people. Sicily had been given her name by parents just hoping she would marry well: "Beautiful as a blossom tree" was fitting for a royal marriage, but it was purely by chance that she had caught my eye when I was casting about for my successor. And once Sissy had visited the lodge, well, she'd settled comfortably into the role and never looked back. Just as Crowea would.

So it was on Sissy's fingers that the heavy crystals sparkled and glinted now. But for a few years I continued to accompany her, enjoying the stay in Helvia as a holiday and a chance to escape court. I always loved being there, and the trips kept me going and gave me something to look forward to.

The summer I was sixty-one I stayed behind at the palace rather than face the journey, but I regretted my decision and returned to the lodge the following year. I found the journey very hard and did not go the year after, but it made me all the more determined to make the effort when I was sixty-four. After that I reluctantly decided it had become too much for me, but I still delighted in hearing reports from Sissy and loved to catch up with any gossip or news from Helvia.[89]

89 I could have gone by sea and been taken ashore by the local fishermen who

I had grown frailer as the years went by, and I found life at the palace ever more tedious. I attended the ceremonies at the Great Temple, and still enjoyed the Thanksgiving for the Grains, but slowly somewhere deep inside I began to give up. I knew I'd never go back to Helvia, and I started to fade out of life.

My name had meant "Rich as spices, life enhancing," and that was how I'd tried to live. I'd been weighed down by the laws, but not been afraid to go my own way when I could; I'd been lively and good company to be with, and I was kind to my servants. My name had even literally given me a love for herbs and spices once I'd learned its meaning, and I'd taken quite an interest in learning about them. But I was no longer full of life now. I'd become a shadow of myself—there, but not really present.

It was shortly after the harvest ceremony in the year I was sixty-eight that the morning came when I failed to open my eyes.

When the emperor was told the news, he sighed. I had always been a dutiful daughter, never a cause for concern, and in that moment he realized he would miss me. Because I'd never caused him any trouble he'd always taken me for granted ... and now I was gone.

Everything changes, he mourned, and he felt the weight of his years pressing on him a little harder than before ...

My maids dressed me in one of my favorite dresses, fussed me, perfumed me, and arranged my hair for the very last time. I was lain in an open casket amid a sea of flowers, with spices and the leaves of fragrant herbs, like those I'd loved and had in my garden in Helvia, strewn all around me.

My bodyguards bore the open casket to the Great Temple, the Temple of Hera, and there I lay in state for the people to come to pay their respects to me.[90] I was to be presented to Hera at dusk.

---

knew the treacherous rocky coast well, but it was simply not allowed, because everything had to be done with pomp and ceremony to keep the status of the royal family high. The rules were a cage I had to live in when I was Ayesha; I also had to live in the palace instead of being allowed to retire to Helvia as I would have liked.

90   The news of my passing was proclaimed in the streets by town criers, so people would know to come if they wanted to.

As dusk approached, a priest climbed steps high within the temple and blew on a conch shell directed through the open dome, to summon Hera and Zeus, to tell them Princess Ayesha was waiting.

The priest's words rang out as he made the invocation to the gods, entrusting my departing soul to their care for the coming journey back to the Divine:

"**Hera**, through whom we embody,
Giver of Life and the days in which we live it,
Holy Mother divine at whose breast we suckle,
Whose hands enfold us in life,
Who delivers us into the care of Zeus each night,
Who unceasingly collects us each morning until our last day,
Who with Zeus gathers us up and takes us back to the Divine,
To rest outside of Creation in the divine womb,
Before rebirth once more,
Princess Ayesha awaits you now."

When dusk became night, they felt my soul to be safe in Hera's care, gathered up with the last of the light of the day.

Then came the care of my body. This was to be entrusted to Poseidon, to rest with him in his kingdom with the dolphins forever. My guards carried my casket out of the Temple of Hera and took it into the Temple of Poseidon.

The priests there received me and presented me to him.

In front of his great bronze statue with eyes of flame, I was anointed with seawater, as though kissed on each cheek by him in greeting. Then my casket was taken out of the temple, carried down steps to the water, and placed on the burial boat filled with the fragrant seasoned hardwood of a funeral pyre.

And this time it was the priests, and not I, who called out the incantation to Poseidon as I floated out into the waters of the night.

My boat had flaming brands tied aloft that pierced the darkness, and it was pulled by a boat manned by oarsmen. Boats carrying the mourners followed on behind.

The stately procession of vessels made its way down the main waterway out of the city, and into the wide river, down to the estuary mouth. The waters glinted with the broken reflections from the flames of the brands, and the pale moonlight made ghosts of mourners and rowers alike.

When the boats reached the ocean, the fire of the brands was used to light the funeral pyre, and the rowing boat disengaged. The mourners watched from their vessels as the tide and the winds took the burial boat out to sea. My body was sent into Poseidon's embrace on a sea of fire that burned fiercely into the night.

In death, I was released from the weight of the world.

I was light.

I was free.

I watched. I wanted to comfort Sissy and Crowea as they wept, to say, "I'm alright, I'm free, I'm light, I'm blessed and in bliss," but there were no words. And as the boat burned and grew tiny on the horizon, I passed on, rising up through the dimensions of the universe on my way to the Divine. I passed through the frequencies of light that were Hera, through the higher frequencies of light not yet manifest that were Zeus, until I came at last to rest in the heart and mind of God, in the very depths of the Divine. My eternal spirit had returned to its home.

And all that was left was for those in the boats to return to the city.

They retraced their route, with teams of oarsmen bringing them safely to the Temple of Poseidon. Here the mourners disembarked and were taken back to the palace, back to the comfort of mulled wine and strong herbal draughts designed to restore them from the effects of the cold winds and the cold hands of grief about their hearts.

Chapter 6

Chronicles of Atlantis 5

Why We Have Darkness and Light

Feeling life draining away while waiting for others to do things is something I recognize, and I've often joked about "losing the will to live" in such circumstances, and that literally is what Ayesha did. She lost the will to live.

I still can't resist picking up sea shells on beaches. They fascinated me as a child holidaying in North Wales. Mostly it was razor shells and cockles there, but I remember finding a little pointed one once, just like a unicorn's horn, and I carried it in my purse to school for a long time and really treasured it.

But by this time the prophecies of doom had begun. The things that made Atlantis strong had begun to break down, and from now on the sense of unease deepened. Distrust spread. The emperors did not trust the priests, but what was worse, the priests no longer trusted one another, and there was rivalry between the temples. It was as though the very bones of Atlantis had begun to weaken and crack. In the dimensions known as the astral levels, this weakness manifested as the smell of decay, an odor that heralded impending death. This was soon picked up by the vultures of darkness, primordial beings who hated all life except their own kind, and it wasn't long before they left their home in the Abyss of Chaos[91] and circled our world,

---

91 Imagine throwing a stone into a still pond. The ripple that spreads out is like a circular wave. Well, when the universe was born in the "big bang" scientists theorize about, light poured forth like just such a wave. The light chased the darkness before it, until its energies were spent, until "the wave" broke on a distant shore. And so just beyond light's reach, darkness festers in the Abyss of Chaos, in the void that surrounds Creation, on that "distant shore." Darkness still

ready to pick at the bones of Atlantis and finish her off completely.

The next chapter is set in the time of decay, and this is where I learned that the skulls are slap bang in the middle of a war between the forces of darkness and light.

After my experience of enlightenment,[92] detailed in *Spiritual Gold*, I had wondered what came next—and within a year I was to find out. I was given an experience that taught me to understand the forces of darkness, the devil, and the black god: "endarkenment," you might say, and it revealed the other side of the Creator.[93]

Dr. Francesca Rossetti, my soul therapy and regression teacher at the time, had suggested I clear any ancient satanic links from my heart during my next routine soul therapy session—but I have to confess that if I hadn't previously seen the light of God within me when I had my enlightenment experience in Spain, I would have had great difficulty integrating what came up that summer's day in 1993. Well, we had asked for it! But somehow I imagined it would be in a more abstract symbolic form …

The session began in the usual way, with the journey to the divine essence before Creation, and then when I was above my body we began to clear my heart. As I was sifting through the things held there, searching for what needed to be released in response to

remembers that it ruled unchallenged and supreme before the emergence of light, and so it plots and waits, sensing opportunities to wreak its revenge, longing to reassert its primal supremacy.

(As it says in the Bible, Genesis 1:3, "And God said, Let there be light." There was a time before light.)

92 In *Spiritual Gold* I give the full story of how on a therapy retreat in Spain, at Cortijo Romero in 1992, after three days of fasting and an evening of connected breathing I literally had the light of God enter me. I remembered that I was God (like we all are), I danced with Death and saw my lives on other worlds, and laughed at the joke of Life—I saw how we set up our karmic lessons, and then try to avoid them when they come up in our lives! It is hilarious! You can't avoid yourself! We are God and we want to know about sorrow, pain, loss, and death— all things that are not part of our Divine nature. That's why we come here, to experience them! And then we try to duck the lessons!

It was my experience of enlightenment.

93 "Lucifer," "Satan," and "the devil" are used interchangeably here, because Lucifer was the angel who fell from heaven and became Satan the adversary, the devil who presides over hell. Lucifer means "light bearer," and this gives a clue as to how things will work out in the end, when at the last he is finally restored to his place in heaven.

Francesca's questions, I went deeper and deeper. Looking for animal influences that needed to go I found a black raven. Suddenly I *was* the raven. And I knew I was Satan visiting his kingdom[94] in this guise, and then I went back further ... and I was in the consciousness of the black god.

There was no time to be scared, and to my surprise the black god was in a sorry state, frozen and fixed.

My body had become his, and as I looked down upon it now it seemed to be made of a black ice-like substance ... and then I remembered, and then it all came flooding back to me. He'd been born from the Creator first, and only when his cold, fixed energy had been released from the divine consciousness could Light burst forth. It was the black god's energy that had held everything in balance. Only when it had gone was Light able to expand, radiate, and shoot out into Creation and become physical light in the material world. So, the light god is younger, and his arrival in Creation had really annoyed his elder brother.

Light hurt the black god. Light caused him pain. Being ejected from the bliss of the Creator, the black god's energies had plummeted. It was as if he now had a terrible hangover. And as the universe began evolving with light fizzing about all over the place, pouring forth from suns and giving rise to life-forms, it gave him the most monstrous headache. To ease his pain, he tried to smother and crush the light—with terrible curses he tried to destroy the worlds and all the irritating life-forms on them ... and the black god's war has been going on ever since. But without help it was an unequal struggle.

The Creator, the father of both, loved both his sons because each embodied a part of him. To help his first son he caused war in heaven and sent him his finest angel with a third of the angelic hosts. These became the fallen angels. This meant Lucifer was now chief of active dark forces, and so the fixed energy of the black god had active black energy to help him, and the fight became fairer.

Both his sons collect the fruits of Creation for their father, and without their fight the fruits do not form. We are stuck in the middle of their battle, and it is a very uncomfortable place to be. But although the battle rages on around us it also rages within us,

94 Visiting his kingdom *in our world*.

for we are also the Creator: *we are infinitely small droplets of His consciousness, infinitely small droplets embodying both darkness and light.* **And although there is no escape from the battle we will all share in its fruits.**[95]

The session had been profound, but afterward I did need a very strong coffee and a walk in a leafy sunlit park to recover!

Francesca had found it disturbing, although to her credit she hadn't show it and so I felt safe.

Afterward, she told me she had used a rattle given to her by Joseph Rael, Beautiful Painted Arrow, one of the Native American shamans with whom she had studied, and a feather had fallen from the shamanic tool and settled upon me as things went deeper and darker. I think this was a comforting sign that the angels were with us; and at the end of the session, as I was about to come back into present time, I distinctly heard Michael, Uriel, Raphael, and Gabriel saying, "Thank goodness, someone else has remembered," and they did seem pleased about it.

Understanding the duality of life—good and evil, darkness and light—certainly helped when it came to the next story. It was actually the very first story to emerge when Veronica and I had started researching my links with the skulls, and we were thrown in at the deep end with this one.

The session began as usual, and I entered the inner world and descended a staircase to meet with my guides.

The guides came, and took me to the hallway of doors, and this time I was drawn to a very unprepossessing plain wooden door that I had never seen before. It had an old, tarnished brass doorknob … and it didn't look like much, but strangely enough it pulls me to it.

I touch it. I turn the knob … the door opens and I step through into night.

I'm in a very different consciousness now, a nonhuman

---

95 The microcosm and the macrocosm, the large mirrored in the small and the small mirrored in the large. The Divine sibling rivalry is in our spiritual genetics. Love is the answer—loving ourselves, accepting ourselves, knowing who we really are is where it starts. When we do this, then we can truly love others. Through love we will transcend.

consciousness.

And I am male.

I'm on a hillside, hiding in a forest of rocks. Black, spiky, volcanic rocks like shards of glass rear up around me—and I'm crouching down to conceal myself. I know I do not belong in this place of darkness… I have just arrived, and my craft is behind me…

I'm in danger, **and something is terribly wrong.**

The Pleiadian's Story

DARK FORCES GATHERING

Alive in the electric silence of the night I watch and I listen.

All senses are scanning, on full alert.

Nothing moves, and this gives me a slight feeling of relief.

Good—the thought comes—*then they haven't got here yet— so I still have a chance to get what I've come for and escape.*

I look up. Unfamiliar star patterns pierce the dark sky above me, and three golden moons wreath the mountains around me in shadows. A blood-red stain on the largest of the moons makes me shudder. The strangeness of the sky reminds me I'm a long way from home, and I feel very vulnerable. I'm grateful for the shadows because they're helping me hide, but I desperately need to spy out the lay of the land. So I grip the rocks and pull myself up. I lean out to look down the hillside.

I am now this tall stranger, ill at ease in an alien land.

Veronica asks me a string of questions ... and his story comes tumbling out.

Good, enough light for my purpose, I think, and I study the landscape hard. The red-gold moonlight glints and shimmers faintly on my angular crystalline form as I shift about. I am still trying to get accustomed to the gravity of the world, and these dimensions are always a trial. The only good thing about them is that they make me almost transparent and quite hard to detect—and I know this is going to be an asset in the current situation.

My attention is drawn to the valley below, where pinpricks of bright light are disturbing the shadows and betraying the location of a city.

This is it. It must be here.

By now I am confident that no being knows of my arrival— yet—but exactly **how** I'm going to go about the work I've been sent to do I don't know. The thought troubles me ... but by some means or another I have to retrieve an irreplaceable device. The device has been stolen and has fallen into the wrong hands—very dangerous hands at that—*and it's here, somewhere—oh, yes, it's here ... but where, exactly?*

I steady myself. I expand my awareness and sweep it through the city, trying to sense what is going on. With a shudder, I become aware that there are already those at work trying to use this trans-dimensional tool. It's a powerful magnifier and amplifier of energies, tuned to its home world, and there it is the chief controller for many more of these devices. I know this meddling is affecting other worlds and that they could do tremendous harm. They shouldn't have it, shouldn't even know about it—never mind use it—and what's worse, **others are coming looking for it**. The consequences of it being manipulated by these ancient beings are just too catastrophic to contemplate. If their emissaries get to the device before I do, the first thing they'll do is destroy the hapless world it's tuned to—and that would be another precious seeding planet gone from the galaxy, another tear in the fabric of the universe—but who knows what else they might do, or where the unraveling of the structures of light would end this time—Sirius? Or even … home? The shock would surge down the field lines of the galaxy …

Feelings of desperation flood over me.

I have to get to the device before harm is done. It should never have been transported to this star system as a curiosity and never have been put at risk like this.

It is imperative it be returned to its home world.

There is no time to dither.

And resolute, I race down the mountainside toward the city.

But I still have no plan for what I am going to do.

My elongated spiky body is used to less gravity, but I bound along with huge strides, I almost fly. It feels strange to be here, and I am longing for home, but there is no going back until this task is done.

As I approach the city I adjust the spacing and bonds of my atoms to make myself even more invisible.

I melt into the city.

Beings feel me passing like a breeze and shudder. I try to avoid them.

Where is it? I send the questioning thought out, like a wave, seeking. I become aware that it is being shielded and deliberately hidden. Frantically I scan around me for an anomalous energy.

What shouldn't be here?

What energy pattern is out of place in this city?

I feel drawn toward a temple that is alive with activity. As I draw nearer I scan through the fabric of the building and perceive it has underground chambers. I relax the atoms and molecules of my body even further, and enter. I begin to melt down through the temple floor, wriggling gently as I ease myself through its molecular structure until I am in a spacious room below.

And there it is.

The crystalline device I have come to collect. But there are so many beings clustered around it I can't just take it because they'd notice and interfere.

Whatever I do, I will have to act quickly.

It leaves me no choice.

I'm going to have to stop time and freeze them in the moment—it will be a drain on my energy—but at least that way they won't see what's happening, and they can't stop me. One moment the device will be there, the next it will be gone, as though by a conjurer's trick.

All around me figures freeze, poised in an eerie silence, with mouths open, hands extended, eyes unseeing. I focus on my intention and then create a vacuum within my body cavity, pulling the crystalline device deep into it, deep into my solar plexus. My energy field will shield it from sight ... and with the device safely within me I release the little bubble of time distortion I've created and slip up through the atoms of the temple's floor. As I race out of the building I hear a great commotion ensue.

I bound up the mountainside back to my craft, but I begin to feel more and more uncomfortable. Only in the shelter of the craft do I feel safe enough to release my burden, but I find it much harder to get out than it had been to suck in. I struggle and struggle, and it is only after an enormous effort, a really tremendous push that I manage to reverse the vacuum. The device slips out, but to my chagrin it doesn't come out as cleanly as it went in. Even in the short space of time it has been inside me, some of its crystalline energies have intertwined with my own, and now they've ripped off, leaving behind painful residues deep within me.

I am attempting to release the residues when to my dismay I detect a shift in the world around me, a rippling in the space/time fabric. The subtle change heralds the imminent arrival of the forces of darkness and the agencies of Chaos—*and I know they are almost upon me. I can't stay a moment longer ...*

Swiftly and carefully I stow the device in the place I've prepared for it in my craft, and as soon as it is secure, I leave.

Once in the anonymity of space I begin to relax a little.

It is a relief to be off the world, and despite my discomfort I cheer up because it is almost "mission accomplished." After all, I've got what I've come for, and all that remains is to return it.

I speed through space and time, safe in the energy field that comprises my craft. I know I am approaching journey's end when I can see the luminescence of a world drawing near. This world shines like a pearl, shimmering with a rare and luminous beauty. Such riches of water and atmosphere are unusual in the galaxy. I feel my heart center opening in the presence of so much loveliness, and I'm distracted for a moment from the pain of the residual energies.

Third planet out from a smallish sun, this is my destination. This is where the crystalline device is to be restored to its rightful place.

Lost in the beauty before me my thoughts wander back to when it had all begun. It was the guardians of this world who had called upon my people in the Pleiades for help.

The guardians are vast beings beyond form, higher-dimensional energy fields without substance, just pure consciousness, and they are at too high a level, too abstract, to be able to do this particular job for themselves.

They had come into being when time was young.

Before time and space existed, there had come a point when the Creator, perfectly balanced in bliss, desired to experience a new wave of Creation. In the divine orgasm of his desire to know himself He expelled streams of energy. First, in order to break the stasis of balance, the darkness was sent streaming out, and once the compressing heaviness of its negativity had gone, then came the explosions of light. As the light of the Creator moved away, its frequency dropped and light froze to form matter ... and the universe was born.

Out of this outpouring of divine energy, patterns of consciousness manifested. Those of light became the very highest levels of angelic command, whose purpose was to organize the evolution and unfoldment of this creation wave. It was from the energy of their thoughts that multidimensional crystalline configurations sprang into being, as a means of interacting with the evolving worlds. These were tools fashioned by the power of mind to help the guardians steer the course of their planets' evolution.

Each tool's world of origin was declared by its form, and there were wonderful variants scattered across the galaxy. Not all worlds needed such devices to monitor and steer evolution, because not all worlds offered the complexity and potential that this one did.

The device I had with me had taken the form of the seat of consciousness of the dominant species on the planet, and so it looked like a crystal counterpart of one of their skulls. In terms of the planet's age, beings with skulls of this shape had only been in existence for a very short while—but long before any life-forms manifested anywhere, their blueprints were held within the dreaming seed energies of their world. Their potential was already available at the archetypal level long before they undertook physicality and began the arduous journey of spiritual evolution—they were simply destined to be, and the preparations for them were already in place.

Like me, the beings on this planet were droplets of the Divine's ocean of consciousness, but their species had plunged deeper into matter and while there they had forgotten their true nature. This was their choice because it gave them the opportunity for undertaking the greatest possible adventure as they made their journey back to the Creator. The tool was to help them and to help the forces of light steer them on their journey …

The worlds were formed to be evolutionary platforms, perfect for such journeys to take place on, but they were also evolving planetary beings in their own right. They sponsored the life-forms they accepted, and so their fates were entwined with the evolution of the beings that called them "home." It was not unknown for a world to regret its generosity, and then the species failing to evolve would be recalled, or if it was left too late, the world itself might be damaged or even die.

This planet's crystalline-device skulls were trans-dimensional receivers and transmitters, and in earlier times the guardians had been able to transport them with the power of their own thoughts. However, as time went on and the process of evolution brought changes, the skulls' energy condensed and penetrated the lower dimensions, some of it even dropping down to the three-dimensional level of reality and becoming solid crystal. As a consequence, such a skull could no longer just be thought back. It was now out of the guardians' direct reach, and they needed someone who could interact with that level of the world to retrieve it for them.

It had ever been the custom of my people to help where we could, and so I, as a Pleiadian being with suitable skills, had answered the call of the guardians when it came.

... But at this point the discomfort of the residual energies is almost unbearable, and a sharp pain cuts through my train of thought. It's now urgent to do something about it, and besides that, I can't return an incomplete skull missing the energies that are trapped within me. I feel like I have bad indigestion ... as if I've swallowed rocks, and that is virtually what I've done.

I wonder what to do.

Who can help?

And as I struggle with this, the realization comes to me: I need to visit the sun, where angelic forces will have the power to sift the energy out of me ...

... which means further travel.

Once more I lift up my mind to the Creator, and I focus on my desire to be with the angels of the sun. The energy field that is my craft powers up to maximum amplification—and I rise through the dimensions of the universe, almost touch the Oneness of the Divine where everything that exists in space and time is held within the mind of God, ricochet off the edges of that dimension of singularity, and find myself deposited in the midst of my heart's desire.

I am with the angels of the sun.

Throngs of angelic hands come to help me, coaxing the crystal energies up through my throat and out of my mouth. I burp crystal energy and begin to feel better. The angels are always so happy. They are laughing and clapping and chorus, "You'll live!" "You'll be fine, stop fussing!"

The residual energies are carefully gathered up and angelic beings take all the skull energies into the heart of the sun. There is repair work to be done, upgrading and cleansing of the information that had been absorbed on the other world, in a totally different star system ruled by a sun other than Sol.

The angelic healing is soon complete.

And when I am reunited with the crystalline energy fields, to my eyes they now look shiny, bright, and vital. It is time for me to press on, and once more I travel at the speed of thought to the world that shines like a pearl.

Descending through clouds, I drop down the dimensions and find that I am on the night side of the planet again, just as I had been on the other world.

I land on a dusty plain near an ocean.

I sweep my awareness around the vicinity to make sure it is safe for me there, and as I scan for life-forms, I sense a herd of wild horses in the hills behind me bordering the ocean.

All well and good, I think to myself, the horses are no threat to me ...

I leave the craft, taking the skull with me in its carrier thoughtform. Again, I adjust the spacing and bonds of my atoms, making myself much taller this time, and from this lofty new height I look around to get my bearings.

A large, single moon casts plenty of light on the plain ahead and reveals a city built on a river and surrounded by water. The silvery hued moonlight of Earth lends a delicate beauty to the many fine buildings of the city, and in its center I see graceful towers reaching up to the sky.

I know what I seek is there. This is Atlanta.

With giant strides, I race across the plain toward the nearest of the bridges giving access into the city. As whispering waters ripple and sparkle beneath me, I breeze over the bridge, and on and on I run, past sleepy guards and through deserted streets.

I'm taking the skull home now, to its rightful place in a fine white temple, and as I run I am no more solid in the Earth dimensions than I had been on the other world.[96]

I head toward the center of the city and soon find the temple I'm looking for, but as I stand outside, trying to locate exactly **where** the skull should go, I encounter a problem. I have a dilemma

---

96 In the spectral moonlight I would not have been seen by human eyes. Had anyone been looking they might have caught a hazy glimpse of the skull in the crook of my arm, appearing to travel unaided through the air in its carrier thoughtform.

because I can sense it has two homes, one in a high circular tower area and another in an underground cave. Is it to go in the tower tonight, where it is displayed for important rituals at certain times in the calendar of the days? Or is it to go in the cave where it is otherwise kept for safety?

I pause for a moment.

I scan for the answer.

And then I know—tonight it should be in the tower, because the other skulls are there. There are a number of others, but this one had been at the pinnacle of the tower's display.

I melt in through the walls of the temple and find two priests asleep on duty—and twelve more of the crystalline devices, all soaking up the energies of the night sky as they rest on a stand beneath the temple's open dome. Releasing the energy locked in the carrier thoughtform, I watch until it has dissipated safely, and while the priests sleep on, oblivious to my presence, I gently replace the skull at the top of the stand, making sure it is positioned correctly on its detachable jaw.

Bah Ha Redo is back![97]

At least that's what the sleeping priests would call this crystal.[98]

But "Those That Do" is not how I, a crystalline Pleiadian being, choose to address the skull when I ask it for help in completing the last remaining task before I can return home. No, I address it by its true name, one crystal consciousness communicating with another.

_____I need to get to the bottom of how it had been possible to steal

97 The theft had taken place around midnight, Earth time, and it's now about two-thirty in the morning. Fortunately, the skull had not been missed as the rescue had been swift—I had been contacted by thought, all traveling had taken place at the speed of thought, the angels were outside of time in the eternal now, and it was only while I was on the worlds that I was engaged with linear time in any real sense at all.

98 Shamans who had first found the skulls sheltering in their sacred cave had asked them their names, but had found the vibrating resonance of their signature sounds impractical to warble. And because the skulls' true names had not lent themselves to the Atlantean tongue, they had been given nicknames for everyday use—they simply became known by what they did. **Down the ages the nicknames attained hallowed status. And it was with great reverence that Bah Ha Redo was referred to.**

the device in the first place. It should not have been so vulnerable. The crystal should have had its own built-in protection, an invisibility factor, a cloaking device to prevent it attracting attention from those who shouldn't see it, particularly off-worlders and beings of a negative orientation. This protection had been destroyed ... and I have a feeling it's because there's a traitor in the priesthood.

It must not happen again, I think to myself, *because things might not turn out so well a second time.* I focus on the crystal and enter the request to be shown exactly what had happened.

I receive the information that the country is going through a very unsettled period. There is unrest everywhere, turmoil within the royal family, and a schism in the priesthood. Some of the priests desiring to break with the traditional ways of doing things have been channeling dark forces through the skull, and this is how off-world beings had been able to manipulate them and were able to steal something so irreplaceable and precious.

Satisfied, I reset the protection.

Noiselessly, I set about finding those who had slipped into a treacherous state of mind. I have been told there are five ... and I seek them out.

I melt through the temple complex, sweeping my awareness through corridors and underground tunnels, along passageways, until I find them.

I drift past the sleeping priests, sensing. I begin to read the energy emanations surrounding their supine bodies. Their thoughts, feelings, records of past experiences, are all there for those with the eyes to see: their auras are a mirror to their being. Most have the clear, bright hues of auras cleansed by meditation, fasting, and spiritual practices, but five are darker.

These priests have become tainted by their association with negative entities and energies. Subtle changes have been caused, not only to their auras' color, but also to its smell. The changes, undetectable to human senses, make them smell of sulphur, of rotting eggs to me. The five had thought themselves so clever, and yet, in the end, the traitors are themselves betrayed by their own auric fields.

I find the first, sleeping fitfully. I lean over and my energy engulfs the priest like a soft, thick, dark blanket. It presses down on his chest, it seeps into him, slowing his heart until it is stilled forever. I find the next, and one by one I silence them.

When the last has been dealt with I enter the chamber of the sleeping chief priest. I had learned from the skull that the chief priest had sensed that treachery was afoot, and had asked the gods to send him a dream to reveal all that night. As the chief priest sleeps, I begin to influence his dreams—feeding in the information from the skull, so that he will understand the peril it has been in and be able to take the appropriate actions to safeguard it in the future.

With my task now complete, I am free to return home.

My heart is light as I leave the beauty of Earth and journey back to the Pleiades, to a world of a higher vibrational frequency than Earth.

(In my Pleiadian home I appear black, and much more solid, with a form akin to the Jack Frost of earthly children's fairy stories.) And just as on Earth, the color of your skin has no relation to the polarity of your soul; because I look black it does not make me a being of darkness. I was an agent of light in the battle against the darkness of evil.

EVIL : LIVE

It's the same word but backward, a mirror image, and in our lives we are always having to choose which side of the mirror we are reflecting in. Every day we are free to choose the *evil* of greed, hate, or bitterness or to *live* in the loving, kind way that nourishes ourselves, other people, animals, and the planet. And so our freewill choices are the tool for our own personal spiritual evolution … or devolution.

We have both the light and the darkness within us because they both come from the Creator and we are droplets of the Divine consciousness. There is no locking the darkness up and throwing away the key, it needs to be integrated and thus transformed, and that is our challenge. The darkness may hate the light but the irony is that it needs the light. Beings of darkness cannot spiritualize their own energy, they are well and truly stuck in that dire level of consciousness. Interacting with beings of light may not be comfortable for either party, but without the light the darkness would be doomed never to return home.[99]

The devil does the dirtiest job in Creation, but there will come a time when Lucifer is restored to the right hand of God. Creation was set up for the battle between good and evil, without it there would be no adventure for the Creator. In its essence, Creation is like an elaborate game of Patience for God. The only thing that varies from wave to wave is how long it takes to work out.

But as for us, all we need to do is embrace the adventure that is life, and use our hearts to navigate our way through it.

And as for the Pleiadian, my adventure drew to a close when I reached home and was greeted rapturously by my wife, children, parents, brothers, sisters, their children, and on and on. My huge extended family of loved ones gathered around me and welcomed me back, immersing me in the vibrations of love and joy. Loosening the spacing of all our atoms, we mingled our forms and it was like melting, singing, floating in a sea of love. I was happy, and thought no more of Earth.

* * *

This was an enigmatic little story, a fragment of a past life I knew very little about. The incident spanned only a few Earth hours, and the rest of this Pleiadian existence of mine is shrouded in mystery.[100]

99 And in terms of the first footnote in this chapter—when the wave breaks on the distant shore, all fruits of Creation formed, then it is sucked back into the sea, absorbed back into the ocean of divine bliss that is God. The light is the taxi that takes the darkness home. It piggybacks home on the actions of light. And as the saying goes, "If you meet the devil on the road …" send him love and compassion and watch him transform!

100 The door into the session was unobtrusively drab, as if it was trying to hide and blend in—which is exactly what the being was doing on the alien world. The old, tarnished brass doorknob referred to the skull—it was old, it had been tarnished by the way it had been misused and by its experiences on the other world.

I seem to have made a bit of a habit of incarnating elsewhere in the universe—I've had other Pleiadian lives too, and plenty of lives on worlds I couldn't say where they were—but unless a life is relevant to the theme of this book I haven't

When I tried to understand who the enemies were that were coming after the skull, the information was well shielded, and it took all Veronica's skill to help me penetrate the reflective layers of blankness that were wrapped around it. Dark forces prefer to operate in secrecy. It makes it harder for you to stop them when you can't see what they're doing.

It had been a very close call, **and now we knew that throughout the universe agencies of evolution and devolution battle for success, and that the skulls act as lenses through which the energies that bring change are intensified.**

I like to think that as the black god is less than half the Divine's consciousness, darkness can never win in the end, even with all its additional helpers … but as the old saying goes, "For evil to triumph (in our world) all it takes is for good men to do nothing." And at some point, we all wander into the dark side as we explore the universe. Even though the Pleiadian's mission was on behalf of light, when I was him I had killed. I had taken five lives for the greater good, but at least it stopped the erring priests from accruing more shocking karma.

Sometimes people considering having a past life therapy session ask me, "What if I've been bad?" And in truth, we've all been "bad," it's part and parcel of our growth. What is important is what we've learned from it, and in past life work not only can you assess that but you have the opportunity to put things right and bring healing. There is no need to feel guilt, because it wasn't "present you" that did it, but "present you" can put it right with the help of the archangels and your guides. There is so much natural goodness in us that most of our lives have been lived with passion and spirit and love. The ones where our hearts didn't open deserve healing.

As surely as bubbles rise to the top of a champagne bottle, so we rejoin the Divine when we have finished our exploration of

made mention of it here. In a private reading with Lilla Bek years ago (National Federation of Spiritual Healers lecturer mentioned in *Spiritual Gold*), she said to me, "When it comes to atoms and molecules, you've shed far more elsewhere in the universe than you have here on Earth"—meaning I've been elsewhere rather a lot! Of course, back then I had no idea where … why, or who I really was. But later I found I was a citizen of the cosmos, a bit of a wanderer—up and down the dimensions, in and out of the life streams, and in the case of my current life I like to wander backward and forward through time with regressions!

matter. Our souls journey through Creation like the tiny bubbles race through the liquid in the bottle. But not all bubbles rush out at once, and some tarry longer in the darkness of the glass—and so it is with us. We all have to experience the darkness but some[101] *choose* to linger there. Our free will enables this to happen, but those who tarry are really only delaying their bliss.

But now, despite corrupt priests and the machinations of the forces of darkness, Bah Ha Redo was back. Had Bah not returned, what was coming would have been even worse;[102] and thank God we still have that crystal skull[103] with us today. Its energy emanations are helping us make a positive shift in our collective consciousness— and thus helping us ground a better future. And the skulls will go on helping us through the challenging years that lie ahead, as the Age of Aquarius unfolds from a very rocky start into what could be a golden age.

---

101 For example, Satanists. The devil has always enjoyed the sport of toying with people who are tempted by the path into darkness. "Making friends with the enemy" may be their rationale, or worldly gain or to make what they see as their inevitable stay in hell more bearable, but would you really trust the devil? Ever?
102   And affected more of the world—because the skulls' energies interplay with the fabric of the world and are a stabilizing influence on it.
103 Although it is now known as the Mitchell-Hedges skull (see chapter 1), it is being taken around the world, awakening consciousness in many countries, in the care of its current guardian, Bill Homann.

Chapter 7

Chronicles of Atlantis 6
Distorting the Divine Archetype

It was Pythagoras, the famous Greek mathematician, mystic, and scientist of the sixth century BC, who said:

> "Know thyself and thou shall know all the mysteries of the gods and of the universe."

And he wasn't joking! He was absolutely right. But it takes an altered state of consciousness to look so deeply within.[104]

    I'd already seen the truth of his words on the therapy retreat in Spain in 1992, when I experienced enlightenment[105]—and although I'd have to wait until 1993 for my realization about the black god, within weeks of my return from Spain a soul therapy session took me deeper into the mysteries of the gods—well, at least into the mystery of one of them! ... The one whose sad story underpins this chapter. It was the first of the rare times I'd looked down to see the blockage I needed to release, only to be shocked to find it was not my human 3D body I was looking at, no, not at all, but a body made of etheric energy—which was a soft, luminous pale blue, very definitely male, and endowed with a huge scaly fishtail where there should have been legs!?!

    Undaunted, Francesca had pressed on and explored the

---

104 Altered states can be accessed through fasting, meditation, hypnosis, entheogens, Sufi dancing, body work, breath work, shamanic work, regression therapy, etc. Altered states help us penetrate the mysteries by making it easier to tune into the unified field of conscious existence, where we all function as tiny, perfect holograms of the whole.

105 As explained in footnote 2 in the preceding chapter.

situation. We released the emotional energy trapped within the body, and as we proceeded with the healing, a story emerged: *Poseidon's view of the events leading up to the destruction of Atlantis was revealed—for that's whose body it was—it was Poseidon.* Now I'm not Poseidon anymore than you are, but we all share that energy within our collective psyche, and it had come up to be healed through the consciousness that was open to it at the time.

So you can see I'd had Poseidon's story since 1992 ... but it never crossed my mind to wonder if I might have had a more personal link with the Atlantean catastrophe ...

The regression for this chapter was almost the last I underwent for *Holy Ice.* I'd breezily thought we'd finished before we did this. But I'd been asked if I knew anything about the end of Atlantis, and with this intriguing thought in my mind I'd meditated and found memories welling up.

Veronica agreed to do an extra session to see what we could uncover. As there was no skull in the life it hadn't come up while we were researching the skulls, but looking back now there was no way I could have missed this session and still had *Holy Ice* making sense. It's a pivotal chapter: the events, and especially the connections afterward.

Veronica had suggested I meet the guides in the setting of an inner-world library. Utilizing such a device is a good way to gather extra information, because you can consult the books held therein—a symbolic means to access knowledge perhaps otherwise even more deeply hidden. So armed with what I had gleaned in the library, and with what I already knew about Poseidon, I entered the hallway of doors.

An azure blue door with four beaded panels attracted my attention. I could see the evidence of men's handiwork in the uneven brushstrokes that marred the finish of the paint work, but I admired the richness of the color, much more vibrant than lapis lazuli, and a color you might find in the sea or the sky. The door had a polished gold knob. There was a keyhole, but the key was missing. It was not there, and there was no sign of it.

I turn the knob and find it isn't locked.

The door yields, and I open it and step through … into clouds.

Armalco's Story
POSEIDON

I am above the Earth. Guides and angels are with me planning my next incarnation. They talk together, while I look down from the clouds and see the lands of Atlantis stretching out below me, basking in sunlight and framed by the sparkle of the Atlantic Ocean.

My soul grows restless as memories stir. I've been to these lands so often. I've been so very happy here that I have forged a heart-link with this country … but it's not all been sunshine and roses. I've been sad here too. A poor slave sent in as part of the taxes, desperate to escape, who eluded the dogs, talked himself onto a ship bound for home—only to be tossed overboard, sacrificed to Poseidon in a wild storm, as the sea captain sought to save his ship and crew …

The guides and angels break into my reverie and tell me it's my last chance to be here—will I take it?

Without hesitation I say, "Yes," and the prebirth contract is arranged.

They show me details of the coming life. I'll be the son of Jonas, a humble fisherman, but I'll be happy and strong. They say male energy is important for me, I have a lot of female energy at this point in my evolution, and a strong male incarnation will bring balance. They show me the potential mother and father, who seem kind. I'm confident they'll love me.

I allow myself to be conceived. I come spiraling down the frequencies of the universe, like a sycamore seed spinning down to the ground. When my energy matches that of Earth I'm sucked into a womb. It is a serene space, peaceful and nurturing. Over the next months I drift in and out of the developing body and spend time in my mother's aura as I get used to my parents-to-be. I note they are healthy, they're always short of money, and they eat a lot of fish!

Birth is straightforward and anchors me firmly in my body. My soul memories fade. I'm a big lusty baby with an appetite for life and no problem feeding. My name is Armalco,[106] but I'm Malco for short—unless I've been naughty and I'm being chastised. Then it's, "**Ar**malco, **no!**" Being mischievous is fun and it's how I find out the rules. I learn to walk early and have a good sense of balance, and by the time I'm three I'm allowed out on the boat with my dad. I enjoy that very much, I like the water.

It's loads better than being stuck at home with my mum where it's boring. I love Mum, but it's much more exciting being out with Dad. Dad is my hero. I want to be like him when I grow up. He's strong and he knows everything there is to know about fishing, and when he comes home with the fish he makes my mum laugh, telling her jokes he's heard and saying how beautiful she is. I like the sound of her laughter.

Another thing I like is the company of the other fishermen. I feel very grown up when they ask me if I'm helping my dad out.

On the boat, I get given little jobs to do, and as time passes I can do more and more. By the time I'm six, I catch fish myself, and I feel very important presenting them to my mum for our supper.

It's a simple life but it's good.

We have nets, fishing rods, and baskets to trap things. What we use depends on what we're after and where we're fishing. Sometimes we go further afield along the rocky coast and stay away overnight. Being away from home is always an adventure.

Our home is in the fishermen's quarter of Atlanta, close by the waterway where we moor our boat. My family are renting the cheapest rooms they can find, at the very top of one of the tenement buildings. These weren't intended to be so tall, but generations of landlords have piled a patchwork of flimsy wooden structures on top of the flat roofs of the original stone dwellings, so five families live on top of each other now, where there was one before. We often talk of moving but we never do, we just talk about it.

Absolutely everything has to be carried up all the way to our rooms, every stick of firewood for the brazier, every morsel of food, every drop of water. Jugs of water from the well are heavy, and it

---

106 Armalco has come down to us as Malcolm. Just as Wama-marma is still with us as William.

is a struggle to carry them up the steps that zigzag up and down the outside of the building. It's hardest for Mum really, because she's there the most.

The first two flights of steps are stone, worn down, but solid enough. They're not so bad. The problem comes with the narrow, rickety stairs clinging to the wooden walls above them. These are dangerous at the best of times and always in poor repair. And of course, when we came along, Mum also had us little ones to look after as well as coping with all the tricky, troublesome stairs.

By the time I am twelve I have a brother of nine, Shen, and a little sister of two, Jena. So although us lads are out from under Mum's feet, busy helping Dad to feed our hungry mouths and pay the rent, Mum still has Jena at home, and there's another baby on the way. But what's life if it isn't a mix of sunshine and rain? And sometimes it's our turn for the gods to smile on us.

It was the day of my dad's birthday.

Mum had gone to market to barter the best of our catch for some meat. We enjoyed meat but could rarely afford it; this would be a real treat to honor Dad's special day.

She had taken a bag of fine lobsters, and as she waited patiently in the queue at the butcher's stall she overheard some women gossiping behind her. There was much talk of an accident that had happened earlier in the day. One of the women had seen heavy logs fall from a cart and go crashing and rolling into a crowd of people. A young lad had been fatally injured. The woman didn't know whose son he was, but she did know he was wearing the clothing of an apprentice from the Temple of Poseidon ...

"The temple will tell his poor family ... terrible ... snatched from life with no warning ... ee, it makes you think ... no chance to say good-bye ... you never know when your last day's comin' ... it could have been us passin' there ... mind, it's them dogs I blame ... poor horses ..."

Mum got her meat and she realized the significance of this bit of information. Of course, it was a tragedy—but perhaps within that lay an opportunity.

Thank the gods, Dad and I had finished early that day, because as soon as she got home I was dispatched to the temple.

There was only a slim chance the position of apprentice would still be vacant, but it was worth a try. There wasn't a moment to lose.

I jump down the creaking stairs, race through the back alleys, cross the bridge over the waterway, and come to the sun-warmed stones of the broad thoroughfare that borders the seaway. The paved highway stretches ahead of me into the haze of the distance, and I know if I follow it, it will take me straight there.

I'm a strapping lad for twelve, big, strong, and well muscled. I cover the ground as quickly as I can, stopping only occasionally along the way to catch my breath.

The temple is near the center of Atlanta, near the palace, and it fronts onto the tidal seaway that cleaves through our city like an arrow, straight to its heart. A private waterway runs round the great rectangular building that forms the main body of the temple, and turns it into an island.

I draw near, and cross over a footbridge to reach the steps of the proud porticoed entrance. Rows of stone columns screen the walls, standing on silent guard like sentinels, and I pass between them and enter the cool darkness within. As my eyes adjust, I step down—into a dim and shadowy world of illusion.

The kingdom of the sea echoes and whispers around me. Seawater is running in open channels around the sides of the gloomy chamber. Tiny light wells hidden in the ceiling beam down narrow fingers of light, which catch on the rippling surface of the water, giving rise to the ceaseless dance of fluid patterns that flicker over the blue-green walls: it's like being under the sea.

With respectful footsteps, I walk past walls covered in scenes of sea life; where among rocks and coral swim fishes, dolphins, and mermen. On the wall to my right a group of mermaids have been drawn, waiting in attendance on Poseidon's consort. There are paintings and mosaics and shells all intertwined to create the pictures on the walls; and though there's beauty here, the place is heavy with a feeling of Poseidon's brooding presence. It's a powerful energy, like a storm waiting to happen. And it emanates from the looming dark hulk of his statue.

The deeper I go into the temple, and the closer I get to the statue, the darker it becomes and the harder it is for me to see—but there's no mistaking the frightful red eyes now glaring down at me. Poseidon towers above me, a giant, taller than five men standing atop each other. His hollow eyes glow a baleful red as the torches set within them flicker.

I bow my head and wait. My gaze falls on the channel of seawater encircling the base of his statue, and I see the angry fire of his eyes reflecting in the watery channels on the floor. As the minutes pass, I study the huge bronze fish-scaled tail in front of me. Eventually, a priest appears from the mystery of shadows to the rear of the statue. He asks what brings me to this holy place, and I offer myself in service.

He considers me.

He looks me up and down and asks my name and age. He questions me closely about my parentage and lineage. I tell him how I love the sea, how strong I am, how hard I will work for the temple, how grateful my family is to Poseidon for his bounty, as he has given us our livelihood for generations.

"Very well then," he says, "We'll see if Poseidon will have you."

He tells me to kneel before the statue.

He bends down, and I hear the scrape of stone on stone as he pulls out a stopper and unblocks a hidden channel that runs beneath the statue, allowing seawater to flow in. Standing before the great bronze image he bows, and begins to ululate the priestly incantation to the Master of the Sea:

> *"Herr-Merrr, Herr-Merrr, Herr-Merrr.*
> *Does it please the mighty Poseidon to accept Armalco,*
> *Humble child of your lands,*
> *Into service?"*

And from the channel under the hollow statue the restless swell of the sea sighs, "Yesssssss."

Had it remained silent I know I would have been dismissed. But now he scoops up seawater with a large shell and anoints me, tipping it slowly over my head. And as cold salty water runs in rivulets down my head and face—making me clench my eyes, running over my lips, dripping off my chin, and wetting my tunic, I hear the words, "Your service is sealed by Poseidon's kiss."

"Very good then," he says, "Welcome to the fellowship of the temple," and he offers me his hand with the hand clasp of brotherhood, and pulls me to my feet.

"I'll get your uniform. Wait here."

He returns. Over his arm lies a white tunic top, rope belt, and navy leggings that will reach down to below my knees, and in his hand he holds a thin white rope for fashioning into a circlet for my hair. I see the sign of Poseidon is embroidered on the back of the tunic—everyone recognizes his trident. God of the seas and earthquakes, he whips up the storms with the prongs, and when he's angry he beats the ground with the staff, until the very earth quakes. It's the symbol of his power, and I never thought to wear it.

The priest says to come back tomorrow, in the uniform, at day's start.

I bow to him, and to the statue, and take my leave. I'm absolutely thrilled. This is more than I could ever have hoped for. You have to be born into the right family to work for the temple, not to be of poor fisher-stock like me. I can't get home quickly enough to tell my parents.

I pant up the creaking steps, gasp it out, and they crow with pleasure and exultation. It will mean more money for us all—and a better life for me, though my dad says he will miss me out on the boat. But he has my brother, Shen's a stout-hearted lad and a good help at that, even though he's only nine.

Our evening meal is a celebration and a taste of better things to come. I go to bed excited, mind in a whirl, looking forward to what the morrow will bring.

"You're made-up for life, working at that temple," my mum had said, *"No more uncertainty about wages ... You don't have to risk your life in storms ..."* The words go round and round, but eventually I do drift off to sleep ... *temple ... wages ... storms ... storm ...*

I'm dreaming. I'm out at sea in a boat. There's a big full moon in a darkened sky, and I'm very, very frightened. The waters rage around me and I'm terrified for my life. The boat is going to sink.

Poseidon rises up out of the sea, clear to his waist.

He is enormous, much bigger and kinder than the statue would have had me believe, and he holds my boat in the palm of his hand and says, "Be safe, my son, I will look after you. I will protect you. Have no fear."

Calm steals over the waters of the deep, the sun comes out, and Poseidon sinks down beneath the waves.

The dream is chillingly vivid and I still remember the intense feeling of terror when I awake, but once I'm out of bed I get caught up in the excitement of the new day and think no more about it. I don my uniform and breakfast hastily on some bread and goat's milk, then set off for the temple.

Once there, I am set to polishing the bronze trimmings along the length of the stately boats.

All the rowlocks, handles, and decorative bronzes have to shine like mirrors, and the boats look extremely impressive lined up, one by one, along the back and sides of the temple—their metalwork flashing in the sunlight, as they bob gently on the swell of the temple's waterway.

And there are a lot of boats. They are solid craft, made of expensive woods, and not at all like my dad's patched-up, small, ancient, and dropping-apart fishing boat ... which had been his father's before him, and his grandfather's before that.

It is a very busy temple. It seems as though every sea captain wants his vessel blessed before setting sail, and money just pours in to the priests. There is a steady flow of funeral work too, and I am well paid for my labors.

I am part of a team of boys and we work away with a will. We share laughter and camaraderie, and we are treated well by the priests. I enjoy my work, and I enjoy the company of the other men. As time passes, I grow bigger, stronger, and taller than my dad.

When I am eighteen, I am promoted to oarsman.

I join one of the rowing teams taking the boats out, and I'm proud to wear the navy-blue tunic and navy leggings that go with this station; the golden trident I sport on my back is much larger than when I was an apprentice. Our teams look spectacular when we are out on the water, pulling on the oars, all bending together in rhythm, with the sun flashing on our rows of golden tridents.

Temple work pays even better now.

As time goes by, some of my friends set up their own homes and get married, and there is certainly no shortage of beautiful girls trying to catch our eye in the hope of marrying an oarsman. But even though I am nearly nineteen I still live with Mum and Dad. I could go drinking and squander my money on the favors of pretty girls in the taverns, like the others do who were born to riches, but I love my parents and owe them everything, even my good fortune.

My dad's boat had been almost beyond mending when I first went to the temple, and so from the very first day we had decided to save my wages and put them toward a better fishing boat, bigger, stronger, and more seaworthy than our old wreck. With this new boat, my dad would be able to have people working for him, and with more money coming in we would soon move to better accommodation.

Well, that was our plan.

We did get to eat meat much more often, which was good; but because of a dreadful storm we had to replace our boat sooner than we wanted, which was bad. By this stage we had only saved enough to buy a small one, not the big boat of our dreams, but at least Dad could continue fishing. It was only after I became an oarsman that we traded this in, with all our extra savings, for the boat that was going to change our lives forever.

I loved my job … and everything was going nicely to plan.

But as it turned out, I didn't get to do my job for very long.

We had recently got the large seaworthy boat we had longed for when fate stuck its oar in our fortunes. It was true that for generations our people had been living their lives against a backdrop of prophecies of doom and destruction. Some had heeded the warnings and left to make new lives for themselves in other lands, but the prophecies had been going on for so long now without anything happening, that many had returned.

We had become inured to the tales of a watery end, and people were so weary of hearing about it they had stopped listening.

Besides, the priests at the temple where I worked declared loud and long, for all to hear, that there was nothing to worry about because they kept Poseidon happy with their ceremonies and sacrifices. *So why should he want to take our land? And why should we worry?* Well … that's what they said.

Yes, there had been signs and portents, there had been comets, but after all this time we had begun to think that the prophecies foretold by the other temple would never actually come to pass, and certainly not in our lifetime. Not even when Dad saw the cloudiness come into the water, and suffered days of poor catches with never a dolphin to be seen, not even then did we think the end-days were upon us.

How wrong we were.

We had gone to bed as usual, with stomachs full after a good supper of skewered lamb.[107] Because although Dad was grumbling about the lack of fish, my wages bought us tasty meat and there was never a need to go hungry—and anyway we were sure the fishing would pick up again soon. There had been plenty of lean times before, but they never lasted long.

It was in the darkness before dawn that the first tremors began to ripple through the tenements.

We were torn from the land of dreams and shaken out of our beds … We awoke to an ominous cacophony of cracking and splintering timbers.

Our home was crumbling around us.

Dad shouted for us to grab our little ones and flee. Terrified, Dad, Mum, Shen, and I staggered over the swaying floor boards dragging Jena and our three youngest with us, escaping down what was left of the steps. We passed the young ones between us across the yawning gaps, and when we reached the ground only luck saved us from what was falling and crashing around us.

Dad yelled out, "To the boat!" And instinctively we headed for the open land around the waterway, leaving ruined and collapsing buildings behind us. Fissures and cracks were appearing, and the land beneath our feet juddered and shuddered like a jellyfish. We ran as fast as we could.

We weren't very religious—and the Temples of Hera and

---

107 Kebabs.

Poseidon were a long way away—so it never even crossed our minds to seek shelter there. We were pragmatic folk, us—and our thoughts had gone straight to our boat. We wanted to save it, because it was all we had. And right now Dad had more confidence in the sea than in the untrustworthy land, so he was planning to see this crisis out at sea.

We would return later, he said, when it was safe.

There were people screaming and running everywhere, but we had only one thought in our heads—*our boat*—and when we got to the waterway we found it waiting for us, and still in one piece, though the angry waters had made driftwood of some of the others.

We helped our four little ones down into the safety of Dad's arms as he stood surefootedly in our rocking vessel. And when my mother, brother, and I were in, Dad cast off the mooring ropes. As we floated free he found eight lengths of rope, one for each of us, and when he was sure they were secured around our waists he knotted them firmly to the boat. We were preparing to sail down the seaway to the ocean.

It was still dark, but the sky was a bloody red over the sea and the ground was roaring.

One minute our boat was bobbing on the water, the next minute the water was being sucked out to sea, taking our boat with it. We floated in the terror of that early morning, and when we peered over the sides to look for the coastline, we could see there were fires in the city and smoke was filling the air.

A huge wave surged beneath us and we were lifted on high with a sickening, sinking feeling in the pits of our stomachs. The little ones cried out, and though we tried to comfort them and held them, there was nothing we could do because the situation was so dire. Wave after wave surged beneath us. We were borne on high, and brought swooping down with a sickening lurch time after time. The children cried inconsolably, and we lay in the bottom of our boat and prayed.

Mercifully it did not overturn. Morning broke but things got worse.

The air was tainted with a stench and there was so much smoke that the light was dim, but we could see that the land was disappearing beneath the waves. We floated through the nightmare hours until they became days and we were faint with hunger and thirst.

From time to time, rain collected in the bottom of the boat. It did not taste good but we drank it. Although there were eight of us and I was the strongest, my strength availed us nothing.

There was just nothing to be done.

And it was hardest on our youngest. Sho-nu was seven, and the poor little twins, Ad-ri and Beno, were only five.[108] We gave them what bread was left on board from the last fishing trip, and perhaps we came by the odd fish—it's hard to remember now. We began to drift in and out of consciousness. As we floated on the sea, so lost and alone, my dream came back to haunt me.

I hoped something would happen.

I hoped Poseidon would keep the word he had given me in the dream. It was true we were still alive, and that the boat hadn't gone down, but there was no land to be seen anywhere. And in truth, *the only thing we could see approaching was death* ... We were almost on our last gasp, expiring as surely as do fishes pulled from the sea, when we were found by one of the huge ships of the Atlantean navy.

The sailors and captain picked us up and looked after us just in time to save all our lives; and fortunately, they had enough supplies with them to make us welcome. They pulled our boat up on board, and we made our home on their broad deck, beneath its up-turned shelter.

They were returning home from a mission, but after hearing our account of the terrible events, and finding that home was no longer there, they set sail for the Lands of the West.[109] Some call them the Empty Lands because so few people live there, compared to our land, and to the lands of our empire to the east—but they are fertile, and full of animals that could be hunted. It would be a good place to replenish supplies, they said.

It was just dreadful—sailing where there should be land, but there was nothing. There was just water. They had maps with them and they could tell from the stars what should be where. We

108 Ad-ri and Jena were my sisters; Sho-nu, Beno, and Shen, my brothers.
109 North America.

sailed right across what would have been the northern part of our continent, right over where the great lakes had been.[110] We passed the tip of a mountain here and there, barren and rocky, you couldn't call it an island. There were lots of things floating, dead bodies, dead animals, bits of things, bits of wood, broken things. We didn't see a living soul. It didn't mean there wasn't anybody else … I wanted to think there were other people who had survived.

Like everybody else, we'd heard the legends and the prophecies, we knew all about that, but working at the temple of Poseidon you felt safe because Poseidon's the one who calls the sling shots, after all. He's the one who makes the earth quake and looks after the sea, so if he's happy you're alright. And we thought to keep him happy, as we'd always done before. We worked hard for the priests, and they'd said there was nothing to worry about—***but something had gone terribly wrong.***

When we reached the Lands of the West, there they left us.

The captain explained he hadn't enough supplies to take us farther, and he wanted to go south to see if there was any part of our land left remaining.

He gave assurances he would be coming back.

The sailors came ashore to get water and meat, and they took us with them. They left us with a little camp, our boat and the means to fish, as well as knives and bronze implements so we could hunt. They kindly made sure we had what we needed to look after ourselves, and after helping them hunt, we'd learned enough to be able to get meat for ourselves.

Before they left, the captain said, "If there's any land, when we come back for you we'll take you there. So give us about a moon, and then start lighting bonfires on the high ground," he gestured to a nearby cliff top, "Then we'll see the smoke and we'll know you're alive and wanting to come with us. It will help us to find you. We won't let you down."

He meant what he said, and he was as good as his word.

---

110 As the lakes were well below sea level, when the mountains around them were breached the sea made short work of claiming them for its own. This contributed to the northern half of the continent disappearing very quickly. And as Atlanta was on a low-lying floodplain, she was soon beneath the waves too.

When they returned, they brought the welcome news that there was still land to the south. But although they took us there we did not feel safe. The tremors continued, and so we, like many others, journeyed further to the Lands of the Sun.[111] There we settled and began again.

I married and still made my living by fishing, but the young ones never really got over it. They'd wake screaming in the night, thinking they were living through the nightmare time again. And for sure it hastened Mum's death.

But in time I had children of my own, and we got by, that is until I reached my forty-eighth year. I was not ill then, but just utterly worn out. It had been a very hard life of graft.[112] And looking back, I could see that Poseidon had been good to us—he fed us and kept us safe—and we were blessed and fortunate when you think how things might have been.

I slipped out of the life and reached the point in the regression session where it was time to consider what I had learned:

- **It was because of love we were saved.** Because I loved my family and wanted to help I dashed to the temple, and because I loved them I gave them all the money I earned— so **love bought the boat that saved us**, and love tipped the scales of karma in our favor.[113]
- **Because we worked as a team** we saved all the children.
- **You need to be in the right place at the right time, and if you follow your heart you will be.** That was how my mum overheard the conversation in the market and how she knew there was a chance for me at the temple. Jobs there were very sought after and hard to get.
- **I came to understand the camaraderie of men, that male energy, and how seductive it is when you're in that sort of environment.** You enjoy the company of men and you're all very hearty and bluff. But that's not what the world needs

---

111 Central America.

112 A far cry from the long life of a pampered princess.

113 The dream was part of the prebirth contract, but we have free will and so I might not have fulfilled my part of the bargain. We would not have got the boat soon enough to save our lives if I'd spent half the money on myself.

now. Not in the places of power, in the boardrooms and governments of the world, where the decisions are made that affect all our futures. That "gentlemen's club," as it's been, needs female values to come in to bring balance, and this will be explored later—*because it is the missing key to unlock the door to our future.* And without it, the door stays locked.

Next, it was time to consider the healing I needed to do. The most important thing was to release the terror from the time Atlantis went down—the energy was black and dark red, the color of the sky at sea and the smoke. And when I looked to see where I was holding it, it was everywhere in my body. After I released it with the help of the angels, I visualized pale-green and diamond-white light flooding through me, healing and rebalancing my entire body.

This is such an important chapter that all three guides who were involved at different points in the research came to help me to understand its significance: Francis, Jesus,[114] and Hera. They said there needed to be a simple but effective healing included, because many people reading this chapter will have been there. So many people died in shock, horror, and terror at that dreadful time that they gave me the words written below to help let the pain out of our psyche. It's because of the sheer size of the wound that the memories of Atlantis never disappeared, and the myths and legends persist on down the ages to this day.

Intention is everything. Please give it a go in a quiet moment, it need not take more than a few minutes. Settle down as you would for a meditation, or just read it like a prayer and say to God in a heartfelt way:

---

114 Jesus came for sessions in *Spiritual Gold* and *Divine Fire*, but not for the early ones in *Holy Ice*. The gift of being aware of the presence of your guides is one of the loveliest aspects of doing inner work. To meet them yourself in meditation I recommend Edwin C. Steinbrecher's book, *The Inner Guide Meditation: A Transformational Journey to Enlightenment and Awareness*—I first met Francis through the suggested meditation in this book. Try it! It is simple. Remember we don't choose our guides, they choose us. We simply find them when we make time to go and look. Besides our main guide, it is quite normal for specialist guides to be drafted in for certain things from time to time, depending on what is needed.

**Deliver me now from the sins of the past
and the wounds of the world. Cleanse my spirit and
my soul. Renew me. Renew me with the Creator's
light and fill me now with boundless energy. Wash
me in light, make me whole, and may I be blessed
and an instrument in thy service to bring about
the healing of the world and myself.**

Then visualize divine light flowing down to you from God, flowing into your crown and all around you, dissolving any darkness and shadows of pain within you. Breathe in the light until you are filled, and then continue for a little while longer as you visualize the light still flowing down from God to you, becoming a fountain now, that flows out to bathe our cities and our lands with light. Nourishing and strengthening, bringing healing and cleansing, you and the Earth washed and made new with light.

And when you have done as much or as little as you have time for, finish with:

**I accept that it is done.
I thank you.**

Doing it in silence is fine, but the spoken word carries more power.

If everybody reading this were to do it, even just once, I'm sure there would be a shift in the collective consciousness of humanity. So many of us are carrying that wounded traumatized energy, and the Earth is carrying it too. She lost a continent because of an imbalance on the etheric level of cause, created by those of mankind who should have known better.

Of course, on the physical level of reality the trigger for the earthquakes was pressure being released in the Earth's crust. Volcanic activity vented gasses, and chambers that had honeycombed the rocks underlying the continent collapsed.[115] It's possible that a meteorite

---

115   Col. James Churchwood's *Cosmic Forces of Mu, Volume 2,* gives a good idea of this process.

may have struck the already unstable seabed and precipitated this,[116] but there are many people who say that an abuse of crystal energies was the catalyst.[117] But whatever happened on that fateful night, a

---

116 Otto Muck makes a good case for this in *The Secret of Atlantis*.

117 **Abuse of crystal energies:**

Imagine how useful it would have been to the priests of Poseidon to be able to whip up a vortex of energy at will, use it to create a whirlpool, and sink a targeted ship. Was it so tempting they experimented? I wondered this as I was finishing *Holy Ice*, and so in January 2017 I was regressed to see if I could find any memories that would shed a bit more light on things—because up to this point it was nothing more than a hunch.

I found a shepherd's life. He had witnessed things he should not have seen. There was an area of coastline north of Atlanta that had been sequestered by the priests of Poseidon. Fishermen in the local villages were forbidden to take their boats there, and clandestine things were going on in caves that ran beneath the sea. It was a crystal-rich area and they had large crystals in the caves.

What came up in the regression was supplemented by additional information gleaned in a later meditation, and so I became aware of more than that which the shepherd had been able to see as he watched, hidden, from the cliffs overlooking the bay where the priests were conducting their experiments in using crystal power. He saw a cloud of haze hovering over the sea, and in it hung lightning bolts. It looked very unnatural. The sky was blue, there was no storm, it was just a very localized small disturbance over the water. But day after day the priests persisted and repeated the phenomenon. The lightning bolts got bigger.

They had huge piezoelectric quartz crystals in the caves which they repeatedly struck to release an energy charge—this was collected in accumulator crystals from which the energy was targeted and released involving telepathy. On the fateful night they had targeted a ship that hadn't paid them for a blessing, the lightning bolt had penetrated it and sunk it, but had carried on down into the seabed and kept on going until the seabed ruptured and all hell was let loose. It was a major miscalculation, much more energy had been released than was necessary to do the job.

Well, that's what I saw in meditation, so I will leave it with you. We can only speculate, but in esoteric circles the crystal hypothesis has been embraced for a very long time.

The shepherd was a parallel or sub-incarnation of mine; such is the power of our spirits—our True Selves—that we can sustain several incarnations in the same time frame. (As a part of God, our TS is outside of time.)

At the start of the regression session (a psycho-regression session, conducted by my husband, Ye), I was as usual told to visualize myself in a beautiful place in nature, somewhere I felt relaxed and at peace … And I found myself on a riverbank. I felt relaxed there, but then I found myself looking round for places to hide. I considered the river. There were reeds at the edges, and I said to Ye I could crouch down under the water, make myself disappear from sight, and

rift opened up on the Atlantic bottom, and this was so great that it stretches all the way from Puerto Rico to Iceland even today. This was the rift that Atlantis dropped into.

Atlantis was situated on the junction of continental plates.

The Eurasian and African plates abut the North and South Atlantic plates, which rub shoulders with the Caribbean plate—

breathe through a hollow piece of reed stem(!) This was so bizarre, to be thinking like this. It had never happened to me before, to be scared in nature, before we had even looked at anything … (but I did go on to complete the shamanic journey that eventually took me into the shepherd's life). But it was as though I was subconsciously afraid the priests of Poseidon were coming after me. And Lord knows what they'd have done to me if they found me. **Because the cat would be out of the bag—I knew they cheated! They did not have Poseidon's ear. They were faking being able to make him do their biding!** If it got out, the flow of money to their temple would dry up, and they would be discredited. **Their temple thrived on tricks and deceit.**

In the space of time it took to drink a cup of coffee after the session, I began to feel ill. I had been absolutely fine before. It just came on out of the blue. And for the next month I experienced the most terrible flu. My bones were like ice and I did not want to eat. I just slept, day after day and night after night. I have never been so ill in all my life. Coincidence? I began to suspect I'd taken a vow of secrecy concerning the activities of the priests of Poseidon. Obviously, the shepherd hadn't. He had no dealings with the priests, or their temple. But either Armalco had a formal induction into temple life which did not come up in the regression when I found his story, or there may have been yet another life involved. Like the Official Secrets Act, even today at work it is routinely expected that you will sign a form forbidding you from disclosing your employer's secrets or bad-mouthing the company you are working for. Neither Armalco nor the shepherd gave away secrets, but I was planning to! Thousands of years later I was preparing to share them with the world, when I was struck down. When I thought about it I was so sure that it was punishment for a broken vow, that the next time Ye regressed me I asked him to check it out before we finished the session.

There was a vow, and a subconscious belief that I deserved to die because I'd broken it. The belief lay behind the terrible "one-foot-in-the-grave flu," I had actually called it that at the time! The symbol for the vow was a black trident spearing me through the guts. It was the reason I couldn't eat—and if I'd followed the feeling right through I would have starved. As it was I lost half a stone in weight.

Releasing vows and curses is quite routine, but somehow this one had slipped under the radar! Ye used the usual rattles and sounds to help me release the old stuck energy, and when the black had cleared I rebalanced my body and aura with golden white light. Poseidon came to help me and he was angry because they did it in his name, but it was nothing to do with him. He took out an etheric energy that was part of the trident.

and Atlantis lay over or touched on all these junction points. As these large pieces of the surface of the Earth move separately, their movement creates stress that seeks release. But when you consider that the physical world is an out-picturing of the spiritual reality that lies behind it, the spiritual reality will have its own answers about what provoked such a massive disturbance in the fabric of the world.

In just the same way that emotions and thoughts can be psychosomatic triggers for disease in a physical body, so imbalances in the world's subtle energy will show up, eventually, as changes in the world of form.

The world had been stable for a long period of time prior to this, and as surely as winter is followed by spring, some sort of a change was coming. But it should have been a shift in the political landscape, with Atlantis being overthrown by an empire united against her. Or the earthquakes that drowned her could have merely changed her coastline. There's usually a recovery after earthquakes and tsunamis, but for them to wipe out a whole continent something has to be seriously out of balance. And that something had been detected by those who worked with the skulls in the Temple of Hera.

Hera came as a guide for these sessions because she knows her children need healing from this trauma. The trauma took her temple from her and she's never had an anchor point in the world like that since. Hardly anybody gives her a thought these days, but she still cares, and she still watches over us because she's part of the Creator, she's caring female energies shaped by human thought and personified as Hera, Her-Ra. She was a mother for the people of the ancient world and she weeps for her children still.

To understand why this disaster happened I'm going to use an analogy. It was as if Atlantis had grown old, become stiff and rigid with traditions and rules, and then contracted a fatal disease. The deadly disease in question was the dis-ease that had sprung up between the two Great Temples.

Rampant male ego and stubborn pride had inflated the cult of Poseidon. It was an all-male temple dedicated to a powerful male god; there were no priestesses of Poseidon. And because of the importance their society attached to him, his priests came to think of themselves as more important than those who served all the other gods in the Temple of Hera.

They fell prey to a spirit of rivalry. They ceased to undertake the rigorous training provided in the Temple of Hera, and when they took control of their own training they abandoned many of the priestly disciplines such as scrying.

A spiritual blindness set in.[118]

They saw no need for divination or anything not directly required for the functions of their temple, which were simply:

- **ceremonies at sea**—giving Poseidon **living people** as sacrifices, in the hope of gaining his favor
- **funerals at sea**—being paid to give **dead people** to Poseidon
- **blessing the boats** of superstitious sea captains—and the more fearsome they made Poseidon out to be, the more money they raked in.

As their wealth and power grew, greed came to seduce their integrity. They ceased referring to, or as they saw it, *bowing to*, the priests and priestesses of the Temple of Hera *over any matter*.

So when the skulls showed things needed to be different, they would not listen. They refused to reintroduce the old ways from the time when all they'd had was a chapel in Hera's temple: they wouldn't bring back the worship of the Queen of the Sea,[119] or remove the scary statue—renowned the length and breadth of the empire— because this would cause great loss of face and loss of revenue. They considered themselves to be the experts on Poseidon, and they did not want to be humbled and told they'd got things wrong. They certainly did not want the central point of their temple to be reduced to a simple altar to Poseidon and his queen, Amphitrite.

This refusal to reintroduce the worship of both the male *and* female energies of the sea meant that balance was not going to be restored on the etheric levels of cause. And like all imbalances, it

118 They hadn't got the crystal skulls, so they downplayed their worth.

119 I feel this loss was symbolized by the missing key to the door at the beginning of the session, and that the poor painting technique equated to the poor job the priests had done at the Temple of Poseidon. Without the key to lock it, the door yielded easily—just as Atlantis yielded easily and was swept away. With the key gone, her defense was gone. (The key being reverence for the Queen of the Sea, a symbol for honoring female values.)

would seek to right itself when it grew too great.

If you will, they had been distorting the soul of the world for their own gain, and in their blindness they were determined to go on doing so. The temple's huge program of human sacrifice was what was fueling the distortion.

The reasoning behind it was that they believed if they gave Poseidon the lives of lots of slaves and prisoners he wouldn't take the lives of the Atlantean sailors and those who had paid them for a blessing.

But it wasn't lives Poseidon was after, he simply wanted his queen.

Because Amphitrite was of no value to them, the priests had ignored her. They had reduced her to a vague mention among the murals on the temple walls. She was no longer included in their ceremonies, and this had gone on for so long that the energies in her archetype had grown faint, while the psychic energy of all the sacrifices they had made to Poseidon had inflated his archetype. He had been puffed up and distorted, and as his wife faded away from him he had grown lonely, irritable, frustrated, and ever more angry. The imbalance between the male and female energies was growing bigger and bigger, and a dangerous tipping point approached.[120]

The emperor was caught between the two factions. He was concerned about the prophecies and had no reason to doubt the visions of the future that the skulls were showing, but he couldn't

---

120 The priests had meddled. It would have been better if they'd done nothing. Life on Earth had begun in the seas long before humankind strode the planet. The energies that had been translated by human understanding into the king and queen of the sea had happily seeded the seas with life in their joyful and fertile union. But now they were trapped in the archetypes, and distorted by the power of human thought. This was purely an Atlantean problem because the empire had been educated by the scrolls from the Temple of Hera, and so recognized Amphitrite in her rightful place. The empire did not pay the price because it did not make the mistake. They say pride goes before a fall … but even today she must be the least known of all the goddesses, even though all life began in the sea. Without her we would not be here. In their union, spirit had impregnated matter. His body had been of transparent, blue, etheric spirit-energy, while hers—as I saw her—had been more solid, the flesh from which all things are born into the world of form. Her upper body was the color of pink-white flesh, while her tail was a turquoise sea-green. When they were restored to each other in the session I experienced a great charge of energy in my base chakra.

control either of the temples, they were both far too powerful. He couldn't send the troops in to resolve things by force, because there would be uproar. The priests were considered essential by the people and there would have been a total revolt. He couldn't touch them. It had been alright when the two temples got along, but when the rift happened they were like two titans fighting.

Hera's was a temple of light, open to the heavens, a place to find truth and beauty; it was somewhere you went to know, to divine, to be healed, or to give thanks for favors received. There were both priests and priestesses there. In sharp contrast Poseidon's temple was dark, intimidating, and all about power. The unbridled and unbalanced male energy was destructive. The hollow bronze statue, so huge it had been carefully assembled from many parts, often concealed a priest who frightened the living daylights out of sea captains. It was fear of death that brought people to Poseidon's temple, and in time the momentum of that energy became so great that what was feared came to pass.

Poseidon's priests were very, very wealthy with all the money pouring in from blessing the boats, and it was money they had come to care about. By contrast to their greed the priesthood of Hera's temple had kept the purity of their spiritual traditions. They were more altruistic, and they had a greater ability to see the truth of things because they held the skulls. They could see what was going to happen and why, but try as they might, they couldn't force change on the Temple of Poseidon.

All they could do was save the skulls.

Some priests chose to stay behind in the temple out of service to the people of Atlanta. They knew that in the final hours the people would be traumatized and would be streaming into their temple looking for succor and respite. They didn't want them coming into an empty and abandoned temple although they knew it was doomed.

The rest of the priests fled with the skulls to other lands. Sea levels were lower then and it was easy to go south, by way of large islands linking to Central America, and it was easy to go to the northwest, where there was almost a land bridge to Canada. Most of the skulls were taken to North America that way and are still there today.

America is the new Atlantis, or more accurately could be called "child of Atlantis," heir to the Atlantean knowledge and power. Americans have called one of their major cities Atlanta, and its seal and flag show a phoenix with the word "resurgens" meaning "rising again." Purely by chance? Or did the Masons, who were instrumental in the early planning of the cities and who have wielded covert power ever since, know more than you might think?

There is a hidden well of the old knowledge buried inside the name given to the country itself. A "mericum" was literally a "well of knowledge" and that's what Hera's temple was, it was a mericum. It was a place where things poured forth to bless the land—prophecies and knowledge, wisdom and truth. And when I see pictures of the United States Capitol Building in Washington, DC, I see a descendant of Hera's temple; far bigger and grander, yes, and more complex, but with the same central dome rising above a rotunda pierced by many windows.

However, it is the Native Americans who hold the lineage of the priests of Hera. They have descended from those who took the skulls to safety, and they look after them still. The new priests of Poseidon are in the Pentagon and in the military-industrial complex. Those in the Pentagon see everything as a threat, and want to be in control and still don't want to listen—and the military-industrial complex is fixated on making money. They are the ones likely to bring the next catastrophe. Not necessarily a physical one, like the Atlantean inundation, but a catastrophe for us all nonetheless, affecting our quality of life, health, and freedom.

Arms companies want profits from sales, and they benefit from wars thrown in other people's countries. War, money, oil, and greed are inextricably linked. The Pentagon is hardly in the business of balancing male and female energies with its phallic rockets, bombs, planes, and weapons. Hearts and minds? It's not something they're good at. Shock and awe, and a steady flow of computer games and films to glorify destruction and rope in the next generation of young men is the order of the day.

There is only one thing weapons can do. So there is one thing you can absolutely rely on, that no matter where the war is, there will be an ever-growing tally of the dead. Like the priests of Poseidon, the rich and powerful have never had a problem sacrificing others, and so the program of human sacrifice rolls on … just like it did in the Temple of Poseidon.

This Atlanta is built on land taken from the Cherokees and Creeks, and it is a center for germ warfare labs. With the tax dollars of ordinary people, they have created deadly organisms to which we have no **natural** immunity. Why? I can't help but wonder what they are planning to do with them.

We are at the eleventh hour before the next cataclysm. We're facing a similar time of reckoning, a time when things have to change because the old ways aren't working.

The forces of greed have a shadowy web of power with plans of control, wanting to establish a new world order. Sinister undercurrents have been building for a long, long time and there is a lot of information out there if you want to go deeper into this side of things. A good place to start is with the books of David Icke and *The Truth Agenda* by Andy Thomas. But it's what the vast majority of people think and do that will affect our future in a very fundamental way.

If we follow our hearts and do what we know is the right thing, the few can't control the many. It's only if we're kept distracted that the shadowy elite will get away with it. They profit when we are kept fearful by one thing after another: bird flu, swine flu, the financial crash. Drug companies profit from the pandemic fears and there are always people in the know who make money while the ordinary folks are left impoverished. It is all part of control and a shifting of the money away from **us** to **them**.

Money was what was important to the men who ran the Temple of Poseidon. But did it help them when the end came? Did their piles of gold save them?

As the Native Americans have already pointed out, after the last fish has been poisoned you can't eat money.

Truth or greed, it's time to choose again.

But the skulls survived …

Chapter 8

Atlantis Had Gone, but Her Legacy and Her Children Live On

The epicenter of the earthquakes had been out at sea, off the east coast. On that terrible day in 3114 BC destruction had come with the dawn—and although Atlanta and the northern half of the continent perished in a single dreadful day and night, just as Plato says, the south of the continent lingered on for many years longer. But the earthquakes continued sporadically, until only large islands remained above the waters of the ocean, and Atlantis entered the archipelago stage. As time passed, further quakes reduced the islands in size and the map of the Atlantic and Caribbean took on its now familiar form.[121]

The pre-classical civilizations of the Mediterranean which had traded with Atlantis and been part of her empire perished much later, after the eruption of Thera in 1628 BC.[122]

121 Traces of Atlantean buildings are to be found under the seas off Bimini and other Caribbean islands.

122 The Minoan civilization based on Crete, and named after Minos, their most famous king, had grown rich trading food and supplies for goods from the shipping sailing to Atlanta. In alliance with Atlantis, they built up a powerful navy which policed and taxed the shipping lanes and upheld her rule. I believe they were an outpost for Atlantis, that they were "cousins" of the Atlanteans, and that those we think of as the ancient Cretans were well represented in her population. After Atlantis's demise in 3114 BC, the Minoans on Crete took over her trade routes, sailing as far as Canada for copper, and to Britain for the tin they needed to make the copper into bronze. For information on the mineral analysis of copper ingots found, and blood group types, that provide evidence for this, see the book *The Lost Empire of Atlantis* by Gavin Menzies.

In 1628 BC the nearby island of Thera erupted violently and brought all this to an end. It finished off the Minoans—the ensuing tidal wave devastated Crete, destroyed their ships, and brought an end to their power. The subsequent poor harvests (due to volcanic dust blocking out sunlight) brought famine so severe

But so great had been Atlantis's influence on the world that their survivors did not forget the gods she had taught them to worship, nor what a temple should look like. So when civilization flowered again in ancient Greece during the first millennium BC, the same gods were worshipped in temples that echoed the Temple of Poseidon. (Every king and sailor alike had visited there, seeking to ensure their safe journey home, and the design had become imprinted on the Mediterranean psyche as being what the temple of a god should look like—rectangular, surrounded by stately columns and housing a bronze statue of the god or goddess.)

When the Romans came to power in Italy, they also built rectangular, colonnaded temples just like Poseidon's. They worshipped the same gods as the Greeks, although by different names, their Poseidon was "Neptune." But being great engineers they had the skills to build the Pantheon in Rome. This was a great circular temple dedicated to all the gods, roofed over by a dome with a central eye open to the heavens ... and doesn't that sound very familiar? It was, in its essence, a replica of the Temple of the All, Atlanta's Great Temple, otherwise known as the Temple of Hera— and the name is from the Greek for "All the Gods."[123]

So, the Romans had copies of both major Atlantean temples, and they too established a mighty empire. When the centuries turned and BC became AD,[124] it was a world ruled by Rome. By the early fourth century AD, Christianity had become the official religion for the Roman Empire, and the Pantheon was used as a church and

---

that archeologists have found evidence of cannibalism. These were dark times indeed, and civilization ebbed away. But as the centuries passed, it flowered again but this time on the mainland of Greece, when the classical world was born.

123 It did not have windows like the Atlantean temple, because the drum on which the dome rested was not pierced by any openings but was made up of solid wall. The Roman dome was based on the semicircular arch—but the Atlantean dome was a beehive shape, as found in many ancient tombs and buildings attributed to the third millennium BC. This vaulted dome was taller than the squat Roman hemisphere, and better accommodated the painted figures of Hera and Zeus. Like the Atlantean temple, the Pantheon also had a checkerboard floor. A different design, but nevertheless, a checkerboard floor.

124 We count centuries from the birth of Jesus Christ, so BC is **B**efore **C**hrist, or sometimes BCE is used meaning **B**efore **C**ommon **E**ra. AD is anno Domini, Latin for the year of the Lord.

rededicated to the Virgin Mary and all the martyrs—an update on Hera and all the gods!

It is still in use to this day.

However, as time passed, Rome's power waned and the empire split into two; the eastern half, with its capital at Constantinople, was to last longer than the western half. In Rome, as the fifth century AD drew to a close, the last of the Roman emperors was deposed; and after that, Barbarians ruled there. Northern Europe sank into the Dark Ages.

For a long time, scholars thought "dark ages" referred simply to the eclipse of civilization, but from recent studies of ancient tree rings dendrochronologists have found that it really was a time when light levels were poor. The age was literally dark, and this affected both plant growth and climate. There's nothing like scarcity of food to destabilize populations, and this was a factor in the Barbarian hordes migrating and pressing on the Roman Empire. The culprit was volcanic ash in the atmosphere, which screened out sunlight and had a cooling effect on the weather—*affecting events not only in Europe ... but in North America too.* And this is where we are going next.

Ruins at Teotihuacán showing the Pyramid of the Sun

So, northern Europe was slipping into the Dark Ages, and Atlantis lay buried beneath the waves, but her legacy, and her children, lived on. They may have been snatched by fate from an advanced Bronze Age culture[125] and thrust back into the Stone Age—forced to make their home in foreign lands, but they had not forgotten who they were and what had been ... as I was about to find out!

The next session began, and once more I entered the hallway of doors.

You never know what you are going to find, but this time it was an extremely short corridor. The first door I came to was black. I passed it by. I didn't like the feel of the energy coming from it. I sensed there were things I needed to learn before I'd have the armor to face what was in there ... it could wait for another time, and I shuddered.

Instead, I went to a big, solid wooden door that was waiting at the end of the hallway. It had an attractive polished finish that revealed the natural beauty of the wood grain, and it was a little old fashioned, with panels and a brass lever handle and finger plate. I felt comfortable there until I noticed there was a spy hole—arranged so those on the other side could see me, but I couldn't see them. At this point I just knew that in the coming life I had a fear of being observed—and so, without further ado, I blocked up the spy hole. I wasn't having that, being spied on in *my* inner world!

There was a big brass key in the lock and it took two turns to open. The door had been well maintained[126] and I heard it going

---

125 I'm aware there are many accounts of Atlantis having enjoyed a very advanced technology, with flying ships and the like, but I found no evidence for this—I'm not saying it didn't exist, but perhaps it was part of the earlier culture, before the disaster that led to the skulls being taken to the sacred cave for safety. This would be before 10,000 BC.

"Visits from the stars" may have accounted for some marvels. There were hints of this even in my lives—in Ayesha's "star metal" rings, and a feeling that some of the divination in the Great Temple of Noni's time was to ascertain the timing of the next visit from the "stars that landed," as they would call a UFO. One of my past life clients reported seeing a light display over an Atlantean temple, and said it was "their friends from the stars saying good-bye."

Or possibly people have accessed parallel realities where these things happened.

126 Like the legends of the tribes, as you will see.

smoothly "clonk, clonk." Not wanting to be locked in, I visualized handing Veronica the key.

I was still feeling a little nervous and a bit jumpy, so before venturing further I checked that it really was alright for me to continue. The Archangels whose protection I seek before all inner work gave assent.[127] So with Michael, Uriel, Gabriel, and Raphael happy for me to continue, I open the door.

It swings toward me on well-oiled hinges ... and I step through.

Into darkness.

Into night.

... I'm on a high mountain plateau, standing beneath an overarching firmament of twinkling stars.

I am reading the stars ... night breezes swirl gently around me, bringing the scents and sounds of the night.

I'm "Moves Like The Clouds."

I'm a tracker. I melt away before others know I'm there. This is very important to me.

My life depends on it.

Moves Like The Clouds's Story
Vision Quest

In the Rocky Mountains of North America there lived a very troubled people.

We were used to enjoying a simple life in the land of our ancestors, but our land had grown cold. The buffalo had changed their routes of passage, snows lasted longer and fell where no snows should fall, and year on year life was becoming harder to live. For long ages past, our land had supported us and been like a mother to us, but

---

127 I write about angels in *Spiritual Gold.*

now we feared she no longer loved us and that was why she had grown cold.

With the patience of hunters, we waited, hoping things would get better. But they didn't, and now our tribe faced the unthinkable decision—should we abandon our ancestral homelands? We desperately needed to know how long this was to go on, if things would get worse, or if there was any more that could be done to placate the weather spirits and restore balance to the seasons.

Our legends told of brothers in the south with the powers to help, and so a questing party was sent out to find the brothers and bring back the answers that were needed. It was the importance of the quest that led my tribe to choose not one, but three brave men to undertake it. There was safety in numbers, and the two extra braves were an insurance that at least one would get through.

It had been essential to choose the right men, and to give the tribe's chosen heroes a good send-off. Custom had been observed. A big fire had been lit and the best feast possible under the circumstances had been prepared. That evening our tribe hummed with speculation as to who might be chosen, and after we'd eaten, the choosing began.

All the braves knew it would be an honor to be asked and almost impossible to refuse, but it would be a dangerous quest, lonely and hard. It would take several years of their life, and possibly end in death. There was a tense silence as the chief spoke.

My father, the tribe's medicine man, was highly respected and he had seven sons. The chief did not ask the eldest three, sons one, two, and three, as they had families to feed. He did not choose the youngest two, sons six and seven, because they were too young for such a quest. But he had asked me, Moves Like The Clouds, son number five, because I was a good tracker, old enough, and as yet without wife or children to support. And he had asked my half-brother, son number four. From the tribe's point of view, we both had the advantage of having been at least partly trained in the shamanic arts and healing skills of our father, and it was thought this would help with the coming challenges of the journey. The third brave to be asked was one of the chief's own sons.

We all accepted.

The chief's son welcomed the adventure, as he knew he had too many older brothers to ever be chief, but I did so with a heavy heart. I loved Soft As A Deer and had wanted to marry her.

We set off the next day.

This was a time of peace for the tribes, so we did not have to conceal our presence while crossing the lands of others. We could trade to replace worn-out moccasins, and we generally enjoyed cooperation from those we met along the way. But this had an unexpected effect on the chief's son.

While negotiating for moccasins he had fallen for the charms of their maker. He wanted to marry her, change tribes, settle down, and abandon the mission. He knew this would be considered such a disgrace by our tribe that he could never go back to his father, but he could not be dissuaded; and so my brother and I continued onward without him—until the accident.

We had to hunt for food as we went, and not all hunts go right.

My brother lost his footing on mountain scree and fell and broke his leg. A tribe nearby was willing to look after him, and so he told me to go on without him, vowing to follow as soon as he was able.

The questing party was now down to me. Along with my arrows and bow, stone knives, and bedroll, I carried an extra weight of loneliness and sadness for those who were no longer with me. It was a dangerous quest and by the time I reached the highlands of Central America I'd faced bears, snakes, rock falls, and mountain lions to come so far, but each time I'd had luck on my side and survived.

* * *

Each day was the same.

Dawn came and the hours were measured out in footsteps until dusk. I would eat and sleep and begin again. Then came a night I stood on the hard rock of a high mountain plateau, studying the stars … In the kingdom of the night I surveyed the world around me—all that was above me and below me. I smelled the wind to see what was coming … the wind was cool against my skin. Through my moccasins I felt the strength of the mountain, and though the Earth held me, my eyes were in the stars. I could read the stars—and they were telling me I was nearly at my journey's end. I was glad, so very, very glad. And, for the first time in a long while, I smiled.

I looked down on the moonlit treetops below me and saw a sea of trees swirling around the mountain's lower slopes. Tomorrow I would be down there, surrounded by the dangers of the jungle, but tonight I could get some rest and go to sleep happy, happy in the knowledge that my quest was nearly at an end.

I made myself as comfortable as I could.

And before falling asleep I lay still, looking up at the beauty of the sky. At this time every night, my thoughts went out to my people. I missed my companions, oh, yes, but most of all I missed my beloved—and I tried to remember her face, her smile, her voice. My face grew sad, my eyes pricked with tears, but it was a comfort to think that the same moon was shining down on both of us.

There was no going back without the answers, this I knew, but as soon as I returned we could be together. I had hopes that our union would be blessed with many children, sons to teach my tracking skills to and daughters as beautiful as my love. As I drifted off to sleep I could feel the spirits of my unborn children pressing around me, I could almost see them. Their voices whispered to me in the wind and they comforted me.

The next day I traveled warily through the jungle.

Before I started I made offerings to the spirits of the new land, so they would help me rather than trip me up and hinder me—because in my experience this was always a wise precaution; it helped to smooth the energies of passage. And I took the same care when hunting. I used certain herbs and incantations and had ways of blessing my arrows so they flew true and pierced the heart of my prey.

And my precautions paid off, because the jungle allowed me safe passage.

Within a few days I arrived at my journey's end, and here I found a city—but nothing had prepared me for the sight and sounds of such an enormous mass of habitation. My people, the Deer Foot, part of the Shonee[128] nation and distant cousins of the Pawnee,

128 Probably Shoshonee, but "Shonee" was what was on the session tape.

numbered only a few hundred. We lived a simple life, our tepees were our shelter, made of skins and poles, but here there were throngs of people beyond the counting, and buildings spilling everywhere. There was not a tepee in sight, but solidly built homes that could not just up-sticks and move.

Men, women, and children, dogs and animals were all noisily going about their daily business. People were engaged in activity everywhere. So very, very many people who looked so different to me in their simple cloth garments with their dark shiny hair chopped short, always in the same style and with a short straight fringe.

I still wore the soft skin leggings and tunic of my people and kept my hair long and in braids. Sharp stone-bladed knives rested in a bag at my waist and I carried my bow and arrows slung across my back. It was hot here, and as I stood watching I could feel sweat trickling down between my shoulder blades beneath the quiver.

There were plenty of traders and other travelers, and amid all the hustle and bustle few were looking at me, even though I was so obviously a stranger.

The city was uncomfortably noisy after the quiet sounds of the forests and mountains. My ears were accustomed to the sighing of the wind or the snapping of a twig that could signal danger. But here, crowds of people with loud voices were shouting a strange language to each other. I couldn't understand a word of it; and I knew I would have to rely on sign language from now on.

I felt overwhelmed.

I breathed deeply to steady myself.

I said to myself, "Remember who you are. You are Moves Like The Clouds, such a good tracker that animals and people don't know you're there. So silent you can disappear and appear out of nowhere—and a son of the medicine man with knowledge, training, and powers." My fingers strayed to the talisman my father had given me to wear around my neck, a gift of powerful magic to keep me safe.

Of course I was safe.

And now with curiosity, I began to survey the city that sprawled away before me into the haze of the distance. It was extraordinary. I'd never seen anything like it … and my eyes were inescapably drawn to the long, wide, and remarkably straight road that ran right through it, that ran past huge pyramids of stone … (because this was Teotihuacán).

The simple houses of the people were everywhere else my eyes looked, *but it was their medicine men I'd come to find … as only medicine men would have the answers I was seeking.* Medicine men were important people … and the most important things I could see by far were the pyramids—*so that's where I'd start my search.*

According to our ancient legends they had possession of an oracle, a talking head of crystal. And although other, nearer nations were said to have such skulls of beauty, this was the chief of the skulls, and so it was from *this* one that my people sought their answers. And as it would not be to these lands we would be moving, if we had to leave our homeland, we trusted that the answers here would be true.

With the sun beating down on me I followed the road.

In front of the largest of the pyramids I found an imposing stone carved with a skull set within a sun disk. It was hot, I was tired, and this was the nearest I'd found to what I was looking for— so I sat down beside it, to wait. Wait to see what would happen.

It felt good to rest.

Before long a man came up and asked me what I was doing. I tried to make myself understood by signing. Pointing repeatedly to my eyes for "see," and then to the skull carving for "skull," I began to get my message across.

The man took me seriously. He was a priest, and he led me to his house nearby. In the welcome shade of a cool room he offered me water to drink, and then we continued trying to communicate.

I attempted to explain what had brought me, and the reason I'd come to see the skull. To show I was serious I produced a small gold artifact that I had carried with me on the journey, a gift from my tribe to their brothers in payment for the answers they sought. The priest took one look at it, his face grew grave, and he sent for an interpreter.

It soon became apparent that although the interpreter didn't speak my language he did speak languages with an affinity to it. He was a friendly, open man with a ready laugh and very white teeth.

He was full of life and joy. Nothing was a problem to him, and against his lightness I became painfully aware of just how heavy was the burden I carried because of the troubles. When the snows had come to our lands it wasn't just the lakes they'd frozen, but the spirit of my people … and I saw that now, quite clearly.

The priest arranged lodging for me with a humble family in one of the little houses nearby, and there I stayed for the next few days.

Over a meal at the house the interpreter and I had a laugh and set to, finding words for "food," "cold," "hot," "weather," and so on. We got on well and found we enjoyed each other's company. The interpreter was fascinated by words and enjoyed a challenge. He was pleased to be learning a new language, and the time we spent together passed swiftly.

Over the next two days we established communication in the nearest language that he knew to mine, and I began to feel confident that I was being understood.

I was assured that my questions would be conveyed to the priests.

The next morning, I was taken to speak with them. And that's when I found to my surprise they had not just the one, but three skulls of crystal, including the chief skull, and later that day they were going to search it for my answers.

I had feared I might have to wait until it was time for a big festival before I'd be able to see the skull. So this was welcome news indeed, and it meant I would not have to hang about in their city for very much longer.

There, I felt like a fish out of water.

Although they had been good to me I just wasn't comfortable having to rely on the goodwill of others for every mouthful of food I took, and for every drink of water that I sipped. In a city like this I couldn't go hunting for my food because every animal already belonged to someone else.

… The conversation whirling around me was far too fast for me to understand, and perhaps other pressing matters were being spoken of as well. I felt sure many would have need of the priests' services in one way or another, and also of the interpreter's skills.

The priests seemed to know the interpreter well.

As I stood waiting patiently while they talked, my mind slipped back to the gift my people had sent in payment for their answers. It was metal. Pure gold and very old, it came from the Age of the Skulls. And like the skulls, it was from a homeland beneath the sea. It was a precious relic my tribe had brought with them when they'd first fled west to the shelter of our mountain home.

We had only a very few things of such antiquity, and giving this signified how important the answers were to us.

It was beautiful.

It had been worn and smoothed by the passage of time and by the caress of many fingers. Its shape was long and curved, like a great fang, or claw. I remembered how it had felt, lying in my hand; its pleasing weight was not heavy. It had been as big as my palm, with a loop at the top, which made it look like it wanted to be threaded on to something.[129] At night before sleep I had often looked at it and run my fingers over the worn carvings that were chased around it, where figures and animals intertwined with the sun, stars, and hieroglyphs. It was said this golden talisman was to do with the gods of the old land.

When the ancestors had escaped a great flood, they brought with them what they could carry. They intermingled with the people they met in the new lands, and though we looked a little different now, their blood was still there, flowing in the veins of their descendants. There, but just mingled. There, within me.

These things were known from the legends and the stories that were handed down. The old stories were held in high esteem and were retold down the generations at the festivals of the year. They always began:

> There was once, long ago in the
> beginnings of time, this land,
> And this is where the people were,
> And the people lived,
> And the people grew,
> And the people learned,

129 It was hollow, so it wasn't actually that heavy. I think it was filled with a solid resin to help prevent it being dented.

> And they learned many wonderful things,
> And they built wonderful buildings,
> And they could do all manner of things,
> And it was a time of great wonders …

They always ended:

> … Then there came the end of the wonderful time,
> There came storms, hurricanes, and tempests,
> The earth did shake,
> And the land was rent into pieces,
> And the sea came over it.

The legends said that this catastrophe had been foretold by the seers, but some people didn't listen, some didn't believe, and others simply did not want to go. Those that did, left; and those that didn't, stayed.

The earth quaked its warning and the lands to the north went very quickly, taking a Great City with them. But the lands to the south took longer. Only after a whole series of cataclysms, over the lifetimes of kings, were the lands to the south no longer there.

All that was left were islands.

The city I'd come to was not far from the south of the old land, and this was how the chief skull came to be here. When the ancestors were leaving they had carried some of the earth here too, literally transporting the old land to the new. The legends said there had been time to move a lot of things from the south of the homeland before it was covered by sea. The ancestors in the north had much less time, and so brought less, but every tribe had something from the old land, and these were well-guarded treasures.

The priests had access to the holy things, so when they left they brought them with them. The sacred skulls were the most important of all the holy things, and were dispersed for safekeeping among the tribes. There were skull-bearing tribes and there were many tribes like mine that were not skull-bearing.

Things were split between the different tribes long ago in the Great Dispersal, but even as that was done it was understood there would be a Coming Together in long ages yet to come. This would start slowly like a trickle, then happen faster and faster, until like a great wave all that survived would reunite and the wisdom of the skulls would once more steer the path of destiny.

And this was how my people came to have the golden relic, once part of a great ceremonial necklace composed of many such pieces, each piece dedicated to a different deity. At its center had been a golden sun disc, and according to the legends it was worn by the one who presided over the ceremonies held in the Temple of All the Earth in the Great City in the old land. This temple was where the chief skull and the other crystal heads had had their home. And it was where they gave their warning about the flood ... because in the time of great wonders, *the sea god had grown angry.*

The people had tricked him into doing their bidding. They'd played the coyote and made bad magic. And they'd hidden his wife, so she would not tell him. And dazzled by their own cleverness, they did not see how foolish this was.[130]

Through his labors the City had grown Great.
But then came the time he grew lonely, and remembered his wife.
She was not to be found.
He saw he'd been tricked—he'd made their City,
And in his anger, he broke it.
He took the broken City down beneath the waves,
And searched its shattered stones looking in vain for his wife,
His salty tears swelled the oceans' tides.
And when he couldn't find her, he took the rest of the land.

---

130 The wealth the cult of Poseidon generated enabled them to experiment—the **"cleverness"** is a way of saying that the priests of Poseidon were the scientists of their day. Poseidon's temple was the source of their income and their front to the world, but other activities went on elsewhere. Armalco had too lowly a position at the temple to be involved with any of this, and so it did not come into his story— but absence of evidence is **not** evidence of absence—the shepherd in footnote 14 in the previous chapter had certainly witnessed something strange and unnatural. And I do believe they experimented with crystal energy to create storms and whirlpools—to be able to demonstrate their power over the sea, **to make it do their bidding**. A massive miscalculation in the "Large Hadron Collider" of their day ruptured the seabed, when an energy vortex got out of control.

He had punished the cleverness of a people who had become too clever and caused him pain.

Those from the north who escaped with their lives took care to bring none of the **dangerous cleverness** with them. They had lived a very simple life ever since, to keep the gods happy, to protect themselves from catastrophe repeating.

My people had run a long way from the wrath of the sea god, and only when they reached the Great Mountains[131] did they feel safe, and far enough away from the sea to make their home. The land there gave them shelter, accepted them and supported them, and they felt love and gratitude for her bounty. The ancestors had settled in the new homeland, and there our tribe had been for ages beyond the counting until now. We did not want to move, but we could not stay … What would the skull who knows all things concerning our peoples have to say?

I was lost in my thoughts when I was brought back to the present abruptly. One of the priests placed a hand firmly on my shoulder, and said, "Return this evening for the answer."

When the words were translated for me, I let out a deep sigh.

I straightened my shoulders and stood taller. I smiled. *Soon I would know*, and soon I would return to my love.

The day was still young, but the hours of waiting passed pleasantly enough and did not weigh heavily upon me. The interpreter took me to places of interest because he was proud of his city, and there was much to see.

We ate and we laughed and it felt good.[132]

I was taken to meet the interpreter's family, his wife and his children and parents. The little ones were excited by the presence of a stranger and kept running in and out of the house, hiding and peeping at me. I liked children and I laughed and pretended to join in their game. I was invited to share in their evening meal, and so I ate with the family, and after that it was time to return to the priests

---

131 The Rocky Mountains.

132 I liked the thin, bitter drinks of hot chocolate they made, and perhaps this is where my love affair with cacao, cocoa, and chocolate started! I still like it bitter and dark.

who would be waiting for us at the pyramid, at the Temple of the Sun.

The evening was warm. The pink light of sunset was draining out of the sky and the first stars were coming out. As we walked past the homes of the Teotihuacános, we could hear the sounds of children being put to bed. It wasn't too far to the temple, and soon the looming bulk of the pyramid began to blot out the stars ...

The priests we had met earlier fetched the head priest to meet us.

With flaming torches to light our way, we were taken down into a dark passage that eventually gave out into an underground cave beneath the pyramid.[133] The torches were put to rest in stands at the back of an altar table, and the soft light shone on three skulls of crystal set in a line. The chief skull was set in the center of the altar, and to its right lay brother skull Ra Nan Sa and to its left lay sister skull Sha Ran Sa. The skulls glowed in the light and looked unearthly and magnificent.

There was a sharp intake of breath from me.

In that moment I knew my journey had been worth every step and every bird and rabbit I'd had to hunt to sustain myself on the way. There was strong magic here ... these priests knew a lot, you could see that from the city ... strong medicine and a lot of knowledge ... great cleverness. I was in awe of their powers and wisdom. I could see why my people had sent me here for the answers.

And to my great surprise I was given the chief skull to hold.

It was heavy and very beautiful. I had to be careful how I held it because it was in two parts, the lower jaw being formed separately. I held it firmly and looked down into the depths of the lustrous, polished quartz, but all I could think of was its weight.

No answers came to me.

I felt honored to be entrusted with this treasure, but after a polite amount of time I passed the skull back.

The head priest smiled reassuringly and then spoke slowly, as the interpreter translated. "My friend, there is nothing to be done

---

133 Archeologists assumed the cave was natural, but it has been found to be manmade. Bearing in mind that the skulls lived in a sacred cave under the Great Temple in Atlantis, I think making the cave here was an attempt to give the skulls a suitable home: a cave with a temple on top.

to change the weather. There is no doubt that your people must move and leave their lands, but there will come a time when you will return. You are to keep the memory of your beloved homeland alive, so that after generations yet to come she will be ready to be a mother to your people again."

Then his dignified face grew sad. The chief skull had told him more than he had wanted to know, and he had been charged with passing this information on. He said the skull had told of a bad time to come in the future, when it would be a very bad time for all their peoples.[134] This time was so far away they did not need to worry about it, but it needed to be known about in preparation. The knowledge was only for the chiefs and the medicine men, and it was imperative it be passed down the generations so that when the time came it would be recognized.

The skull had said they must meet the end with dignity, but it wouldn't really be the end, it would just seem like it. It was necessary, just as without winter there is no spring, without death there is no life. As the old land had gone beneath the waters and they had traveled to the new one, so all things change and all things have a season. Without that, there is only stagnation and death. Rain is followed by sunshine, and there is rain coming in the future for their people, but it will lead on to the fertile growing of spring … It is just part of the pattern of unfoldment for this world.

The skull's message ended with me being told I would return safely to my tribe, and most surprisingly, that the skull had been expecting me. I had only been entrusted to hold it because it had asked to meet me, and not because I was expected to read my own answers. It had wanted to read *my* energy and tell me something, in the form of a message that was now hidden within me for a future time.

The other two skulls had not asked to meet me, and nor did they have detachable jaws.

The answers had been given.

And the palpably charged energy that had filled the place began to soften. Everyone relaxed a little. I was curious and asked the priests where they normally kept the skulls. I was told they went

---

134 I just knew this meant the coming of the Europeans, with all the bloodshed and diseases, the trickery and the stealing of their lands that would follow.

into safe places most of the time but were brought out when they were needed to be worked with, like this, or for big ceremonial events.

I guessed that these big ceremonies were probably very much like they had been in the old land, the motherland beneath the sea. After seeing the city and meeting the priests I was convinced that much more of the ancient culture had been brought here and still remained intact than with my people. In the face of all this I felt humble. My tribe were just a very simple people, they hunted, ate, and got by. All they had were their legends, and they kept them alive around the campfires at night, but they had no cities and stone temples, they were not even skull-bearers.

Then I was told that though the priests had welcomed my gift, they had been told to give me something in return to take back with me.

They had needed his gift to help complete something they had, but the chief skull had decreed that I be given a clear quartz crystal point from the old land. The head priest picked it up off the altar and took hold of my hand, pressed it into my palm, and closed my fingers over it.

When I opened my hand to examine the polished crystal, I saw there were carvings of people and symbols around the middle of its parallel sides. I examined it and thought it very beautiful. I was told it had the ability to link my tribe's medicine people to the chief skull and so would enable them to ask questions from it directly in the future, without need of a physical journey. It would tell my father, when in trance, how to use it, and then he must pass it down to his successor and keep it in the tribe, but he must also share it if other tribes had questions, and assist them in their quest for answers.

I thought this a most wonderful gift.

I was told that my people had earned it because consulting the skull had been important enough for them to undertake this huge journey.

And I was also given what looked like three small stones for my father. These were divination balls, made of vitrified clay and stamped with symbols. When the balls were thrown to divine, the answer would be given by reading the symbol on top when they landed. The symbols were ancient, and these were from the old land too.

Then a magnificent sacred necklace of great beauty was taken carefully out of protective cloths and held up for me to see. Its many pieces shimmered in the soft light, and there I saw the golden relic, back in its rightful place among its peers.

The head priest spoke to the interpreter, who then turned to me and said, "Tomorrow, my friend, you will be leaving us, we know, but we will be giving you food and currency[135] for your journey. The skull has spoken to us, and it must be so."

I felt they had been very kind and helpful and had looked after me well. I was impressed by the way they took anything to do with the skull with the utmost seriousness. I had come to consult it as an oracle and had been treated with respect, because it was respect that had drawn me to the skull to ask my questions. *I'd been looked after because of the power of the skull.*

Standing in the flickering light I felt elated, yet a sudden sadness pierced me. I felt a powerful bond with these men. I'd known them such a short time, yet my life had been changed forever by their help. What united us lay in front of us, the lumps of quartz shaped like human skulls, inert, but the energy that moved through them was what bound our hearts.

The next morning I was escorted out of the city by both the interpreter and the priest from the first day. They wanted to make sure I got off to a good start on my journey home.

Before I left I told them about my brother, so they would be prepared for him if he came. It would be obvious who he was, as his clothes, language, and story would match mine, and they both promised to give him the answers.

We walked together through the area of cultivated land surrounding the city, then said farewell, and I retraced my footsteps through the jungle to the plateau of the stars. And from there, the long journey of my return was made a little easier because I was now familiar with the terrain, and my heart was lending wings to my feet.

---

135   Perhaps shells, beads, things to trade.

Life was stirring in the tepees the morning I walked into camp, and there was much excitement when my people saw I was back. A big feast was immediately planned and the fires were lit. This was their usual enthusiastic response to any special occasion, no matter how scarce food had become, as they all loved a feast!

First, I sought out the tepee of my father, and was warmly welcomed. My father called out thanks to the spirits and the ancestors for returning me safely to him, and then he told me that two nights earlier he had dreamed I was back with him in his tepee, and that I had often come to him in his dreams and told him how things were progressing.

This was all news to me, but indeed my thoughts had gone out to my people as I drifted off to sleep each night, so perhaps it was so. Proudly, my father took me to the chief's tepee, where at last I could recount my experiences and share the answers.

I was warmly greeted and made welcome, offered refreshments by the old chief's first wife, and made comfortable. Then I told them everything. It was painful for the chief to hear that he would never, ever, see his son again, and hard to come to terms with the disgrace. I tried to be diplomatic about it, but there was no hiding what had happened.

The chief and his medicine man spent the rest of the day mulling over what they'd heard, and working out what to tell the tribe. Everyone else busied themselves cooking, hunting, and getting things ready for the evening meal. But as soon as my duty had been discharged, I'd sought out my love.

We had had an understanding before I left, and I had dearly wanted to marry her then, but I felt I couldn't as it wouldn't have been fair to leave her on her own. I hadn't even wanted to hold her to a promise in case there was someone else for her, as, after all, I didn't know if I was coming back. You just couldn't tell what might happen on a journey like that. There were so many ways to die.

When I found her, she was waiting for me in her father's tepee.

Our eyes met and time melted.

That very evening, after the feast, I, Moves Like The Clouds, and Soft As A Deer were betrothed. Of course, I was now He Who's

Journeyed And Returned, and when the entire tale had been told to the tribe after the feasting, I was also He Who Spoke To The Skull. To be fair I had said, "Hello" to it, and I was reliably informed by the head priest that it had spoken to me, even if I had no idea what it said. But I kept that bit quiet unless I was talking to my father or our chief!

My people had to move quite a way to find their new lands. The skull had given landmarks to guide us and signs by which to recognize the new terrain. The land was lower and flatter, but there we prospered.

My brother returned safely, and for Soft As A Deer and myself, children came and life was good. We had a graceful daughter and sons to be proud of. In time we were blessed with many grandchildren. Our hair turned silver and we grew old, and by now my ever-growing name ended with Old As A Mountain.

I never took another wife. I used to tease her that I would, but then she'd smack me playfully and we'd laugh. We never forgot how lucky we were to be together, and just how precious we were to each other. I knew it would have broken my heart to have found her married to another man on my return.

We lived long and happy lives until one winter her laughter was heard no more. Things were never the same after that, and I began to feel I had less to live for. Of course, I loved my children and grandchildren, and even the great-grandchildren that had begun to appear, but I began to feel very tired. Two years trickled slowly past me, and patiently I met the days until the dawn of my release, when she came to take me with her.

* * *

And that is the story of Moves Like The Clouds, He Who Has Journeyed And Returned, He Who Spoke To The Skull, Husband, Father, Grandfather, Great-Grandfather, Old As A Mountain. And this is the message he carried for us from the chief skull at Teotihuacán. That skull was Bah Ha Redo, now called the Mitchell-Hedges, the Skull of Love (the other two are now to be found in the museums of Paris and London. London's skull is Ra Nan Sa, in the

British Museum).

It is time now for the world to become aware of the skulls once more. Many already know of them, but there's many more that need to know. They can help humankind steer toward a destiny of joy, peace, and love.

We have reached a critical point in our evolution when things could go terribly, terribly wrong or very, very right. We need to wake up to our power and realize we have that choice, and we need to make it, or others will make it for us without being asked. The forces of greed and power need to be kept in check by the good-hearted mass of humanity. It is a stand-up-and-be-counted time for everybody.

The skulls may look scary because they're skulls, but it's the beauty and purity of their crystal that reveals their true nature. The universe is unfolding all the time all around us. We have an important part to play in this great cosmic unfoldment. We have the choice as to how we unfold. We can make the right choice, the one that makes our heart glad, or the choice that brings the destruction of our world. It is up to us. If we would leave a future for our children and a future for the world, it needs to be the right choice.

We can do it. We can remember and wake up to who we are. We can be true to ourselves and not be swayed by fear, greed, and sloth. We don't have to give in to not bothering, not caring, not feeling important enough to matter. We just need to be the magnificent beings we truly are. The skulls are here to remind us of that. Just as they are perfectly formed, so are we.

We can have a very successful outcome. We can do it. We have a lot of allies trying to help us. There are many beings in the nature kingdoms, the angelic worlds, and higher dimensions all really, really trying to help us.

If we can remember who we are and get back to the blueprint of our true essential nature all will be well. The skulls' message is one of encouragement: we can do it. We need clear communication and we need to awaken.

My book has to help people to awaken to their hidden selves, their treasure, and the deep, beautiful places in their spirit so they know we are all eternal beings on an endless journey of wonder that takes us into the heart and mind of God and back out into the world, and that it is our universe. We create it, we live in it, and we can make it what we wish.

Chapter 9

The Legacy of Pyramid Temples

The races from the south had traveled to Central America and built temples in the new lands. Living a long way from Atlanta, they were less familiar with the temples of the capital city, and they drew upon the designs of their healing temples for their inspiration.[136] This was a very different tradition of building based on the pyramid form, and it can be seen in the temples at Teotihuacán, which provided such striking landmarks for Moves Like The Clouds.

Pyramid Healing Temples

In Atlantis the elements of earth, water, fire, air, and ether were accorded separate temples, and diseases were classified by which element was out of balance in the body. Local physicians set broken bones and dealt with most things, and crystals were abundant and extensively used in healing,[137] but if the local physicians could not affect a cure then people would be referred to the temples to have their balance restored. Element healing temples were scattered around the continent and located at places where Earth energies

---

136 They may not have had the skills to recreate the Temple of Hera, nor the desire to build the temple of the irascible sea god Poseidon, who had treated them so badly.

137 Close your eyes and imagine walking into a room where the walls and ceiling are covered in crystals, like a crystal cave lit by soft light. Feel your cares lifting and melting away as you relax in comfort, lying down, as kind hands work on you with crystals, spiraling them through your aura to draw off disharmonious energy blockages, laying warm ones on your skin, balancing your chakras, and bringing your energy bodies back into alignment. In the spacey state that ensued, spontaneous pictures might come to mind—past life memories surfacing to explain the roots of a problem—or dreams might be interpreted, revealing the key to deeper healing.

were strongest.

The pyramid form drew the energy in, collected and focused it. It was stored in a shaft beneath the pyramid forming a self-charging rod of Earth energy that rose up through the pyramid to the apex, and served to balance the heavens and the Earth. And as these are the energies that meet within us—we are heavenly spirits in earthly bodies—they were regarded as places that could restore balance to the sick. Flat-topped pyramids provided an energy-enhanced platform for healing to take place on and were also used for religious rites, particularly at key points in the year like solstices, equinoxes, and eclipses.[138]

In Europe and elsewhere, the stone circles and mounds of the ancient world served the same function—drawing to them, collecting, intensifying, and discharging energy for the purpose of balancing the heavens and the Earth. Spiral processions around the sites built up the energy,[139] and any sacrifices made were intended to release even more energy into the process. The energy shot up through the sacred site and jetted skyward to join bands of protective energy that circle the Earth;[140] it was like strengthening the Earth's natural aura, if you will, and was designed to help keep us safe from any negative extraterrestrial interference—guarding against asteroids, and maintaining our place in the cosmos. It's well known that the sites were aligned for tracking the stars and making astronomical observations, and this was all part of keeping the balance of the heavens and the Earth.[141]

---

138 The Great Pyramid at Giza in Egypt is not flat topped, and was used for initiations into the mysteries of life and death. It provoked out-of-body experiences, and the granite "sarcophagus" in the king's chamber acted like an isolation tank. No mummies or human bones have ever actually been found in the pyramid to support the accepted pyramid-as-a-tomb theory, and as far as I know, nor have they been found in any other pyramid either.

139 Clockwise in the northern hemisphere (counterclockwise takes it down); reversed for the southern hemisphere, as water flows down a plug hole in response to Earth's spin. (There's more on this topic later.)

140 When I saw the bands, they seemed to be strongest around the tropics of Cancer and Capricorn.

141 Although they are in disrepair, people are still drawn to the ancient sites today—which is good, and visitor numbers are constantly growing. They are places where we can recharge ourselves, and they speak to us on an unconscious level, while their energy affects the water in every cell of our bodies. In England,

Pyramids, temples, stone circles, and sites of power are all linked via an energy grid made up of ley lines, along which Earth energy flows.[142] This grid was strong on Atlantis, but the last two thousand years of neglect has seen the European grid weaken and break.[143] However, ley lines are not hard to repair and within dowsing circles it is understood how to renew them.

Element Temples

1. **Fire temples** were located in the north and south of the continent, where hot springs like those in Iceland—the land of fire and ice—were to be found.

2. **Water temples** were built on rivers on the coast, so both fresh and salt waters were available for treatments.

3. **Earth temples**: I had a life where I trained in an Earth temple. I was a quietly confident young man with long wavy dark hair, I looked very Cretan. Honestly, I could have stepped out of one of the frieze paintings on the walls of Knossos. We wore tunics of natural raw silk, because we understood that this was what best suited the electromagnetic properties of the human body. The pyramid where I worked was divided into four, as though cut into quarters and pulled slightly apart. The square space at the center was a sacred garden.

Stonehenge and Avebury are UNESCO World Heritage sites, but it is amazing just how many smaller sites there are.

142 There are plenty of ley lines throughout Great Britain; dowsing reveals them, and most churches have been sited on them. *The Old Straight Track* by Alfred Watkins is the original book on ley lines, though many other very good books have been written since. The author is reputed to have had an experience when he saw "the lines of the world" (as Castaneda calls them), shining like gold and silver threads (rather like the meridians that acupuncturists perceive chi energy flowing along in the body), and he went on to research the phenomena and its link to ancient sites.

143 Two thousand years ago the Romans persecuted and killed the Druids (the Celtic priesthood who used the sites and maintained the energy grid), because the Druids' power was a destabilizing influence and a threat to their rule. And when time had reduced the Romans to the dust of history, the Roman Catholic Christian Church continued in the same vein, with its zeal to get rid of all things pagan. Some great stones were tumbled, others broken up with fire and water.

Herbs were grown here to make our remedies, and they were grown in soil dressed with powdered gold, through which the energy charge of the pyramid surged. The potency of the land and the herbs was further enhanced by crystals buried in the soil. The quartered pyramid contained rooms where we were taught. We gathered other plant materials from the countryside, and sometimes took trained sniffer dogs out with us to dig up roots and find fungi by moonlight. We learned to make poisons ... but I think that's a tale best left for another day ...

4. **Air temples** were flat-topped pyramids built on high ground. Bonfires of aromatic herbs were burned on the top so people could air-bathe in the fragrant smoke, thus cleansing their bodies and auras, and purging disharmonious energies from their being.

5. **Ether** is regarded as being the first element, and is above the other four, which all have to pass through ether to come into being. There was only one **ether temple** in Atlantis—Hera's temple, classified as such because it housed the thirteen quartz skulls. These were placed in the category of ether because they could transcend time—they could look into the past, and see the future that was not yet formed, the potential of life. They were regarded as gifts from the gods, as coming from the heavens. The skulls brought healing by restoring harmony, and if the other temples did not succeed in healing people then they could always turn to the skulls.[144] This made the Temple of Hera a great focus for pilgrimage.[145]

---

144 Princess Sahaara had been taken straight there, bypassing the water temple because her father was so worried about her.

145 The Spanish Camino pilgrimage route is a relic of this, and the path is still walked today, although it has been Christianized. Originally it would have ended at Hera's temple in an audience with the skulls, but now it ends at Finisterre (meaning "the end of land") on the Spanish coast. Today it is still customary to burn your dirty and tattered pilgrimage garments there and put on new raiment. (Then you would have been suitably attired to board the boat for smart and fashionable Atlanta, and to have been received into the temple there.)
Walking the route strengthens the ley lines, and in turn because you're walking

There were other quartz skulls in temples dotted around the continent, but they had been found elsewhere, and not in the sacred cave. Some had been sent in with the taxes from foreign lands, while others were survivors from Mu and Lemuria—taken to safety before volcanic activity had pulled the ancient lands beneath the Pacific Ocean. Any extra skulls were given a period of training under the thirteen, and then they were sent out so they could link the priests and priestess in the peripheral temples with Hera's temple.

Atlanta was surrounded by pyramid temples. There was an air temple in the mountains to the west, where the tributaries of the Atlan's river flowed down to the plain on which Atlanta had been built. Auspicious days were those when the winds blew strongly (for wind was seen as the Divine-Creator-God's breath cleansing the world), and the wind caused the smoke to rise obliquely. Days of ill omen were when the Divine withdrew from the world, so his breath no longer blew the smoke. It was an ill day to be born or married if the Divine was absent and the smoke from the temple was rising straight upward; and on such days, there was no healing because, with no wind, the smoke would not blow over you. From Atlanta, the angle of the smoke was clearly visible on the skyline, and so the nature of the day was revealed.

Stonehedge, England

along a ley line, it makes the journey less tiring, it strengthens you.

* * *

Although crystal skulls had been taken west, and south to the Lands of the Sun, others were dispersed east and north. Their stories come next.

The climate disturbance that led Moves Like The Clouds's tribe to seek a new homeland caused problems elsewhere in the northern hemisphere. Around this time there was a wide-scale displacement of peoples, with those the Romans called "Barbarians" eventually bringing the downfall of the Roman Empire and setting in motion a trail of events that have been immortalized in the legend of King Arthur!

There cannot be many people today who have not heard tales of King Arthur and his magician Merlin. The Arthurian legends are set in Britain's Dark Ages, in the period after the collapse of the Roman Empire, at the time when Saxon tribes were crossing the sea to steal the land; Arthur was a native Briton and the Saxons were his enemies.

Down the centuries the legends have remained very popular—even among the Saxons' descendants! The legends tell tales of bravery and chivalry, of the Knights of the Round Table, of Arthur's magical sword Excalibur and of Guinevere, his queen. Countless books have been written, many films made. Today there is an International Arthurian Society with branches in different countries.[146][147] For an obscure British king who lived around 1,500

---

146 www.internationalarthuriansociety.com.
147 In early 2019 while I was readying this chapter for publication, Merlin and Arthur were in the news again. Twice!

On January 31, 2019, news broke that thirteenth-century parchments had been found in Bristol University's special collections library. The seven parchments discovered by Michael Richardson were Old French texts of the Arthurian legends that had been hidden in sixteenth-century books deep in Bristol Central Library archives. (The find was reported by the BBC and in the *Metro* newspaper.) Wales and the southwest of England are closely bound up with the many locations made famous by the legend—and as Bristol is in the middle of this "Arthur country," it was regarded as a very appropriate place for such a find.

Then only two weeks later (on February 13, 2019, in the *Metro*), I came across a review for a new children's film, *The Kid Who Would Be King*. Described as "Modern-day magic in a contemporary Camelot" it was an update of the Arthur and Merlin legend. In the film twelve-year-old Alex plucks a sword from an

years ago (and there are those who doubt he actually existed at all), Arthur has made a big impression on the world. The myth lingers on undiminished by time—and I was about to discover the reason; one I would never have guessed.

The life in this chapter follows that of Moves Like The Clouds.

This time I was born in southern Britain at the time Arthur was still alive.

The backstory to the life is that it had taken the Romans nearly one hundred years and several attempted invasions before they finally managed to subdue the land and its people and add Britain to their empire, which covered most of the known world. The native Britons were Celtic people whose warriors had successfully resisted the might of Rome for a very long time. The Britons' priests were the Druids who worshipped in sacred oak groves and revered ancient stone circles like Stonehenge, which were part of the landscape throughout Britain. The Druids had helped the warriors to withstand the Romans, and so they were slaughtered mercilessly after the Roman conquest.

The Romans ruled Britain for almost four hundred years.

But suddenly the Romans left Britain, and by AD 410 they had deserted the hard-won lands completely because Rome itself was in trouble.

Things had first begun to go wrong for the Romans around AD 300, when restless tribes they disparagingly called "Barbarians" had started to cause trouble on the borders of their empire. But by AD 410 the situation had deteriorated much further—and things only got worse for the Romans after that. In AD 476 the last Roman emperor, Romulus Augustulus, was deposed and from then on it was Barbarians who held the power.

But what is important here for this past life, is that Britain had been disarmed and then left undefended when the Romans abandoned building site and goes off to fulfill his destiny, aided by a young Merlin and leaving a note for his mum: "Gone on a quest to save Britain. Don't worry!" The reviewer commented that given our current level of #BrexitShambles despair, it's a timely tonic to have a film extolling hope in an age when "hearts are hollow and the land is lost and leaderless." Strangely enough, Arthur and Merlin never seem to go out of fashion. (Brexit was Britain's impending exit from the European Common Market.)

deserted her shores—the forcibly Romanized Celts had simply been abandoned. After four hundred years of brutal suppression, during which time all their weapons had been confiscated, their swords of legend destroyed, and Celtic smiths forbidden on pain of death from making anything more dangerous than a farm implement, and for so long that generations had come and gone many times over so they'd forgotten the skills to do more—**the Celts had been left like a lion whose teeth and claws had been destroyed.** They were still lion-hearted but they had little to defend themselves with.

They were abandoned and vulnerable.

They needed Arthur—because sea wolves had found them and had come to take their land.

Johannes's Story

Merlin's Legacy

For me this was to prove the most emotional session I have ever done. A chance question had uncovered this life's existence, and the regression work exploring it was the very last for *Holy Ice*. I'd already signed the contract for the book by this stage, but thank goodness it was not too late to be included. This is such an important chapter that perhaps there is no such thing as chance because it's hard to imagine the book without it.

The regression session starts off normally, and Veronica and I prepare to journey into the past. This time I know I'll meet Merlin, because we've had a preliminary encounter, and now it's time to explore the life. Relaxed and comfortable on the therapy couch I enter the inner world. To go deeper Veronica tells me to visualize descending a staircase.

My subconscious responds with an amethyst crystal staircase. It has polished treads like amethyst wands and white quartz spindles and a golden hand rail … I have to go down barefoot or I can't grip the crystal steps, and it leads me down to a cave. As I enter I feel I'm stepping into a giant geode, a sacred space with crystals shining on the walls, quite small crystals but there are lots of them reflecting light. The cave has a white, quilted velvet floor, soft and beautiful … which forms a pathway that guides me into the center of the cave and takes me through, into a darkened corridor beyond.

I meet guides.

There is a sense of guides observing, come to watch what unfolds. Guides I haven't worked with before. And for this session Merlin has come. He's here and he takes me to the doors. I am drawn to a big, old, wooden one with an iron ring for a handle. The wood is dark oak. It looks strong but battered—and like the Celts—it has weathered tough times! I have to use both hands to turn the ring and lift the latch, but it swings open easily enough.

I step through …

… And find myself in a big hall.

There are people here … lots of people and I'm standing watching them.

There's a fire pit in the center of the hall, and the floor I'm standing on is covered with rushes. Dogs lie in the rushes, gnawing on bones thrown down for them. They're our hunting hounds, short haired with long legs and longish ears … they are very graceful, with slender white or beige bodies. Some are spotted. We love the dogs.

Veronica asks my name.

I'm Johannes, son of Carolus.[148]

Someone brings me a drink of thin beer and I sit down.

I'm tired and thirsty. I've been out in the forest all day and I've earned a rest. Around me people are busy preparing food for the evening meal. But there's a strange excitement in the air.

Veronica asks me to describe the hall.

It's longer than it's wide and two long rows of old wooden tables run down the length, one row to each side of the fire, and I'm sitting at the tables. The king's table is down the far end, it joins the rows together. Our king and his family will sit there tonight, but workers like me always sit on benches at the two long rows of tables. We come here every day to eat.

It's the end of the day now, and we're swapping news—what we've done, what we've seen. We want to hear what the scouts have seen, and the shepherds on the hills—because we need to know if

148 (Said Yo-han-iss) Medieval Latin for "John" son of "Charles."

the enemies have come—what the movements are in the land.

Forty soldiers live here and we call them **the guardians**, they're our king's fighting men, his hearth troop, and they sit up near his end of the tables with the important people. If enemies were to burst in they'd keep him safe ...

Veronica asks if I'm one of the fighting men.

No. I'm an adviser. I'm in charge of the king's diary. I plan when he's going to have a hunt, and if people want a private audience with him they come through me, and I arrange a time. I'm a bit of a fixer. And I take messages—if the king wants to talk to somebody I'll take a message to them and set up a meeting. I smooth things out so he can get everything done and still have plenty of time to go hunting.

My dad did the same job before me. I started out as his runner, running messages for him. Later he trained me up with who's who and how to handle things, how to be diplomatic. I was sent away to learn how to bend people to your will without them realizing it ... you make them think it's their idea—that's a skill I've been taught!

Veronica asks about my appearance and what I'm wearing.

My hair's down past my shoulders and slightly wavy, but Roman-style I've no facial hair. I've a hooded tunic with a belt, and a cloak, and trousers tucked into leather boots. Lambskin socks keep my boots warm. I've an eating dagger on my belt and a leather pouch filled with coins and herbs and things I find—magical things of power from the natural world—stones, shells, feathers. You never know when you might need them, you never know when you might need to make an offering to the gods, or open a (telepathic) channel for communication.

I've more layers of clothing underneath. It's very cold in the winters—you don't take off your underlayers then, and you don't often take off your outer garments either ... perhaps your boots for sleep although not always that, because the lambskin keeps your feet warm, and should you be woken up because there's trouble—with your boots on you can just take to your feet and join the fight. There's great unrest in the land and it pays to be vigilant at all times.

We always post guards, even when there's a feast. Say one of the other kings is visiting and there have been animals roasted and we've got a feast on the tables, some of the guardians keep watch outside to avoid the hall being burned down around us.

Veronica asks how many kings there are.

Twenty-seven, each tribe has its own. We have two because we are the Cornovii, and we hold the Welsh Marches. Our lands stretch from the Severn estuary in the south, where we are right now, up to the Welsh coast in the north—too far for one king to ride if there's trouble. Our kings are brothers, and I'm in the Great Hall of King Cedrych, son of Cardew. A five-day ride north from here takes you to his brother-king's lands in the Marches.

We have a high king, Artur,[149] because with so many kings somebody has to be in control. Not that the other kings always listen to him! People get far too big for their boots thinking they should be high king instead—and there's always plotting going on. I try to find out about it. I visited the other kings' courts when I was younger, when my dad sent me with messages. One of my sons does that for me now and my eldest son is bodyguard to the king. I learn a lot from that one, because being in close company with the king every day he overhears many of his conversations … and things slip out.

So officially I'm the king's diary keeper and smoother-over of diplomatic meetings—but I've also a secret job. I'm an intelligence gatherer, a spy. I pass on information and knowledge to the most important person in the land, and my task is uncovering plotting.

The kings have a social network that brings them into contact with each other and with the high king at least once a year, but it's when they meet up privately that anything goes. So it's always good to know who has visited who, even if it's just to go hunting or marry their daughters to each other.

Veronica asks how the high king is chosen.

The kings vote. The high king is the only one with the power to command other kings. They have to swear an oath of allegiance and send him fighting men so he can coordinate an army if somebody tries to invade—which is what's happening now. The people we fight come in boats from the big lands across the sea. That's why we set guards.

---

149 The world knows him as Arthur so that's what I'll call him. Artur means "bear-like." Merlin was Myrddin in the old Celtic version of his name. I found myself wanting to pronounce it Merd-idin. Cedrych is pronounced Cedrik.

Veronica asks about the boats.

They've been coming to the east coast and the south coast for years. We've not been too troubled here in the west—but we've had to fight off raiding parties.

Veronica asks what the invaders are like.

Big, strong, well armed, fierce, brave, skilled—they are bad news. They are land-hungry sea wolves, not just chancer-pirates, and they have families and big family networks, so they want the land. They bring their own families and settle them, and then they bring more of their relatives and take more land. They've been doing it for years, from before my father's time, and it's getting worse. We make agreements with them but it's never enough. They take more land and then there's more fighting. And every year brings more boats.

Oh, we remember the Romans. We use the roads they left us and the stones they cut, but our people didn't like it when they came. They were cruel and rapacious, and they stole our food and our women. They were here a long time but some of the things they did were helpful, and by the end a lot of our people had intermarried … things had softened. So they were missed when they went, and we had no one to protect us, because they had destroyed the part of our culture that supported our warrior class. It takes a lot of skill to make weapons. When your smiths have only been making farm implements for generations, it's not easy to get the skills back, so we were left at a disadvantage when they went.

They'd tried to break our spirit deliberately, systematically, cruelly because they never thought they'd leave. They thought they'd be here forever, that they owned the world. They thought the world owed them taxes. And then they found some serious challengers! Well, we didn't get to hear all the ins and outs of it, but we did get to hear from the traders that they were in trouble. That they weren't the powerful, untouchable elites they had been. Things rather began to fall apart for them. We weren't sorry to hear that. We were sorry they came and troubled us and tried to smash our ways of doing things in our culture. We had fine weapons, weapons of great legend, of great power, and we still sing the songs about the heroes and what they did with their wonderful swords. Nowadays you're lucky to have a weapon of that caliber. And as a people, if you haven't got your weapons, you haven't got a sound future, have you?

We were wonderful warriors, and we have the legends and the songs that our bards still sing to us, so we know what was, and what has been—and how different it is today. And it wouldn't have mattered if the Saxons hadn't been coming across the sea with their really good weapons and their hunger for our land. We are just seen as easy pickings.

We love to hear the old stories because they give us hope and help keep our spirit alive. We still fight for our land though it's been going on for as long as I can remember. High King Arthur has won many battles and he's given the bards much to sing about, as they travel from king's court to king's court, bringing news and entertainment, bards like Merlin the Wise. (That's when I realize there's a bard coming here tonight—to King Cedrych's Great Hall. That's what all the excitement's about—it's for Merlin!) He's got a wonderful singing voice, and officially he comes to entertain. It is always good to see Merlin.

He is the one I spy for.

I finish the beer and join the jolly throng outside waiting for him on the road, beyond the palisade that protects our homes and the Great Hall. A cheer goes up when we see him, and we crowd round his horse welcoming him. We lead him over the drawbridge and across the deep water-filled ditch encircling the protective palisade.

We help Merlin down from the saddle. He is tall and very robust, with well-muscled shoulders and powerful arms; adept at protecting himself on perilous journeys. Though his hair is gray, it's as thick and long and wavy as mine, and he has the youthful air of a much younger man as he unfastens the saddle, slinging it over his shoulder and carrying his bags in his hand. His horse is taken off for some hay and a rub down, but he keeps his bags with him, refusing offers of help. I know him better than the others do, and though there's a twinkle in his eye and he's trying to look merry, there are signs of strain on his face.

He strides into the Great Hall where the king is sitting on his special king-chair, a Roman-style curule chair. Merlin bows, then drops down on one knee before the king and makes the formal vow of allegiance. He promises to bring him the news, in a fair and true form, accurately representing the state of the kingdoms. Then he goes for a rest, a wash, and a lie down, and we look forward to seeing him at the meal.

* * *

The meal is on the tables, drink is flowing, and for once we are relaxed and happy. Merlin sits in the seat of honor by the king, and when we've eaten and are full of good food and alcohol and feeling mellow, Merlin unwraps a harp from a traveling bag at his feet. He rests it on his knee and coaxes some beautiful music from the quivering strings. With his rich voice, he sings some of the old songs, but he's also good at making new ones. He sings a song of the latest news. He sings about the major battles Arthur has won, and he sings about the ones yet to come—***reminding us we have to be ready***.

But tonight, it's time for enjoyment.

After the song, there comes a point when the buzz of conversation dies away, when in the course of a few minutes heads begin to nod and are laid to rest on tables, cushioned on arms and hands. People slump on benches and others roll off into the floor rushes, curling up with the hounds dozing by the bones they were gnawing. The whole room goes still apart from the crack of the fire and sparks from the logs. I can hear the wind outside. It gusts through the smoke hole, sending the smoke into eddies and spirals. Merlin makes a sign to me and gets up and walks down the hall toward me. Silently I rise, and he and I sweep out of the hall, past the fire burning low. Together we light a torch and walk through the doors and out into the dark night.

It was as though Merlin cast a spell over the feasters in the Great Hall.

I knew he had.

He had projected the thought they were tired, and suddenly they were. I used a blocking picture in my mind and the spell did not touch me.

We shout a friendly greeting to the guards and pick our way along a well-trodden path leading through trees toward a small lake.

The lake is in a clearing. We often meet here to talk, away from prying eyes and listening ears. Mossy lichen-covered rocks set around with ferns and golden bracken ring the lake. The wind that has been tugging at our hair eases, and the air falls still. The black water is calm and reflective, mirroring a hazy sickle of old moon and glimmers of stars above.

We sit side by side on the old talking stone shaped long ago by the hands of our ancestors. It's a comfortable stone on this cold evening at summer's end.

He asks about me, my family, and the king: what visitors he's had, what news we've heard. He wants to check my report against other people's stories. Any discrepancies may need looking into. But there's been a change in him, a little bit of the fire has gone out of him.

And then he sighs.

He tells me he has been looking into the future and seen things he wished he hadn't, and this is what he's come to tell me. He's only told the king a little, he says, but he wants me to know the truth … that he owes it to me.

He tells me Arthur is old and Arthur is ill, that he is too ill to fight much more, just one more battle. The end is coming because we cannot stem the Saxon tide.

No one is fit to be high king in Arthur's place, though too many think they are, and it is harder and harder to get the kings to work together. Those far away from immediate Saxon threat no longer want to field their men, and those nearer constantly squabble over who should be Arthur's successor—instead of coordinating a plan to fight the enemy.

He tells me the end is coming. That it is over for us, that we will be picked off kingdom by kingdom, our fighters slain, our children and women enslaved and carried away.

Tears stream down my face. I can't stop them. I'm consumed by grief. All the years of struggle, all the schemes and plans to outwit our enemies have come to nothing. My father's struggles and his father's before him have come to nothing. My life is turned to ashes. My sons will be killed, my daughters and wife enslaved, my dear little grandchildren too … the tears come

to wracking sobs. I feel destroyed. Dead inside … but Merlin goes on. He says, "It might seem like the end but it will not be so. At least not in the way the Saxon threat thinks it will be … for we will be inside their stockades then. We will change them in ways they will not realize. We will do it slowly, down generations. They think our women their slaves but our women are also our warriors. They will take the fight on now. They have always been fit to lead men into battle, as Queen Boudicca did when she caused the Romans much grief. Our women are the equal of men, but in subtler ways they will win another battle, for they take our blood into the Saxon blood and our blood will transform the Saxon tide from the inside.

"We *will* change them.

"But alas the time is short when we live in our lands as we do. I have seen the future and it has broken my heart. Enjoy what days are left to you, my son. You and your father before you have served me well, but soon I will have no more need of your services. Arthur knows. He will rally his strength and fight to the end. But the end will soon be upon us. I ride north now to gather what support I can muster for Arthur, there is little time left."

Merlin's eyes are wet. Tears still slide down my face and I brush them away.

That it should come to this … our people crushed, our lands taken.

Wind sighs in the treetops. An owl hoots.

* * *

Map of the British Isles
The Fragments of Ancient Continents (Footnote 16)

Map of the British Isles
Places in the Story

We walk back. People are still asleep; the fire has died down to glowing embers. Everything is as we left it. But the world has changed.

We go to our beds.

Merlin goes north next day.

A little time passes. I cannot tell my family. I want them to enjoy what time we have left. I feel destroyed … I go through the days—hear my wife singing, see my three strong sons sharing a joke. I feel sad for my beautiful daughters and the sons-in-law that make them happy. I watch my grandchildren playing, and take part in family life, which is always full of little celebrations—like children's birthdays. I do love my daughters. They always made me smile, but now it's tinged with sadness. They brought joy and sunshine into my life, and would say, "Oh, Dad, don't be so serious. Come to this …" whatever little social event they'd be arranging. They'd get excited when traders brought cloth, and they delighted in turning it into new things to wear. And what they say is true, I have always been very taken up with the serious side of life, with what's happening in the kingdoms. They show me a softer side of life, one that revolves around their own homes.

Your home's for your domestic life, but the Great Hall is also very much a part of life. The Great Hall is set in the center of our settlement, in the most important place on the highest ground. It is our king's court where he metes out justice and entertains visitors, but more than that it's *his* home. His private rooms are at the far end, near his table. His soldiers' homes are built outside the back of the hall, protecting his private rooms, and protecting him, because he is the most important person here.

If a woman was giving birth, she'd be in her home. If you have children, they're usually just in your home, the king doesn't want them running up and down in the Great Hall making a mess and making lots of noise.

Home is a circular building, with a post in the center, and thick earth walls at least four feet high on which timbers are fastened and then secured to the central pole. Rushes and reeds thatch the roof and keep home warm, and there is provision for a fire. Sometimes we sleep in our homes, sometimes we sleep in the Great Hall.

* * *

The days slip past, winter comes, then spring, and each morning I pray Merlin was mistaken.

I send my son the runner away on many more messages than are needed, hoping to spare him our fate, but I can think of no good reason that our king would countenance to allow myself or my family to leave. For sure he heeded Merlin's words and sent to his brother-king for more guardians, until the eating benches couldn't hold them or our women feed them.

But sure enough, one night boats come gliding silently up the Severn. Saxon scum crawl over our land toward the Great Hall where we are asleep. Our sentries wake us, and grabbing weapons, helmets, and shields from their places on the walls, we pour out and form a line to defend our hall and we are cut down by the thieves that come in the night. I know what will happen to my loved ones. I died inside the night Merlin came, but I fight on until a blow to my head makes my helmet ring and knocks me to the ground. I lose all sense. I barely feel the slashes that take my life blood, barely feel it pooling from my wounds to stain my tunic and trousers, soaking into the layers of clothing beneath.

It's the end of my king.

As our shield wall crumbles and even the guardians fall, the doors to the hall are forced open and I hear the women shriek … and then I hear no more. I slip out of my battered body and look down on the world below.

I'm aware Merlin still rides north. He has worn out horse after horse and changed them many times over since he left us on his mission to raise help for Arthur; but he also weaves magic as he goes. He is weaving his legacy into the land—and I can see the tools he uses. With my telepathy skills, I had seen two stone skulls in his aura as he spoke the fateful words to me by the lake. In the extreme emotion of the moment we had opened up to each other in a way I had never experienced before. I'd never been party to his thoughts before—though he could always read mine. The stone skulls were in his thoughts. I did not understand why, but I knew they were important or they would not be in his mind. **I just had no idea how important.** But now that I'm free of my body I have greater understanding and vision.

I see Merlin. I see the skulls: one blue as lapis lazuli, one clear as rock crystal, and I intuitively know this one is a scrying stone. It's the size of two fists, and in this he saw the future he told me about. The blue skull is smaller, but it's at least the size of one fist, it's an amplifier and grounder, used for summoning elementals of air, water, and earth. He had used this one for weather manipulation—a well-placed storm can hinder sea wolves, mists can be summoned to hide warriors or let them slip away, and good weather before a harvest always helps boost the yield, especially valuable in these times of poor harvests.

Hunger is part of the whip that drives the Saxon scum to our shores.

I see that Merlin takes the blue skull to the ancient places of power. He travels from stone circle to stone circle channeling energy, thoughts, and commands through the skull into the earth and stones there, and thence into the lines of power that flow through them into the veins of our land. He channels energy into the very rocks that underpin all. The rock crystal skull is a generator and amplifier, and set beside the blue skull it enhances the work that Merlin and its brother skull do. The three are working together as a team.

I realize the Isles of the Britons have rocks which have brother and sister rocks all over the world. And I see that the rocks of our land will speak to their brother and sister rocks, as Merlin uses the blue skull to put energy into the land, and from thence it flows out into the veins of the world. This is why Arthur and Merlin are never forgotten—they are encoded into the lands beneath our feet. It's a subtle energy that pervades, that has become a part of our psyche, an energy that has entered the collective consciousness of the people who live upon the land. And because of the brother and sister rocks, Arthur and Merlin are loved by people all over the world.[150]

---

150 I checked this out and they really do have brother and sister rocks all over the world, because they are bits of different ancient continents that mashed together.

The northern part of Britain which bears Scotland was once part of **Laurentia** (and Laurentia now bears North America); the southern part of Britain, including Wales, was once part of **Gondwana** (Gondwana now bears South America, Africa, Asia, and Australia). Southern Britain and Scotland met millions of years ago when **Avalonia** (bearing southern Britain, Wales, and Ireland) broke off **Gondwana** and drifted into the bit of **Laurentia** that bears Scotland's rocks.

More recently **Pangaea**, a super continent, formed and "Britain"

I see that Merlin has gone everywhere from Cornwall to Scotland putting that energy into the rocks—which is why so many places have legends associated with him, because he passed through them on his mission to weave magic into the land.[151]

I see Merlin make his way up to Scotland … traveling from king's court to king's court. And I see that at the end he died there of <u>a broken heart, at a Scottish king's court in the Borders.</u>[152]

(comprising the Laurentia and Avalonia continental fragments) found itself in the middle. Eventually **Pangaea** broke up and split into smaller continents, leaving "Britain" on its own.

But new research shows that Britain is formed from **three** landmasses, and not just Laurentia and Avalonia.

On September 14, 2018, the *Guardian* newspaper reported that new research by geologists at Plymouth University (who had run chemical tests on solidified magma that welled up long ago from a depth of 100 km) indicated that the rock underpinning Cornwall and south Devon was linked to Europe, and is in fact part of **Armorica**. This fragment of the European continent had attached itself to "Britain."

I was recently astounded to learn that Serpentine rock in Machu Pichu is also to be found on the Lizard in Cornwall—one example of brother and sister rocks all over the world.

151 For example, Alderley Edge and Stonehenge: Alderley Edge is an outcrop of sandstone rock in Cheshire overlooking a plain. It is an ancient place of power associated with a legend about a wizard. The legend goes that Arthur and countless knights with their milk-white horses sleep in a cave beneath the rock, and that when Britain needs them they will wake and decide the fate of a great battle on the plain below and save their country.

Merlin is supposed to have magicked Stonehenge onto Salisbury plain in southern Britain from Erin.

152 Merlin's grave is most likely near Drumelzier, a village in the Tweed valley where Scotland borders England. Legend has it that Merlin was at King Meldred's sixth-century Celtic hill fort nearby, which now lies under the ruins of Tinnis Castle. "Drumelzier" is a version of the older Dunmellor. "Dun" means fort, I suspect the Fort of Meller was the Fort of Meldred.

Merlin's grave is said to be marked by a thorn tree and to lie at the confluence of the River Tweed and a stream once known as Powsail, but is now called Drumelzier Burn. However, a site that was marked as his grave today is upstream of the original confluence, because the stream was diverted in the 1800s. But if you follow the path further, it will take you to the original water course and thus to the original grave. This is now a field with sheep grazing. The Scottish tourist authorities have placed a sign on the path to say that the grave is in this field. Ye and I went in May 2019 when the hawthorn trees looked beautiful covered in creamy-white May blossoms. It is nice to think that the old thorn trees overlooking the Tweed near the original confluence could have descended

Freed from the bonds of time I see into the future and realize that though the Romans had an empire, the Saxons will have one too. But because our women warriors mix our blood with theirs, we dilute the Saxon scourge, and the world will see more fairness and justice as a result; that when the empire falls there will be a kindlier outcome—for in the end it will simply be given away, given back to the people to form a Commonwealth of Nations. The twentieth-century gift of freedom is a result of spiritual evolution.

They will call it the British Empire ... but WE were the Britons! They will call the lands by our name, but they pushed us out, into the mountains of Wales, the mountains of Scotland, and the rugged lands of Cornwall. But Merlin imbued the lands with energy so the Celts would rise again through those who came after, as long as the names of Merlin and Arthur were kept alive. He wanted us to remember the bravery of Arthur, and that the British Isles are magical, sacred isles whose rocks have brother and sister rocks all over the world. **We need to switch the energy on and boost it higher! That's our job now.**

---

from the one that marked Merlin's true grave.

There is a local legend that Merlin was the son of a Scottish king of the Picts, and that he converted to Christianity before his death. A stained-glass window in the local church there depicts his baptism by Saint Kentigern. Well, perhaps he was baptized to please Meldred, or perhaps he had a crisis of faith as everything he held dear was lost, or he could have simply been muddled up with some other historical character ... but he was certainly not born a Pict. I can see where the confusion might have come from, because Merlin had tattoos, and one was the Pictish royal tattoo. He got it while on a diplomatic posting during his youthful training when he went round all the various kings' courts; a king of the Picts adopted Merlin as a "son" while he was visiting him. Remember, he was trained to be a charmer, trained to make people like him, all part of influencing them. So it would be quite understandable that the old Pictish king might have warmed to him during his stay. At the end of Merlin's life, when his desperate mission to gather help brought him north once more, the tattoo would still have marked him out as royalty. Though the Pictish king was long dead, his gift of the tattoo would have ensured Merlin a respectful burial and a place in legend. Merlin's tattoos were not ornaments, they were his passports into royal circles and also his certificates to prove his Druid qualifications, initiations taken, skills acquired. Even if he drowned in the Tweed as one legend has it, when his body was found the tattoos on it would speak for him.

* * *

The tears I shed in the session (at the point by the lake) were very plentiful and real. I had body-responses as the memories unfolded and emotions that had burdened my soul for centuries were discharged. Wild tingles ran up and down my legs and all through my body as I saw the truth of Merlin's magic and what he'd done with the stones in the land.

It was a relief to reach the point in the session where we do healing.

Veronica helped me release a black energy from all over my body and aura that held negative energies from the life—the sadness, grief, and sorrow for what my family would endure, a sense of loss and feelings of failure because I couldn't protect them, hate for the Saxons. I healed and rebalanced by visualizing white light and a sunshine energy flowing in to take its place. We checked for curses and vows, and I had cursed the Saxons and vowed to get even. We did soul retrieval because there had been spirit and soul loss at the points of trauma. Soul loss had affected my third eye, which to my inner vision now looked like a cracked, gray, glass lens. Once that was repaired, the spirit energy was reclaimed and cleansed, then reintegrated as a white crystal shaft strengthening my spine from base chakra to head.

Looking back, the crystal staircase at the start of the session linked with the healing, its white crystal spindles symbolizing my spirit energy. The rich purple amethyst of the treads offered protection, and at the end, amethyst offered itself in the place of a power animal during the healing.[153] My higher self/soul level/ subconscious that assists in this inner work always has the whole picture from the outset, knows the end before I have started at the beginning, and is not tied to time as I am.

It took a second session before I was ready to forgive the Saxons!

And that's when I found I had been hypnotized.

---

153   Past life healing is covered in *Spiritual Gold*.

Chapter 10

Merlin's Children

Singing the Stones Awake

We did a second session because the tapes had mysteriously malfunctioned—from the point I met Merlin they were blank. I was buzzing from the experience, I could never forget the story, but I was hoping to recapture the power of the words and find more answers.

The staircase that presented itself this time was not crystal but old oak wood, an exact match to the door I need to find. I descend and enter a cave where the walls are lined with books. It's a study cave—Merlin's library, and he's there. He says, **"Go back into the life because you missed a lot. I knew you would. And that was why the tape malfunctioned."** I'm still thinking about that as I go to the corridor of doors, and there it is! The same door. I step through into the Great Hall.

This time, after healing my third eye, I see more.

I go back over events and see what was hidden from me.

I see Merlin casting the sleeping "spell." After the entertainment, when he'd put away his harp he had palmed the quartz skull out of his bag. Balanced on his knee and hidden beneath the table, he'd put his hands around it and stroked it awake. It was a powerful skull which amplified his mental command, and with its help he sent the whole room deep asleep.

I now realize when we go to the pool Merlin has the skulls with him concealed inside the pockets of his cloak, and he has lots of things in the pockets, lots of tools that he uses. As he walked, he'd stroked the lapis skull awake, then directed it by thought to calm the air elementals around the lake, making the wind drop.

This time I see the owl's significance. It did not just hoot as we left. I understood how birds were Merlin's friends. The owl had acted as his eyes in the countryside earlier that day. He'd sent it out to scry the land, to fly around so he'd know if it was safe for us to be out that night, and as he rested he'd seen what the bird was seeing. At the lake, he'd slipped it some meat from the feast as a reward, and the owl had settled down happily to watch us from the branch of a tree.

Merlin was a man of secrets, a surprising man. He was entertaining and amusing, he knew how to charm people and he was always very popular. Children loved him, he had great sleight of hand and could make things appear and disappear like magic— could produce acorns, berries, and crystals from behind their ears! But now I could see that as we sat by the lake he'd hypnotized me.

I had been shown things and told things, and commanded to forget.

There was a gap in my memory of events—between giving my report, so he could find discrepancies in his intelligence gathering—and the point where he sighed.

In the gap, I see him bringing out the quartz skull to show me, for that was where he was planning to look for the truth of the discrepancies.

He shows me the crystal skull because it's important.

He shows me the lapis skull because it's important.

And he places them side by side on his thighs as we sit on the talking stone. The lapis is on his left, and the quartz on his right, facing out to the lake. He takes my hands and lays one on each skull. They feel cool and smooth.

He says, "Remember these, because you need to write about them. You need to record for our people." Then he tells me things.

He says the skulls are very old … they're from far away and long ago. They were so important they were saved from lands that went beneath the sea, lands reached by the golden path of the sun on the ocean, and for thousands of years they have been journeying through the world as tools to try and help the people they are with. He tells me that the people they are with have changed. The skulls were from the lands beneath the sea, but they were brought there from even earlier times and earlier places … They grew in the earth—

they were gifts from the earth—gifts from the elemental kingdoms, the elementals of earth and air and water, the elementals to do with harvest and growth, and the energy in the land and the weather.

To improve a harvest, to improve the weather, he says he works with the lapis skull. The quartz skull amplifies, so whatever he's doing he can use the two skulls together because the quartz will make the work more powerful. He has to switch them on with his hands by stroking and thought. He communicates with them, then puts them side by side and the quartz one amplifies the work that the lapis skull is doing.

That's when he tells me the skulls will always work with me.

Not just these two, he can see in the records of my soul that I've had contact with them before, but also others—and that's why he's sharing this. He tells me he can see future events in the quartz skull, so he uses that for guidance on his journeys, and it's one reason why he's always been safe—he's been able to foresee trouble and avoid it. But if anyone were to find the skulls or try to rob him of them, he would tell them the skulls will bring their death, and that's always been a good protection for them …

… But with the mention of death he puts the skulls away and brings me out of the trance and sighs. And that's when he tells me he's been looking into the future and seen things he wished he hadn't.

Everything else was as I'd seen it.

I did forgive the Saxons, and felt a great weight lift.[154]

154   The angels who assist with this healing work bring me the Saxon king. It's King Aelle, and I talk to him. I understand why he's come, that they have to have somewhere to live and they've been displaced. I forgive him, put arms round him, saying, "We will work together better than we did with the Romans." I told him that they think they've won the land but the land is stronger than them—and it will change them. And our people will change them. That the land will claim the Saxons—it's not the Saxons claiming the land. He said, "We didn't quite know what we were getting when we took your lands. There was a price to be paid that we hadn't reckoned with, but we are happy to pay it." I liked him, which surprised me. We shook hands on it, and then I let him go. From now on I will think of them as being part of the team of guardians for the land.

I released a lot of gray "cotton wool" type of energy that had been deadening me, muffling me, and I rebalanced with a pink-and-gold sparkly divine energy in my body, heart, and aura. That felt better! (Lack of forgiveness

* * *

Merlin was a striking figure, Druid staff in hand, well muscled, hale and hearty, with Celtic mustaches and tattoos! A warrior Druid and not at all what I was expecting; no tall, thin, pale, fey character dressed in black was he. But as he said, he needed to be able to look after himself on his travels because even bodyguards could betray him. His "cloak of invisibility" had often saved him, but it was no more than illusion, and like most of his magic it was wrought by influencing what people *thought* they saw, because he could "hack" into their brains using telepathic skills learned in childhood. I learned a lot more about Merlin.

He was descended from a long line of holy people stretching back to Atlantis, which is why he had the skulls—they'd brought them with them when they left. These people were the Druids' forebears; and they had clothed the British Isles with stone circles, dolmens, and standing stones, and brought the knowledge of earth energies with them.

Merlin's parents were descended from Druids who had sheltered in Ireland until it was safe to return after the Romans left. He was born on the Druids' sacred isle (now Anglesey), and all the wisdom, skills, and resources that remained to the Druids had been channeled into his upbringing. He grew up in the courts of the kings with Druid tutors to prepare him for his mission. **He was the last hope of the Druids, the pinnacle of their aspirations, and the lever with which they were trying to change the outcome of future events.** *He was raised for a single purpose—to defend the land of his people now the Romans had gone.*[155]

---

only ever hurts you, not the intended recipient, but it can be hard to let go. We tend to polish our hurts and hold them close as if they were jewels—which they so obviously are not! But I am sure I still have more work to do on this. I forgave them as much as I could at the time. I made a start. In the future, I can build on that.)

155 I think the name he was given reflected this task. One meaning ascribed to "Myrddin" is "Sea Fortress," which is what he was asked to turn Britain into. Other sources give the meaning of "Myrddin" as "Hawk"—a fierce bird and a good hunter (of Saxons). Merlin (which is also a bird's name when you think about it) had a natural affinity with birds, and was trained to astral travel with

And like the Atlantean priests of old, Merlin wore a gold circlet to aid telepathy—it was enhanced by a tiny golden circle that lay over his third eye which housed a small piece of crystal: he had several interchangeable crystals that fit there. It depended on what he wanted to do, quartz for telepathy, lapis for weather work with the blue skull, amethyst for protection. The tiny crystal amplified his link with the skulls.

To send Merlin a message by telepathy I also wore a crystal in a gold circle over my third eye, but mine was strung on leather rather than a full circlet of gold. This I kept folded in my pouch. When I used it I had to focus, hold a larger quartz crystal in my hands, and put the message into that crystal by thought. Then I entered the Otherworld (inner world) and went to a designated sacred place (usually a stone circle). Then I would visualize putting the crystal I was holding on the altar stone there and leave it for Merlin to find next time he was meditating and visiting the Otherworld. Or perhaps I'd visualize a symbol and leave it for him to find, or hold feathers and use them for my message—the type of bird, the exact arrangement of the feathers, held the meaning. Only another Druid would know. It was our secret code.

It was whispered he had the secret of eternal youth, because both he and Arthur had the stamina and verve of much younger men. He knew the properties of herbs and mushrooms and how to use them, and he was adept at healing. He gave Arthur medicinal herbal draughts and healing with the skulls, and he also did healing Druid-fashion, which meant Otherworld-work. He would visualize Arthur in the inner world and lay him on the altar of a stone circle like Stonehenge—then visualize healing energies flowing into him from the land, from the stones and the energy networks that flow through the world. Different places held different energies and that was the secret of their youthfulness. Armor and swords were heavy but Arthur was still strong enough to bear arms well into his seventies. As I remembered it in the session he was seventy-seven when he fought his last battle, the Battle of Camlann. He was mortally wounded, but his friends spirited him away and the Saxons never took him, never dishonored his body. Amid secrecy he was buried in the grounds of <u>*Glastonbury Abbey near his wives. His sword was seen to be*</u> *thrown* them so he could scry through their vision.

in a lake to deter Saxon grave robbers from trying to claim it.

AD 537 was the year we both died, Arthur and I, but he outlived me.

My father, Arthur, and Merlin were of the same generation, born in the years AD 460–465. (I had been born in 490.) In life, Arthur had forged a reputation for invincibility in twelve major battles between AD 485–496. Periods of comparative peace followed ... until agreements were broken and fighting broke out again. The 530s were very troubled years. Halley's comet was seen in the skies like a portent of doom. The extraterrestrial dust it trailed blanketed the upper atmosphere and screened out sunlight; the 530s brought dark years of famine.[156] Our rich farmlands were all the more coveted by the Saxons, with yields boosted by Merlin's weather magic.

Arthur had many swords. His famous sword Excalibur/ Caliburn was a new blade made by master smiths in Frankia. It was brought to Britain by traders and gifted to him by his father, Uther Pendragon—but only after he passed a test of bravery as a young man. He had to spend the night in total darkness sealed in an ancient stone tomb. He had to find the sword and draw it out of the stones where it had been hidden. When the tomb was opened at daybreak Arthur emerged victorious, sword in hand.

He'd first married at sixteen, and over the next sixty-one years he had seven wives. Guinevere (Gwenhwyfar) was number five and the one Arthur was married to longest. They had girls who

---

156   Scientists examining ice core samples from Greenland have found that cometary dust (regarded as most likely being from the Eta Aquarid meteor shower associated with Halley's comet) had loaded Earth's atmosphere between AD 533 and 540, causing solar dimming. As far away as China, historical records for AD 536 report this solar dimming "as the years without summer."

Cosmic dust in the upper atmosphere takes longer to settle than volcanic dust, which tends to be in the lower atmosphere. The northern hemisphere has its own volcanoes, but even the dust from those around the equator drifts north. The ice samples from Greenland contained cosmic dust, volcanic dust, but also tropical marine microfossils and aerosol-sized particles indicating a low-latitude explosion in the ocean. Perhaps a large meteor hit the ocean bed, but this was a catastrophic three-pronged attack on the climate. The ensuing food shortages made people desperate, affecting their health and immune systems. No wonder the plague of Justinian in AD 541 proved so fatal. Recurring plagues were a feature of life for a long time afterward.

died young. Mordred was his son from an earlier marriage but he was a bad lot, and drowned his own brother. Nobody believed it was an accident, except perhaps Arthur. He caused Arthur much grief and made many enemies, and in the end one of his enemies poisoned him. We always thought Arthur too soft with Mordred ... but he hoped he would change. Arthur left behind a young widow when he died, still hoping for a suitable heir. His other wives died young, either in childbirth or possibly poisoned by rivals. We all wondered. Such was the jostling for power of the kings.

*It was the Celtic kings' rivalry that caused Arthur to have a "**round table**." When the kings came to a war conference there was no other way to seat them without fighting breaking out over who was sitting where in the hierarchy of the normal table set-up. Class and position in society were very bound up with where you sat at the tables—we all had to know our place then. So the tables were pulled out of place and arranged in a circle around the fire pit. The kings sat where they chose, having brought their king-chairs with them, and Arthur took the last vacant place. A brilliant solution; nobody was above anybody else.*

* * *

Merlin's work ensured that he and Arthur were never forgotten, and so the legend was born. A legend that has defied time and traveled round the world and even—ironically—been embraced by the descendants of his enemies the Saxons!

So that's the story of King Arthur, high king of the Britons and now the darling of the world, and his faithful magician Merlin, who died of a broken heart with his lord dead and his cause lost. Merlin engendered such loyalty and love within me that I am still moved to tears by his story and its ending.

I read somewhere that "When it comes to Arthur what is not known outweighs what is known. But everyone wants to claim Arthur as his or her own king." It is quite extraordinary! And even today royalty claim legitimacy through Arthur. Prince William, Britain's future king with no known genetic link to Arthur, is William Arthur. But then that is Merlin's legacy. He was incredibly loyal and gifted, he did his best for those he loved, and that "best" is still with us even now.

And "now" is the place to focus.

The flow of information shifts to the present day.

We are living in times of great peril, we are living at a watershed moment in the history of the world—but like Merlin we can help the future fall out in a better way. The legendary Knights of the Round Table were **the guardians** of Arthur's Great Hall in South Cadbury Castle (Camelot). Today we can be part of a worldwide army of "Knights"—Knights for Justice, Knights for Truth. We can slay the dragons of greed and pollution and profit before people, and all the things that have gone wrong. **When ordinary people become the guardians of the planet, that's when we will win.**

And you don't need a sword now! You need the Internet—the weight of public opinion is a weapon. A weapon that can bankrupt companies ruining the soil with chemical poisons, selling seeds with terminator genes spliced in, and all the other dreadful, disgusting things that greed has tried to foist on the world.

Within "sword" is "word" … your name on a petition may be all it takes.

There's still a chance where things can all go wrong—but there's an awfully big momentum that's going to help it go right because it's in the rocks under our feet. We've caused problems but with a willing heart we can put them right. The younger generation has that willing heart; they are the most awake and aware generation there's ever been. It's in the news now (March 2019) that children all over the world are taking part in globally coordinated protests— taking days off school for demonstrations about saving the planet— because, like Merlin, they want to help the future fall out in a better way.[157] We can't have business as usual, not if we want to survive.

* * *

Veronica wraps the session up by telling me to go to a special place for guidance.

---

157 April 2019 went on to see events organized by Extinction Rebellion, an international movement where people come together for peaceful protests. London was disrupted for days that Easter.

It has been a strange session with little action but a lot of information which flowed through me in response to her questions. Now I find myself at Stonehenge.

Veronica asks why this is important.

Because of the energy in the land; there is very strong amplification in the land here. Stonehenge was very important in ancient times because **it is a real power point. Whoever has Stonehenge, or the control of it, rules the land.** Thousands of years ago there was a huge city there, built of wood. We've got the capital city in London now, but London is not the place of power.

As the Druids would say, "In the time of the gods ..." there was a mythic event on the land and the land got imprinted. It was to do with the sun god, with encouraging the sun to come into the land to bring good harvests and good fortune. The place was famous long before they put the stones up. There was a Woodhenge before the stones, and before that there were trees. It's been very important for a very long time. It was important when Britain was attached to Europe by a land bridge, and that disappeared 8,000 years ago.

Veronica asks if there are any other parts of the world with the same amplification.

Yes. Places like Uluru (Ayers Rock), Machu Picchu, holy places in the Himalayas, sites in Atlantis and Lemuria, and more—there's a resonance among all of them. All over the world there's a resonance with Stonehenge. It's the etheric energy in Earth's body. We can't see it with our eyes, but these places are like the chakra points on our bodies, and we can't see them. **When you ask, "Why is Stonehenge important?" it's like saying, "Why is our heart chakra important?"** Earth has lots of little heart chakras, all these holy places. All land is sacred, but these are the places that are most sacred because they have more energy connections and stronger etheric energy.

Then I see a link with the skulls.

Because there's very strong amplification in the land there, a connection to the site would enhance the crystal skulls and the skulls would enhance the site, and you would get a massive exponential multiplication of power. There needs to be a crystal skull gathering at Stonehenge in the future. When they

talk about the thirteen skulls coming together in a circle that's where it should be—inside the ancient stone circle of Stonehenge.

But we don't have to wait for that.

Because in the inner world we can all take crystal skulls to Stonehenge whenever we like! It's good to visit sacred places, but not essential to be physically present. Like Merlin, we can work in the Otherworld and use the power of our minds. At the end of the book you will find a visualization to help dream the new world into being.

Merlin and his crystal skulls put energy into the lines of power that made the crystals in the rocks sing, and the song of Merlin and the song of hope and the song of truth and justice is still vibrating in the energy networks of the world, we just need to amplify it, to boost it until the whole planet rings with it and that will bring in the new age, a Golden Age.

We can all be Merlin's children now and sing the stones awake.

Chapter 11

By now it is the end of the sixth century AD, and I was ready to incarnate again. After the sadness and tragedy of solar-dimmed Britain I choose the antidote of sunshine. My deep soul longing to know more of the skulls pulls me into a life where I'll encounter one taken east for safekeeping—but if ever a skull was no longer safe it was this one!

The door into the session was a spanking new, shiny, high-gloss red, with a battered, cheap old doorknob made of dull brass. The doorframe was down-to-earth varnished pine, and a little lacy lavender bag hung from the knob.

Lavender is good protection for me, the guides said, and I made a mental note to drink lavender tea for cleansing and protection over the next few days, and to get another plant for the garden. I do love lavender, with its sharp but soothing scent and soft silver-gray foliage. The blue flower spikes remind me of Archangel Michael's sword … and at that point an angel began spraying me with lavender water so I could take the lavender energy with me when I went through the door! The guides were laughing as they handed me wellingtons and a sun hat as symbolic protection from the elements! They said I needed to lighten up and not take things so seriously.

I open the door and step through.

I find myself in a desert.

Akbar's Story
PHARAOH'S SKULL

A hot sun shone in an empty blue sky, and the shifting sands of

North Africa lie baking in the heat. Desert winds have sculpted the sands around me into sharp-edged dunes ... and as I admire their stark beauty I know I am now Akbar, a sturdy lad of eighteen.

My inner senses are desperately grappling for more information: what is going on? Why am I here?

I become aware Akbar is with a camel train, and traveling in the company of men who are returning from a successful trading mission, their saddlebags stuffed full of metalwork and jewelry.

Veronica asks me what I am wearing.

Loose clothing makes the heat bearable. And in traditional fashion we have wound lengths of cloth around our heads to protect us from the sun. When the stinging winds whip us with sand I know I can adjust this, pull some down to shield my nose, so I can still breathe without choking in the swirling dust. Beneath the cloth my hair is bound up in a top knot, and around my neck hangs a small metal amulet shaped like a hand—a gift from my mother—which I've had a long time now. My mother knows I have an enemy ... has seen the spite at first hand, and it's to keep me safe. Her gift is concealed beneath my robe, the better to work its magic in secret.

Filled with the confidence of youth, and with no thought for her concerns, I look ahead into the distance. Hazy purple mountains rim the desert, and I know our goal is an oasis there, where cool mountain springs flow down to create a precious island of green in this parched red-gold land. The oasis means rest, water, and food for the men I am with; but best of all they will be home with their women, their families, and the rest of the tribe who are patiently awaiting our safe return.

I know the men are happy at the thought of getting back to their women—and in truth I *am* looking forward to seeing my mother again, and even my sisters. But as my camel plods away the monotonous hours of the journey, my mind lies elsewhere: I've had many days for reflection and have come to a life-changing decision.

By nightfall our camel train had reached the oasis and fires were lit for feasting and celebration. The moon was exceptionally close and bright that night, and it shone down upon my tribe as they talked, ate, and laughed in the welcome coolness of the evening. With excited voices, they exchanged their news and celebrated the safe return of their men.

After I'd eaten and spent a little time with my family, I could sit on my plans no longer, and I went to seek somebody out.

My confident footsteps slowed when I caught sight of Safiya.[158] She was laughing with her sisters as they helped their mother tidy up after the meal. Moonlight gleamed on her long black hair and glinted on the silver neckpieces she wore over her belted robe. Safiya was fifteen, and she was very dear to me … It was thoughts of asking for her in marriage that had taken up the journey home.

I greeted her family cheerily, and then went up to her to speak more privately.

As soon as I'd got back I'd brought her a gift from the trading we'd done, and she had accepted it with flushed cheeks and great excitement. The men of our tribe were not given to wearing jewelry but our womenfolk prized it greatly, and because I'd wanted to impress her I had picked out a striking piece as my gift. It was a headband of intricate silverwork from which dangled little pieces of silver, like coins—and I could see these twinkling in the light of the campfire now, as she wore it. The shiny silver lay against her sungold skin giving her a look that was both exotic and charming.

She had been happy to see me return, she had been delighted with my gift, but she grew even happier as we talked … because I told her I was going to ask her father for her in the morning. I knew even if her father agreed there would be the question of a bride price to be settled, in camels and gold—which was daunting, but the important thing was that when I'd asked if she would like to be my bride, Safiya had said, "Yes." In fact, she'd clapped her hands and said, "Yes! Yes! Yes!"—and said she very much wanted to take me as her husband.

There'd be plenty of time to sort out the details later, and everything else could wait. After the long time away, I just wanted to be with her, and we sat side by side in the silvery moonlight, lost in our happiness, wrapped up in each other, talking about our dreams for the future. But somebody who had been watching us from the shadows scowled … and clenched jealous fists in fury.

158 "Saf-I-a."

Kamal was my cousin.

He had been born three years before me and was the apple of our grandfather's eye … until I came along. No longer the only grandson, he grew jealous. I, in my turn, had hero worshipped him when I was young and tagged around after him, which made Kamal even crosser. And although other grandsons had appeared over the years, it had never lessened Kamal's enmity toward me.

As we grew up, no matter what it was, Kamal always wanted what I had, and felt it should really have been his by rights. Jealousy convinced him I had been given a faster camel … and there was never an end to it.

Kamal had not gone on the trading mission.

He had been cunning. He had chosen to stay behind with the tribe, to be one of those guarding the women. He had seen it as an opportunity to woo Safiya, and he had tried to steal her affections while I was away. But as he'd watched us together he could see he'd wasted his time, and jealousy rose within him. He went back to his father's tent with a face like thunder.

Eventually tiredness descended on the tribe and people settled down for the night in their respective tents, and I rejoined my family. Armed guards were posted to keep watch through the night. Because being successful traders we had more wealth than most, and there were bandits and robbers who had very little; who could come like jackals in the night and steal our things; who would ruthlessly burn our tents and take our women and camels. These were dangerous times and dangerous lands, as we knew to our cost. Ours was a big tribe, and there was a certain safety in numbers, but we could not leave anything to chance. Unseen dangers lurked everywhere. If it wasn't bandits and robbers it could be sand storms, illness, injury, or the tricksters and dishonest merchants who had tried to cheat us as we journeyed through the lands of Persia, Arabia, Egypt, and North Africa.

When the union was proposed, both fathers smiled on it. They were friends, and Safiya's father liked me. The bride price was a test of how serious I was about her, and so it was substantial, but when Kamal learned the price he offered more. When his offer was turned down, his smouldering resentment grew.

With my father's help the bride price was paid, and when the wedding took place just over a year later Kamal absented himself and his sour face was not there to spoil the feast.

It was an occasion of joy for both families, everyone else was happy for us, and even our camels got on. You never knew with camels, they could be a lot less reasonable than people. The wedding night was spent in our new tent. Its interior was simple, rugs to cover the sand, small brass and stone oil lamps to provide a little light, and there was a padded bed roll for sleeping. As we lay together wrapped in each other's arms, we fervently hoped we would be fruitful, and be blessed with many children to make our families stronger.

Fertility was greatly valued by our tribe as it increased the chances of survival.

The tribe continued plying the traditional trading routes, so from time to time we found ourselves back at the same oasis. Then Safiya and I would call to mind the night of the big moon, and we would look back over the years that had passed since then. Four boys and two girls were born to us—and though life was hard sometimes, we always overcame difficulties by working as a team. Our families shared in joint trading ventures together, and there was a lot of cooperation all around that helped us get through. But Kamal still watched me through jealous eyes, even though he had a wife and children of his own by now.

My fine, strapping sons grew tall and were everything a father could wish for: they listened to me, treated me with respect, learned things quickly, and they were strong, competent, clever, cunning, and wise.

But it was the year my eldest sons turned seventeen, eighteen, and twenty that things took an unexpected turn.

The trading routes had brought us to Cairo in Egypt. Now Cairo had an enormous market where my people had done some of their most successful trading over the years.[159] A lot of traders came and the market served a very big area. It gave our tribe the opportunity to buy a huge range of goods, and we knew where we

159 Cairo was already a very big city fourteen hundred years ago when this took place.

could sell them as people would tell us what they needed. We got orders for things and would say, "Right, well, we'll get that for you next time."

It was always very lucrative when we came here, and we stayed for a couple of weeks or more to see all the things on offer. We made an encampment just outside the city, and there was never a need to leave our women and children behind when we visited Cairo.

But this time we came across something most unusual in the market. It was a real curiosity. No one had seen anything like it. It looked old, it was a bit scratched and battered, but it was definitely a human-looking skull formed from a solid piece of rock crystal. It was so different from anything else we'd ever seen that we said to one another, "What would you do with that?"

The man who was trying to trade it wasn't saying where he got it. He just wanted to get rid of it, so there was a sense of mystery around it.

My people were fascinated by it and didn't quite know why.

We kept going back to look at it, and mulled over what to do. Perhaps it was stolen? Then we could end up paying for it and somebody coming after us claiming it was theirs and causing trouble. That could be messy, and anyway who would we sell it on to? We kept very little ourselves. Being always on the move we had to have the minimum in our tents and on our camels, so that we had the maximum capacity for carrying the trading goods. So it wasn't like we wanted to be burdened with this heavy lump of rock. It always came back to the same thing: who would we sell it to? Nobody had ever asked us for one. We went round in circles umming and ahing like this for days. But there was just something about it, and although we tried hard to forget it, we kept coming back and having another look.

It was after one of my many visits to the skull seller that I was attacked in an alleyway. I'd been trying to take a shortcut back to my family, but with my head full of thoughts of the skull I wasn't concentrating, and three men jumped me, robbed me, and beat me savagely. Kamal had been following me, snooping, curious to see where I was going and what I was buying, and so he had not been far behind. When he saw what was happening, something snapped inside him. Overcome by the fury of all the years we'd had jackals such as these snapping at our heels and stealing from us, and with a blood lust to avenge his dead mother surging in his veins, he sent them flying.

He carried me back to our people and watched as the blood was washed away and my wounds were tended. Pity pierced his heart and from that moment on he was no longer jealous; he became protective of me, and to everyone's surprise a friendship grew up between us.

That night as I lay resting and bruised, my father had a dream. The skull came to him in his dream and told him he needed to buy it, and that we needed to take it away with us when we left. This was most unusual, as he'd never had goods talking to him in his dreams before.

My father told the elders, the others of his generation, and they discussed what to do. They all felt that there was something about it ... and so they took the decision to take a risk and buy it.

Skillfully, they bartered the skull seller down—as they did every time they bought anything—but when they returned to their families they kept it well hidden, and we were all sworn to secrecy over it. They'd bought it on an intuitive impulse and still did not know what they were going to do with it, and they certainly didn't want their women to think them foolish.

Again, the skull came to my father in his dreams.

It told him they could look into it and ask questions and see the future. Although this sounded outlandish my father told the elders, and the men began to think that this just might, possibly, be a way to make their money back and more, if it were in any way true ... there *were* those who made money from fortune telling, they reasoned, so perhaps they could develop a reputation as seers and soothsayers. Perhaps it could help them avoid danger? Desert sandstorms could whip up out of nowhere and bury them alive, and there were many bad things that could happen.

... And so they came to realize how the skull could prove itself to be of value, and we took it with us when we moved on.

As it was my father it had come to in the dreams, it was given to him to look after. It stayed hidden in his tent and was carried on his camel, but it was not his skull because it belonged to the tribe. All the men had given a little bit toward it, and it had been one of those gambles that the men of the tribe took from time to time. However, nobody had come after us saying it was stolen, and indeed, nobody knew we'd got it as we'd kept it very secret, even from the women. My father did try talking to it, and it showed him things when he looked into it. It quite often came to him in his dreams and gave him information which he shared, and things were working out well.

It began to be consulted regularly about which journeys to make and which routes to take to avoid dangers, and it was found to be most helpful. Although I no longer shared my father's tent I had more access to the skull than most. I was curious, and my father allowed me to look into it.

As my father grew old, the skull began to come to me in my dreams.

It told me I was appointed as the next keeper, and so when my father died it came to be with me in my tent. It was kept wrapped up but it was too big to hide from Safiya. She knew the bundle was there, and so I opened it to show her, but I made her promise to keep it a secret. She didn't feel our daughters needed to know, and they did not pry as it was always kept carefully covered and hidden among my things, and they had always been taught to treat their father's things with the greatest respect.

The boys of the tribe were told about the skull when they came of age, but it was really the elders who had the most to do with it. It was still felt best that the women didn't know in case they gossiped and got overheard, or married out of the tribe taking the knowledge with them, which could lead to it being stolen. Boys did not leave, and having rituals and traditions that strengthened the bonds between the male members of the tribe worked well; and the shared secret of the skull made all the men feel a bit special.

Over time, the skull had a very positive effect on the tribe. Its advice proved right and had helped many times.

The years passed and my hair grew gray and my sons had sons of their own. But I was never ill, and neither was my wife nor any of our children, and I came to suspect that the skull had healing powers, and that it kept us well. And when I thought about it more, I realized we were a very healthy tribe. I felt the skull brought harmony and strength, and I derived enjoyment from being in its company: it felt comforting. One evening as my fingers traced the scar down the side of my face, I realized that it had only been after meeting the skull that things had healed between myself and Kamal.[160]

But as the tally of my years neared eighty, the skull started to talk to one of my sons as he dreamed. I took this as a sign I might be approaching the end of my days, and it caused me to reflect on my life. Safiya had already gone and I missed her. Even Kamal had gone …

I was resting in my tent one night when the certainty came to me that the time of my passing was at hand. My family gathered around me, but I told them I did not want to die inside a tent, I wanted to be out in the desert and under the full moon that was shining down that night, just as it had all those years before when Safiya and I had declared our love.

They carried me out and made me comfortable in the desert as I wished.

I looked at the sea of concerned faces surrounding me and told them all how much I loved them, how proud I was of them, and how proud I was to be leaving them behind as part of the tribe. And as I spoke, my eyes grew wet with tears because I knew I was saying farewell for the last time.

I raised myself up with what remained of my strength because I wanted to leave them the most precious gift I had to give them, the wisdom of my heart garnered over the years of my life. I said,

"Always be kind to your loved ones because their love is the most precious, **the only***, thing that really matters in this world. You can lose gold and break porcelain, fabric can rot, but none of that matters though that's the trading we do, it's the stuff of life, but it's not what's really important. The only thing that*

---

160 This explains the shiny new red door I had passed through to enter this life recall; red stood for the blood spilt, shiny and new symbolizes the transformed relationship with Kamal, while the battered old doorknob which allowed it to open stood for the skull.

really matters is love, love for your family. It's better than gold."

I lay back, at peace.

Leaving weariness and exhaustion behind me, I slipped out of my body. Light and free I began to rise upward, my awareness expanding, my limits and boundaries dissolving. I was floating in a transparent sea of knowledge, of direct knowing, and the mysterious past of the crystal skull whose company I had come to enjoy when I was Akbar entered my consciousness.

I understood that the seller was a grave robber who had come across it while looting a Pharaoh's tomb; but the skull had not wanted to stay with the robber, and so it did what skulls do when they want to move on: it had given him bad dreams and brought him bad luck until he came to believe it was cursed and wanted rid of it.

It had proved difficult to trade. And so he had brought it to the great market where it passed into the guardianship of the tribe. The men's fascination with it had to do with their own past life memories stirring within them. The skull had been calling to them at deep inner levels because it sensed their connection.

It had been one of the thirteen in Atlanta, entrusted to a priest who carried it east to Egypt, where it came to the notice of the Pharaohs. It had been placed in the tomb of one of them to be of service in the afterlife. This had kept it safe for a very long time until the grave robber freed it, enabling it to continue its work as a seeing-healer skull for the benefit of humankind.

I became aware that all thirteen skulls were tuned to a slightly different frequency. They all had the same functions to greater or lesser degrees and they all brought harmony, and so they put the harmony back into you and this was how they healed and how the tribe had stayed well. I realized they could all be used for seeing, that they all held records of information, and they could all be used for manifestation in some way. Each function used a different frequency, and it just depended what frequency the function was on as to which skulls were most in tune with it, and thus easier to use. Male skulls were generally best for seeing or manifestation, and female ones for healing, but they all did a bit of everything, although they had their particular strengths.

I saw the splendor of the thirteen as they were displayed in Atlanta, and I saw the skull we had bought, as she was when she'd been there, set within her family.[161]

I believe the skull may still be consulted to this day by the descendants of the traveling people, and I fancy it is hidden in a desert cave, but my guides said it is not forgotten, nor is it lost.

The importance of this story is that it shows the enduring power of the skulls, and how they have their own sort of life. They can make their needs known, and communicate, just as that skull picked its guardians down the generations and spoke to them in their dreams.

My guides went on to tell me to "Be of good cheer, because there are more skulls in the world than you'd think, and just because they're not all out there on the stage of the world, it doesn't mean they don't exist. They are hidden for their safety and they have their guardians."

Sometime after I wrote this chapter I visited Jordan.

I wanted to see the place where John the Baptist baptized Jesus, and I went to Petra where the camel trains of old passed through a rose-red city carved out of sandstone.[162] But it was the amazing rock formation they call "the Pillars of Wisdom" in the desert of Wadi Rum that caught my imagination and really made me wonder. Although it got that name very recently because of Lawrence of Arabia, and it's a Bible reference, I could just imagine a skull being hidden deep in a cave somewhere romantic like that!

The skulls are just as relevant for us today in our modern lives as they were back then when things were so simple—because *we* haven't changed, although the trappings of our lives have grown more complex. They were a force for good in the past, they are a force for good now, and they will be a force for good in the future.

If you have been drawn to read this book it is highly likely

---

161 Directly below the one used to heal Princess Sahara. (The skulls being tuned to different functions was also mentioned in chapter 4.)

162 Inhabited since prehistoric times, the Nabateaan caravan city of Petra lies between the Red Sea and the Dead Sea. Trade routes have crossed here for millennia. It has UNESCO World Heritage status.

you have been close to the skulls in previous lifetimes. You can visit crystal skulls in the museums of the world, in London, Paris, and the United States, and if they're labeled "fake," make your own mind up. You may find they talk to you; ancient skills may reawaken. It has been said that the consciousness that is the essence of the crystal skulls can be channeled even through modern-day replicas, and if you would like one of your own it is easy to buy them on the Internet—just Google www.crystalskulls.com and they can be posted to you! (All the skulls from this website have spent time in a healing sanctuary with Amar, an ancient Tibetan crystal skull.) They have tiny ones that can travel with you in a pocket, and all sizes including magnificent large ones.

I find crystal uplifting, and small new skulls can be very comforting to hold.

It is simple to establish a connection with the crystal skulls by inviting them into your life for personal and planetary healing; and in any sort of healing endeavor, intention is always the most important factor. During the regression session, I was given these words to use for this:

"Be with me, let me listen to you, let the truth be heard and let your love flow out into the world and into me. May you bring me peace, harmony and healing, happiness and joy, and may our futures be golden. We welcome your wisdom and we ask for your guidance, and may all things be in the perfection for which they were ordained by the Creator."

Chapter 12

The door to this session was another of the old-fashioned-looking paneled ones, but it had an incongruously modern high-gloss finish in shiny white. The transparent crystal glass faceted doorknob had a brass collar, and, like some of the other doors I'd faced, lots of light was escaping from around the edges.

But first I had to put on the protective outfit hanging from a hook on the back of the door. The guides had ensured it was a lurex jumpsuit in a lurid purple to give me a laugh and lighten me up, and there was a glass fish bowl thing for over my head that could have come straight from a comic book space suit.

I open the door and step through. Everything melts away.

I am in space.

I have no body at all.

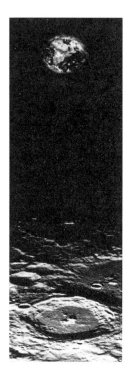

The Watchers and Catchers of Souls

It is one of those times between lives, when it is time to plan my next incarnation.

All I am is pure consciousness floating in the blackness of the void and admiring the beauty of the stars. I can see the Earth below me looking blue and luminous with her oceans and clouds, and the moon looking hard and crusty and dusty. I am not alone, my guide is with me, and there are angels and other guides too. They speak with one voice in my mind.

"We've got a job for you," say the guides and angels. This is not what I want to hear, and I experience resistance. I don't want to listen. It's so lovely looking at the stars and being with the guides and angels, why would I want to go back into a body and have another struggle with living a life? I'd much rather stay with them.

I'm told I'm being naughty, that I must get back on with my development, my lessons and learning. If I don't, I'll be holding other souls back. They promise they'll be there for me, and that I won't be on my own, that they'll look after me. I am reluctant. They remind me that lives are quite short in cosmic terms, akin to watching an episode of a soap opera, or perhaps a play. But of course it doesn't feel like that when you're the one going through the emotional wringer on the stage ...

They let slip it is to be on the moon.

They say a life is part of a series of lives, and just like bricks in a wall, you can't miss a brick out or the wall won't be strong ... they're not letting up. They say this life is necessary, like a foundation is necessary—that I'm to learn determination to succeed, and how not to be cheated of success.

But they say there's always a choice.

There are plenty of worse options for me if I want to do it the hard way. They joke and say I could go back to slime if I preferred, and really do it the long way. I'm aware other lives hang on my decision and that if I delay I'll impede the unfolding of things on a bigger scale. I'm going to have to say "Yes."

"Will I be a life-form? Or will it be more of an existence?" I ask, curious now. "No," they say, "You'll be artificial intelligence with a bio input, a half-sentient machine. You will be the servant of fourth- and fifth-dimensional beings, although your crafted shell will be partly three dimensional as it will exist on the moon's structure. The workings will be thought into form and the programming will be done by thought also." They are failing to sell this to me, and it's not sounding very appealing.

"But you'll learn things you need to understand, and it won't be for long," say the guides and angels. They promise that the machine will have a malfunction and they will pull me out of it when I've learned all I need to know. They say there will be no emotion with this incarnational experience; it will just be a very mental part of me that will be going in. The form will be built for me, and it will be scrapped by the beings after the malfunction to prevent the contamination spreading to other machines.

My masters-to-be have a base on the moon that they visit, but they live elsewhere also. They travel a lot between worlds; they like to keep up with how the worlds are evolving and what the life-forms are getting up to. They're not record keepers exactly, but they like to keep their eye on trouble spots, where beings endanger their world and other life-forms. They get involved, sometimes to make it worse, and sometimes to patch things up. It depends on what they'd get from the world's demise, because as they see it, they *harvest*, and sometimes the worlds aren't ready to give their best harvest yet.

These are the Watchers and Catchers, and the harvest they are after is souls. They have been ever so busy for a very long time, working away like the ants and termites do on Earth. The universe is a big place, so there's a lot of surveillance that needs to go on, and they place energy nets around the planets to catch souls to put to work in their machines. Earth came to their notice a long time ago as there are a lot of souls here, a lot of potential slaves for their mines, and they've been quietly harvesting for sometime. But, as they see it, the biggest harvest of Earth is yet to come.

Not all souls are of interest to them. If you lead a good life, the vibration of your soul will reflect this and will be at too high a level for them to use when you die. Those who have not led a good life may have a vibration low enough to fall into their catchment. It is really that simple. As our religious teachers have always told us down the ages, "Your deeds will find you out."

Their machines are used to mine a higher-dimensional substance, a fourth- and fifth-dimensional equivalent of metal. It is some sort of energy out of which they can form things, and they extract it from the cores of planets or from deep within their crusts. Our Earth metal is too basic, this substance is stronger and finer, and out of it they construct their cities and craft. They don't see themselves as negatively orientated—as bad or evil—no, as far as they are concerned, they are just looking after themselves and ensuring the survival of their species.

My guides and angels tell me that because I make this as a voluntary choice, they will be able to take me out of the machine. But if I was trapped because my true vibratory rate had brought me there, then they would not be able to do so, and I'd have to evolve at my own pace until my energies had changed sufficiently that the machine could no longer hold me.

They say I'd be like an undercover agent or whistleblower in this situation. But it's still not a very tempting option.

It is only when I finally give permission with a grudging, "Oh, go on then," that they tell me it is enough. Only my willingness was necessary, made as a free will choice, and I do not actually have to go any further. I can have the knowledge of those beings and their activities, and share it with others to warn them because I was prepared to live through that experience myself.

I feel greatly relieved when I hear this.

They tell me to make it known, that it will help to prevent people being caught.

I am made aware of the crystal skulls and told that they also try to protect us and prevent the entrapment of souls in this way, as have all the spiritual teachers ever sent by God. We are prey to that net if we live life on a very low level—but the more mindful and loving we are, and the more responsibility we take for our own evolution and progress, then the less likely we are to be trapped.

We've had spiritual teachers sent to us down the ages, we have been given guidance to live by, like the Ten Commandments, and we have been given many signposts to follow. The crystal skulls are one form of that guidance, and there's an energy pattern that emanates from them that goes up through the different dimensions of the universe—to the levels of light and beyond—that makes it harder for the net, that actually weakens the net. While our skulls are with us, those busy "termites" of the universe find it harder to do their harvesting, and if we lose our skulls their job will become much easier, their net can tighten, and more people will fall into its catchment.

The skulls know the Watchers and Catchers are there, and the skulls are a thorn in their side as they emit the energy that weakens their web. The Watchers and Catchers would be quite happy to see the skulls destroyed, except their harvests would begin to shrink because as the world decayed[163] there would be fewer people. So in the past they've had to put up with them, but they're hoping that the time is coming when they can at last have a really big harvest.

They are forces that would like to see the skulls neutralized, removed, or destroyed. We need to beware of any moves that may hasten the destruction of our physical-level, 3D, crystal skulls. They are our treasures, put there for our protection, to protect us in ways we can't even know and are not aware of.

The skulls have a profound and stabilizing effect on the energies of the world, and on our energies. They are in the shape of our skulls and they have a very deep resonance with our species and our consciousness; they are to help us evolve and they are our protection. The Watchers and Catchers are not concerned with sparsely populated worlds that offer slim pickings, but they are very interested in the harvest from our populous and teeming Earth. We are perfect for their machines, and they are anticipating a great harvest from the end of 2012 through to 2048[164] ... but it doesn't need to be so.

This is no time to sleepwalk through our lives, and perhaps we need to think in a deeper and more spiritual way than we have before. Try thinking, "What does love tell us to do here?"[165] And then our hearts would open and flower, and we'd get a much better experience out of our days and years on planet Earth. The days of our lives would be enriched by our actions, our thoughts, and our words if we were to live in the right way, and the right way will keep us safe from that net when we finally come to our last day. We just need to stay fluid and float on the current of love that takes us back to the heart of God, and not get enmeshed in that net to be used in their machines. Not that we'd be there forever, but it's an experience we don't need and it's easy to avoid with a little mindfulness and an open heart.

---

163 Later chapters pick up on the theme of their protective function in more detail.

164 Years that will see great upheaval in the world, explored in *Divine Fire*, book 3.

165 Chapter 8 in *Spiritual Gold* can help with this.

The guides and angels say:

"Only listen, obey your heart and you are safe."

While we're in body, it's never too late.

Chapter 13

Etheric Crystal Skulls

We are crystal beings brought into thought by the Creator, here to guide and help. We can live forever, for we have no bodies to wear out.
—Syphos

The door in the last chapter was old-fashioned because the experience took place in the past, but it had a modern glossy finish because the ramifications stretch into the future. The transparent glass of the knob related to me—my being in the spirit state, having no body, being insubstantial, like you could see through me.

Now, I'd had other lives after I was Akbar, but the next important one to involve the skulls is this one. The life story in this chapter really extended my understanding of the skulls, and it actually came up in the second research session for *Holy Ice*, so I had this information early on. But chronologically speaking—from the point of view of time passing on Earth—it definitely belongs here, which is why this life story didn't go in an earlier chapter.

A thousand years had passed on Earth since I was Akbar, before I embarked on this incarnation—and it demonstrates that the soul's journey is not the straightforward kind of progression that logic expects. On Earth we tend to measure progress as getting cleverer, but we can dip in and out of much older species elsewhere in the universe, and innocence and quality of heart may be developed in experiences in much younger life streams … as I was about to find out.

Working with Veronica again, I entered the inner world.

For this session I was drawn to a huge, matt-black door. It

was ten feet tall and set in a matching doorframe. I only located the knob because tiny gleams of light were reflecting here and there off the perfectly smooth facets on the surface of its black glass. The keyhole was blocked with a key, and I knew the door had been locked "to keep things secret and safe."

It was a big door, it had a very secretive air about it—it was a kind of "stealth door," the black ops version of the door world. I turned the key, put my hand on the cool glass of the knob, and passed carefully through, making sure to close the door silently behind me.

Wherever I was now, it was dark.

It was somewhere enclosed.

I sense stone all around me—and a growing urgency grips my gut.

I am now Ronweg, and no longer alone.

I am not human.

This is what happened.

SYPHOS
& Multidimensional Crystalline Configurations

We came from the swamp and entered by a secret doorway. Time had concealed it with leaves and river debris, soil, and sand brought by flooding. Things change and get hidden, forgotten. Nobody had come here for a very long time, although it had been important once, long ago. We shuffled about in the dark, looking.

I, Ronweg, had come with a party of searchers, and I held up a lantern to give us some light. The old stones of the castle cellars were not for giving away their secrets easily—things scuttled into corners, and all we glimpsed in the dim light were cobwebs, spiders, and bats. We cast huge, grotesque shadows on the walls as the light revealed our hairy, furry forms, long ape-like arms trailing. We were after something that had been stolen from us, and we were urgent and determined in our search. We could hear a faint sound and it led us on.

The Big Old Dwelling of Stone—as we called it—had been built on the tor by our ancestors long ago, as a home for travelers who had come to our world, bringing color, music, and life.

Its cavernous emptiness smelled musty now, but in those days long gone it was full of people and activity, smells of cooking and herbs, full of sound and music, happiness and laughter. The travelers had enjoyed many things. The men loved fine clothing, and their golden-tressed ladies favored bright, pretty dresses that swept down to the floor. There was much drinking of wine and feasting. Their minstrels created beautiful music, and they were much given to singing and entertaining. They were a fun-loving people whose ways had enlivened the quietness of our world and intrigued our ancestors, and so our forebears had indulged them like favorite children. It had been fun watching them, with their different colored clothing, their little concerns, their loves, their fallings out, their busyness—always so busy growing crops and doing things.

Our people just ate fruit from the trees, and for us life was simple and we felt no need to complicate it. Nor did we bother with clothing, for as we said, "If you've got a good set of fur,[166] you don't need anything else." We were a strong and resilient race, and the lifting, carrying, and construction of the stones for the dwelling had been as nothing to our ancestors, they had been glad of the diversion and happy to help their new friends. Our legends told of the building and its construction, and so we had not forgotten the door by which our forefathers had visited their friends in their new home—and we knew where to come to enter The Big Old Dwelling of Stone.

But the happy people were now dust.

There had come a plague, and only their building and their artifacts remained to testify that they had ever been here at all.

Creatures had come to our world prospecting for minerals, and when they'd seen the colorful ones they considered them a nuisance, thought they'd try to stop them exploiting the minerals they found. And whether by accident or design, a plague was let

---

166 By "set" we were viewing the fur on our back, front, head, both arms and both legs as separate items, comprising a full set. It sounds strange, I know, but those were the exact words on the session tape.

loose and radiation unleashed with fatal consequences for the happy people. The two-legged goat creatures had come, plundered, and then gone, with not a thought as to our dear dead friends they'd left behind.

They'd got what they wanted and didn't look back.

But to our ancestors it had felt like they'd been left with an empty world, where the life and soul had been destroyed, where all color had been bled from it. They felt as though they were no more than the caretakers of their world now, and they mourned the passing of their friends.

Our ancestors, like us, lived in the swamps and in the trees above the waters. They were acrobatic in the water and at home in the trees, so they had no need of buildings, and they were so robust that the plague did not touch them. But when the troubles came they had been given something precious for safekeeping. The happy ones had nowhere safe enough. They knew that wherever they hid it, it would be found, and it was too important to be stolen away by the shiny-skinned, black, goat beings.

So it had been kept safe in the watery depths of the swamp, where there were many insects and things the enemy didn't like. The only time the goat creatures came looking, the ancestors were ready. They hid in the trees, pelted them with stones, and made terrifying sounds. They thoroughly spooked them, and the creatures never came back.

The treasure had been safe a long time now; and when, of an evening, we gathered together to sing our shrill, vibrating warbling songs, we would hear the sounds resonate within its crystal matrix, and it would sing back to us. But this evening, when we'd sung, nothing had come back. We'd dived down beneath the waters and it was nowhere to be found.

Nobody had come for it, of that we were certain.

But where was it and what had happened?

We needed to know, we wanted it back. Together we'd closed our eyes and concentrated, we pooled our minds to explore what had happened. As we entered an altered state of consciousness, we began to review the events of the day. We became aware that a beam of energy had been used to locate it. We saw the beam sweeping the swamp and we saw our treasure being sucked up along it, lifted clean out of the water while hidden within the energies of what had become a tractor beam. And ever since then we had been singing the certain pitch and frequency that it had answered to, and had been listening to where the reply was coming back from. We all knew there was a signal, and that was what had brought us to the castle. The crystal was calling to us.

Our ancestors had known all along that it was waiting to be returned somewhere, and that it wasn't ours forever, but *we* knew with a clear certainty that it shouldn't be with those who had it now, and that it was in danger. It was crying out for help and so we had come, all of us, to help the crystal being who had been our friend, generation after generation.

Now we were inside the building, swiftly and relentlessly we climbed the stairways of the castle, working our way silently upward, all the while listening to the frequency that played inside our heads as though in an inner ear.

Our crystal friend was shaped like of one of the happy people's skulls. Although it differed in many respects from the shape of our own skulls, we could communicate with it. It used to talk to us and project pictures into our minds and give us a sense of knowing about things collectively as a group, but right now it was shouting for help. It could read the intentions of the beings it was with—and it knew its very existence was in jeopardy.

It feared it was going to be shattered and eaten, pulverized and ingested. The thieves thought the crystal would imbue them with its powers, and planned to consume it, but first they were attempting to extract information, and when they'd finished with that they would reduce it to powder. The crystal being knew their soft bodies had no use for its hard crystal, no matter how finely it was ground … and the terrible sacrifice would be in vain.

Two hundred shaggy forms surged like a tidal wave up the stairways and spilled into the passages, our concerned faces and kind eyes focused on the task in hand. The corridors whispered into life under the patter of our feet, ancient cold stones now brushed by our warm living flesh.

Higher and higher we ascended, until we were in the upper

reaches of the castle. The six thieves were in a chamber near the top, too busy concentrating to notice the silent tide that eddied and swirled in the passages around them. At a signal, two hundred throats emitted an almighty bone-curdling, piercing, screaming screech that threatened to liquify the very stones, and a surge of large shaggy forms filled the chamber. The thieves were shocked rigid and paralyzed with fright, their puny humanoid bodies pinned against the walls. They were totally out-numbered by us.

The crystal was easy to see.

It was in the center of the chamber in a transparent box of a pressure container, where they had been attempting to take energies out of it, and trying to put energies into it. After their experiments, they planned to split it.

It looked very uncomfortable, and some of us immediately began trying to release it. The primary tool of our species was sound, and this was a job that needed to be done extremely quickly. With one mind, those of us trying to help, focused, searched for the pitch, then together emitted a series of sounds that shattered the box.

Gently, our crystal friend was lifted out.

It began communicating with us telepathically.

"Most important of all," it told us, "nothing irreversible has happened." At that, there was a collective sigh of relief. But it went on to say it had been traumatized, and it was now time it should go, as it was no longer safe on our world. It had a mission. Its time of dormancy and sleep was over, it said, and it needed to be back on the stage of the worlds to complete its mission.

We received the communication in silence, but were puzzled about what should be done. Ours was a collective decision-making process, and together we mulled over the problem. We knew the skull needed to leave our world, it needed to go somewhere else, back to its original home to complete its work. It had been brought by the colonists, the happy people, so perhaps the six thieves could be of use? They were scared witless, but they did have a craft, after all, which was more than we had. Perhaps their craft could take it back? *But they could not be trusted*, and so we decided this needed more thought.

A cage made of branches was constructed for the prisoners,

and they were secured inside it. It was decided to take them back to the swamp, and to summon help, because this had turned into a much bigger problem than we could deal with.

Back at the swamp the thieves were suspended, in the cage, over the water. We didn't want to do anything irreversible just yet, in case they could still be of use. The prisoners whimpered, unhappy, fearing what was to come.

We bathed our crystal friend in the swamp in an attempt to release some of the heat and unwanted energies, but we knew it needed more help than we could give. Its frequency had changed, and it was experiencing pain. As we clustered around it, the skull communicated with us again. It told us it was summoning its guardians for help, and that they would come from other worlds, other levels, other dimensions. It thanked us for keeping it safe until they arrived.

There was no more to be done then, except wait.

I had no further use for my lantern, so I unhooked it from the end of its stick and gently pulled apart the strands of grass and twigs that had been woven loosely together. Taking care not to harm the creatures inside, I shook out the glow worms and luminous swamp insects that had provided the light. I tucked my favorite stick back into its safe place in my favorite tree, made myself comfortable, and settled down to wait. A gentle singing broke out here and there as those with the softest voices tried to soothe their friend. The rest of the colony held back, not wanting to risk further damage. When we all blended our voices together, we could make atoms dance and rocks split.

It was later that night that a beautiful shower of stars began falling on our world, sparkling against the darkness of the sky, their radiance mirrored in the waters of the swamp as they landed. The "stars" were the crafts of the guardians, pure energy fields of light; and from out of them drifted wraith-like beings. They came, silently gliding over the waters of the swamp toward the trees where our people were waiting.

Their faces were kind and gentle and their bodies were of shimmering light. Their whispering, sibilant voices spoke within our minds and said, "It's needed now, it's time," and they thanked us for keeping it safe and for rescuing it. Even the prisoners in the cage were thanked for bringing it to their attention, because the skull needed to be back where it should be.

They enveloped the crystal in their energies of light and began soothing it. Gently they began helping it adjust its vibrational frequency, and it was obvious to our people that the skull was very happy to be with them and that it would soon be restored, and so one problem had been solved.

We asked the beings of light what we should do with the thieves in the cage. "What you like," was the reply. "But they were up to no good," we replied. "Do whatever is your custom for evil-doers," replied the beings of light, as they drifted away.

Then they were gone … and their ships of light were no more than dots fading away into the night sky.

The skull was gone, but not forgotten. We knew our crystal friend was happier and would now be getting on with its work, and we felt privileged to have met it and to have enjoyed all the generations of contact. Our singing and traditions had been enriched, and we still recounted its first greeting, when it had introduced itself to our ancestors with a direct, "I'm Syphos, I have many brothers, we're crystal beings brought into thought by the Creator, here to guide and help. We can live forever, for we have no bodies to wear out."

Oh, yes, we all missed our friend, but, hey, we said to ourselves, we still have the seasons, the changes of the year, food and feasting, and all the things to do that we normally did. And so we got on with life as it was lived at home, on Home.

And if you'd asked us which swamp we lived in, we'd have said The Good One, which was why we were there, as we thought it was the best. Not everyone agreed, of course, and so some lived in the other swamps. But my people thought that the travelers must have thought it was the best too, or they wouldn't have given us the skull to keep there. Although we did admit, when pressed, that it was also the nearest to The Big Old Dwelling of Stone.

The skull began to come to us in our dreams. It would talk and tell us about its brother and sister skulls, and say it was happy and that all the pain had gone; and when we listened we noticed its vibration had become higher and more harmonious. It always seemed so excited and happy, but it hadn't forgotten its friends.

Of course, we had crystals on Home too, but nothing like the skull. We sang to our own crystals, but we did not find them as interesting. The crystals of Home didn't tell us things like the skull did or share information that gave us a lift out of the ordinary level of things. The local ones had only ever been on Home, so their conversational repertoire was rather limited. They just sat and grew, basically, but they were friendly enough, and they could tell of the heartbeat of Home. Like a baby in the womb is soothed by its mother's heartbeat, so the crystals deep in the ground listened to Home's. And so they knew more about the spirit of Home than us caretakers who merely walked upon the surface of the world, and they were very willing and happy to share the knowledge.

The drawback was that it tended to be the same information, whichever crystal you talked to, whereas with our crystal friend it had been different. But we all wished our friend well, and before Syphos had left we'd promised that we would always be of service, and that in times to come, in times of need, we could be counted on to help. True to our word, we passed this promise on down the generations to keep the memory of our friend alive, so should the call come, our people would be ready.

As my people looked at it, it had all ended happily. We had rescued our dear friend and set him free, and it had been a great adventure. And over the years it gave us much pleasure as we remembered it and recounted it to our young when we taught them the legends. But from the thieves' point of view, it was a different tale.

They had had problems with their craft and had landed on the wide, flat, stone courtyard that formed the roof of the castle because it looked a better bet than the swamps. They had not come searching for the skull, but it had shown up when they trawled the surrounding lands with a scanner beam looking for anything that might be of use to them. Its energy pattern had intrigued them, so they sucked it up and tried testing it to discover its properties. One of the properties registered as "healing," and as they were feeling ill they continued probing the crystal in an attempt to discover more. They got as far as healing being linked to consuming crystal energies in water. They were feeling worse with every passing minute, and in their haste their fevered minds took this information to mean that it should be consumed as a medicine. In the desperate state they were in, they were willing to give any remedy a try. They'd had problems with radiation before they arrived because of leaks on their craft, and then they'd fallen victim to the travelers' plague. Their sickness was rapidly followed by death, and we caretakers were spared a painful decision.

* * *

Since that time, life had flowed along from season to season, and the years had treated us kindly. I grew old, and eventually came to the last day of my life.

My eyes closed as I drew my last breath, and I slipped out of body into the freedom of spirit.

I became aware I had a visitor.

One of the beings of light had come, and the being wanted to take me on a journey to see my crystal friend.

Together we drifted back through time to the night of the falling stars, when Syphos had left Home. But instead of staying behind, this time I was taken on the journey.

We traveled at the speed of the light being's thought. Leaving the Pleiadian world of Home far behind, we drew near to a solar system.[167] It was communicated to me that Syphos had been taken to this particular sun, to more fully repair the damage that had been done.

As we traveled, I was told that significant worlds in the galaxy have sets of skulls like Syphos, and that these act as guardians, holding things in place for those worlds. We drifted past the red and arid world that is Mars, and I was told it had lost a lot of its skulls. They had been destroyed or stolen, and this was why the fabric of that world had degraded and it had suffered the loss of so much of its water and atmosphere. I'd liked water, and had enjoyed its fluid embrace in the swamp every day of my life. I'd felt light and agile in

167 It was ours.

water, it had made me happy, and an intense wave of sadness swept over me when I saw a world that had lost its water.

The light being winced at my pain and quickly pointed out that though it looked all dried up, there was more water than you'd think still hidden beneath the surface. Unfortunately, in his attempt to cheer me up, he went on to point out that it showed that not all its skulls had been lost because at least it was still a planet, which was more than you could say for poor old Maldek, reduced to the planetary rubble that formed the asteroid belt we'd just passed. But instead of helping, this had the opposite effect, and I was overwhelmed by grief for a world I'd never known.[168]

We drifted on toward the blue glow of Earth, and I only felt better when I saw all her shining water and swirling clouds. I was informed Earth was a twin of Mars, and that their fates were interlinked. Both worlds had skulls, and Earth's looked like Syphos while those of Mars were more simian in appearance, like the beings there.

We came closer to Earth and drifted down into a volcano. The heat and pressure had no effect on the light being or on my spirit body, but I wondered why we were there.

We continued down and penetrated deep into the heart of the Earth where we found Syphos with the beings of light, now undertaking the final stage of retuning. The crystal had been away so long it had tuned itself to the heartbeat of Home and it needed to be tuned back into the heartbeat frequency of Earth. Without resetting, it would not be in harmony and not be in sympathetic resonance with the other skulls of Earth, and would not be able to link with them in amplifying and channeling the energies coming down from higher levels in the cosmos.

---

168 Kind, simple, innocent Ronweg had never even considered the possibility of Home, or any world, dying. It had been hard answering some of Veronica's questions because his thought processes were different to mine and his awareness of the universe so limited. You get a flavor of this in his response when asked the name of his world: Home. I, as Ronweg, was surprised by this question, and had never considered it. It was simply home.

The events in his life were easy enough to recall when I was immersed in his character, but the additional material at the end of this chapter was gathered when I was in "present me" mode, communicating with the guides, both before and after his story. But I bless dear old Ronweg, he taught me a lot!

The Earth spirit had missed it and was fussing over it like a mother hen, glad it had come back to her, as if it were an adventurous chick that had strayed. And when she was finally satisfied everything was in order, the light beings returned the skull to its rightful place, and took it back in time to when it had been taken.

Just as humans have layers of subtle bodies surrounding their physical body, so also do planets, and Syphos belonged not to the Earth's physical body but to her etheric body. So Syphos, one of Earth's etheric crystal skulls, was put back in place and resumed functioning like a lens through which the energies that bring evolution could be focused onto the Earth and humankind.[169]

I'd been happy to see my friend again, and I marveled at the things I'd been shown. I'd seen and understood how Syphos linked with the other brother and sister skulls, including those that were solid crystal on the physical level below, and those that were formed of light on the higher levels above, levels that stretched right up to the Creator.

Finally I was told it was now time for me to complete my own journey.

With a focused thought, the being of light brought me Home, to the time I'd passed into spirit. The being wrapped itself around me in an embrace and swept me upward. We rose together into a tunnel of light that brought us to a place where swamp and trees grew to perfection. There I was met by friends who had gone before me, veterans of the rescue mission all those years ago. I bathed in the warmth of their pooled love until I was ready to go on, up the pathways of light until I came, at last, to rest in the heart and mind of the Divine, the Creator, God.

* * *

Ronweg's experiences are woven into the fabric of my soul, as are all our adventures in the spectrum of dimensions we explore on our

---

169 Syphos had been solid and quite physically present on Home, but the frequencies at which matter existed there were higher. Our eyes would not be able to see Ronweg's people or Home, because their vibrational rate is higher than our normal spectrum of visibility allows us to perceive. Home is part of what scientists call the "dark matter" of the universe.

journey of spiritual evolution. But I had said to Veronica, "That's weird even by my standards" when we finished the session. It had been a foray into dark matter.

Although it had started out in a way that could have been an ordinary Earth life, it took place on one of the higher worlds that leave their shadows in our universe as the dark matter our scientists know is there because of its effect on what we *can* see.[170] Veronica took it in her stride, bless her, which was just as well—because it wouldn't be the last weird session we'd have.

After Ronweg's story there came more information about multidimensional skulls. We were told:

The universe unfolds at every moment: things do not stand still for long and change is constant. Worlds and beings evolve, or they slip backward into chaos and destruction. Cosmic agencies are involved in these developments, and their interplay determines the fate of worlds. They are the forces in the archetypal battle between light and darkness, and these agencies are beings that barely have form. They are playing a grand cosmic game akin to chess where the skulls are the pieces on their boards.

Chess requires one board, mapped out in squares of black and white, light and darkness, but this cosmic game is multilayered, involving at least three "boards" simultaneously. First, there is the physical level of the game comprising the solid crystal skulls with which we are familiar, dotted about on the chess board that is our Earth, then just above that there is the etheric level of the game with its own set of skulls like Syphos, and above that there is a level of light, set out with skulls of light. Skulls tend to have a feminine or masculine polarity and are arranged alternately. All the boards are connected, and the

170 You can see dark matter showing as the blue areas in the picture of stars on the back cover. NASA's photo of Galaxy Cluster 1E 0657-556 shows the Bullet Cluster, formed after two large clusters of galaxies collided. The pink clumps are hot gas containing most of the cluster's normal matter. During the collision, the hot gas was slowed by drag force, while the dark matter was not, producing an observable effect. If hot gas had been the most massive component of the clusters no such distinction would be possible. Image courtesy NASA/CXC/M. Markevitch et al.

energies of primary cause flow down from one to the other until their effect is out-pictured by events happening in our world. So, the cosmic game is played multileveled, but also on more than one world. Worlds fall and worlds rise, and it is exciting for these beings to watch, as they manipulate the energy flows that lie behind change. We have our brief lives, but these ancient beings experience time on a vast scale and see galaxies born and die. Their game is unfolding in our solar system, where Maldek has already fallen to the forces of chaos and devolution, ruined Mars struggles on, and we on Earth are poised on the brink of a critical and crucially decisive time. Now, more than ever, we need the wisdom of our skulls for guidance, because besides holding Earth's plan, they literally hold the plan for the beginning, middle, and end of the universe.

And we were also given an explanation about how it all came about, and the consequences for Earth of Syphos being on Home:

The travelers/colonists/happy people came from the Iberian peninsula on Earth. Although they looked like humankind, they were an elvish people, and in them were met three threads of existence, the human, the angelic, and the fairy. They were other-dimensional etheric beings displaced by human activity, and when some passing Pleidians offered to take them with them to a new home, they jumped at the chance. They were happy on Home, it was a refuge for them, far from humankind and peopled only by the welcoming caretakers. They'd taken Syphos with them when they left, as a memento of Earth, but mainly because they thought he might come in useful. They didn't realize the impact of what they did.

The guardians of Earth tend to look outward to ward off dangers, and were not expecting the etheric skulls to be endangered in this way. Centuries are but the blink of an eye to beings so old, and so Syphos was hardly missed. He should have alerted his guardians sooner, but he was enjoying his experiences on the other world. He became mesmerized by the slower heartbeat of Home and fell under her spell. It took the pain of the pressure container to wake him up and for him to remember his mission.

Because he had been taken, he was no longer there to hold certain energies in place for us, and the divine principle that shapes our thinking, feeling, and developing was weakened. The divine began losing its power in our thinking, and so came the Age of Reason and the development of Humanist philosophy. Science became a god and everything was reduced to what can be seen, weighed, and measured. A distortion crept into the teaching of Christ's message, and cruelty entered the religious energies. The Spanish Inquisition and the deeds of cruelty and greed meted out to the Aztecs and Incas in Central and South America were all a direct result of the loss of Syphos.

It caused what the Maya call "the mind of separation"— five hundred years of a wrong way of thinking about the world, where each person sees themselves as separate from everyone else and everything around them. This is the mindset that exploits and degrades the environment and threatens life on Earth.

Although Syphos was returned to the time he had been taken, before all the cruelty was unleashed, this created a time anomaly for Earth, as his absence had had consequences. Much suffering had resulted from his loss, while Home and its caretakers had benefited. He had brought an energy boost that accelerated their evolution, but for Earth it had been like having the brakes put on.

Without Syphos, all we valued was what was physical. Now that his etheric force is back, subtle emanations are going out, helping to facilitate change. Although you can't rewrite history, you can change its effects. Subtly, the psyche can throw off the shackles that were put on it, and humankind can enjoy a rebirth as the divine principle is strengthened. People will find it easier to listen to their own hearts and souls and to find divine love and truth within themselves. Given time, this will leave less room in the world for distortions such as extreme fundamentalist bigotry, of whatever persuasion.

It was beings of light who were concerned that the skull be restored to Earth, and not the forces of darkness. They would have been happy if it had not returned. The forces of goodness had been handicapped by its absence, but the fortunate thing is that now it's been returned and upgraded, it is back with more power than ever before, and it will have an enhanced effect. It has had a boost that it otherwise would not have got, and now that it's back in the energy matrix—in its rightful place on the etheric "board"—it will help to bring about a shift in consciousness for humanity. It may be only one skull out of many, but it's going to make a significant difference. It's going to enable positive change to happen, and it's going to amplify the shift we are making in our collective consciousness that will help us all meet the challenges of this crucial time.

If we don't take care of our skulls and use them as forces for good, we could become another asteroid belt. This chilling disaster would not just be the end of us, but would affect others, too. The solar system is a body and the planets are its organs. If one is destroyed or damaged, then the whole body suffers. Mars and Venus would be most affected, but the damage would go much further than our nearest neighbors, for just as the Earth has its ley lines, so the galaxy is connected by an energy grid that transmits such reverberations through space, time, and into other dimensions.

A scenario of tragedy and disaster is by no means inevitable, but those who are fixed in a mindset of negativity—well, perhaps they will have their negative outcome, because there's a time coming when there will be a shifting and a diverging of parallel realities. Earth will have a cleansing and get rid of heavy elements of negativity and shed them like a snake sheds a skin. Those who cling to that because it's all they know, because they're too fearful of goodness and light, will stay there. They will literally create their own hell. But that's their choice for this incarnation, and perhaps they may review their decision when they die, but they can't hold the Earth back any longer. There is a time for shedding that negativity, and that time is upon us.

The return of the skull will help those who are working for the positive energies of change and evolution. We may not know when the split happens, we may well be protected from it. We may wake up one morning and it's already happened! … It really does not have to be a destructive or painful experience. All the suffering and pain resulting from Syphos's loss can be karmically traded for a smoother transition now.

This is an exciting time of great change and potential for the planet, and for us, and we do not face the challenge alone. We have many unseen allies helping us, friends from the past and beings on higher levels that are here to help us create a wonderful future. Each year will offer us opportunities, and each year is very important. As long as we have the hope and the intention, much can be achieved.

It is essential not to be dreaming away the time we have left. Our future depends on what we do. Do the things that you know in your heart really matter and help other people to look within for their treasures, too. Even the tiniest change, gesture, kindness, thought, or action adds up, and changes the sum total for humanity, and can help us all to realize and become the wonderful beings that we truly are. Each and every one of us is a unique expression of the Divine, and if we are true to the wisdom of our hearts, we will manifest the future we deserve.

At the very end of the session, when everything was complete, I came back through the door. Things had changed, and it was easier to see what was there; the stealth and secrecy element had gone. It had been to symbolize the rescue mission, but now I could see flowing elvish script around the doorknob. (It called to mind the way the words were engraved on the ring in the films of *Lord of the Rings*.)

Fortune favors the brave. You need the courage of your convictions and the courage to follow your heart. Be swayed by no man, the words of many are but tricks and lies, but in the end all comes good. Without the journey there is no story, and without the struggle there is no evolution. Judge not the elvish people too harshly, they did not know what they did. In the end the skull came back with more power and an enhanced effect. Rejoice! For all is well. The Creator is happy. Everything in its season, everything in the right place.

And I realized why the door had been so tall. It was big enough for Ronweg to go through! He was a hairy giant, belonging to one of the humbler races of what I can best describe as "Wookiees" because there's no word for them.[171]

We are familiar with them because of the *Star Wars* films, but truth is as strange as fiction in this case—because we are in fact regularly visited by some of Ronweg's more sophisticated brothers. All the sightings over the centuries of Bigfoot/Yeti/Sasquatch testify to this. They look hairy and ape-like and it is easy to think of them as primitive, but this would be a great mistake.

Neanderthal man owed some of his DNA to them, and it is because they live off-world and wisely try to avoid us that few traces of them are ever found. Recordings of their warbling shrieks have been captured on tape, casts of their footprints made, droppings found and a short snatch of film exists that, despite much study, has never been discredited. The Patterson-Gimlin film shows a female crossing terrain in the Bluff Creek area of California, and it is easy to view it on the Internet.

Some years ago, while at a past life conference at Gaunts House in England, Dolores Cannon spoke about her work for MUFON.[172] She had come across accounts involving Bigfoot, and in particular there had been a sighting of twenty or more of these creatures "being rounded up" to board a UFO ... well, that's what it must have looked like to the shocked observer. But think about it, twenty? We've never found as much as *one* dead body. No, in this case ET was going home—they were not stealing a herd of Bigfoot!

And for those who think all talk of these creatures is a hoax—well, there's been a lot of people involved, all over the world, in different cultures, for centuries. And it's no hoax as far as Native Americans are concerned, or for those who live in the Himalayas.

Those who have read *Spiritual Gold* already know why I picked my present life, but there were six other options open to me. These included a life with Bigfoot.

By their standards our Earth lives are very short, and I decided I could catch up with my Bigfoot friends later ... and in fact the guides had taken some convincing that I was actually up to my first choice—to be Paulinne—which was very humbling when I realized it. Apparently, I've messed up missions before now.

171 Bigfoot are seven to ten feet tall.
172 Mutual UFO Network in the USA.

So although I had contracts my soul was longing to fulfill, most especially a soul-deep promise to Jesus to restore his lost teachings on reincarnation to a bleeding and wounded world, another soul suitably qualified could have been drafted in to take on that role. Of course, they'd have done it slightly differently, because we all have our own unique set of past life experiences, but if they'd had enough of the important ones—like hearing Jesus speak, and lives with the skulls—they could have done a similar job to me. You would be reading different stories now, but they would have taken you to the same place in your understanding. It was Shakespeare who wrote,

> All the world's a stage,
> And all the men and women merely players.[173]

And that about sums it up: somebody else would have been cast.

Knowing this has helped me to understand why I've always been very conscientious about things and overly serious: I don't want to let everyone down. Not this time. It's too important.

---

173 In *As You Like It*.

Chapter 14

Three WARNINGS
Extraterrestrial Perspectives

Veronica and I pressed on with our research. We never knew what was going to come up when a session started, but we were determined to find out more. Working with her I relaxed deeply and ventured once more into the inner world. I altered my level of consciousness to meet my guides and went on the visualized inner journey as usual, but this time instead of finding one door to pass through into another time, there were three, and my guides made it clear I would have to pass through them all in the session.

The first had a high-gloss buttercup yellow[174] finish. It was not a comforting old-fashioned door, but intrigued, I opened it and entered.

Other life recall 1

In the darkness of space, I find myself surrounded by wisps of gas clouds, and the pin-point lights of a myriad of distant stars …

Veronica tells me to look at my body.

I find I am no more substantial than lines of energy are. I am an ancient flying creature, a proto-dragon-bat … with a scaly, scrawny body … and with my bat-like wings unfurled I am sailing and floating on galactic tides …

I am coasting through the gas clouds, on the lookout for more of my own kind … and I'm pleased when I come across a small group of them, busy exploring the raw gasses. Because we

174   Yellow is the color of the solar plexus chakra, and is to do with the mental body. High gloss often indicates that what is to be revealed has a bearing on the future.

never know what we are going to find in the clouds, they are always of the greatest of interest to us …

They are busily assessing the gasses, searching and sifting … and in a way that's what I've come to do too—I've come to search, but it's no ordinary sifting I'm seeking. **It's answers I've come here to find.**

It's answers I need now.

In my scaly talons, I grip something tightly—**but as soon as I'd found it I knew I had to find out its meaning** … and for that I'd need help.

The gas clouds are places of social interaction for us. Most of the time we engage in solitary activities, but from time to time we meet up in the clouds for mating … and the gasses provide the ideal environment for us to lay our eggs and for our young to hatch out in.

When alone, we like to explore the energies of planetary bodies. We descend into the gravitational fields of worlds, enter their orbits, and swing around them to see what's there. And it was while riding the energy currents and swinging round a world that my attention had been caught by this thing that I held. I'd heard sounds of screaming—in the frequencies with which we dragons scream—and so I'd swooped down closer to see what was causing the commotion, and as I flew past I picked up the screamer in my talons.

The screamer was composed of light—and so was considerably more substantial and solid than I was, but my energy field was strong and I simply wrapped the powerful energies of my talons around the screaming configuration of light and pulled it with me.

Of course, there had been beings trying to stop this from happening, but their efforts had only made me chortle more. I'd found it funny that I was just so big and so "not there" to them—so insubstantial—that they couldn't assess my whereabouts or even see what I was. But the screamer had sensed my presence and had shouted to me—shouted that it had been stolen, screamed that it had been taken to the wrong world, that it was lost and far from home … and I had known with great certainty that it didn't want to stay where it was. It wanted "to go back."

It had screamed, "Take me back," over and over again.

But the problem was that I did not know where "back" was.

I was puzzled.

But I wanted to help.

And so I'd decided to go along to a gathering of my kind to see if anyone there could work out the meaning of the thing I had found.

I'd headed for the nearest gas cloud, and once there I'd begun asking if anyone knew its meaning, but those I asked were baffled too; we were used to energies more abstract than this, as we usually dealt with potentialities, with things before they actually formed.

But some of the dragons in the group I'd found had gathered around me and given good counsel. They said, "Well, listen to it. If it was calling for help, it *will* tell you what to do."

So we listened intently.

We could still hear it saying it wanted to go back ... and then the tone changed. The alarmed screeching eased off ... and it said it would tell its rescuer where "back" was.

To my great relief the others were so intrigued by this they decided to fly in a flock, all together, to see "back"—and I'd got what I needed when I came: I was no longer alone with the problem.[175]

We soared up from the gas clouds and rode on the energy currents of the universe (just as migrating birds ride on the winds of Earth). With the screamer in my talons emitting impulses of direction, I was out in front, and the others followed on close behind. We were usually such solo creatures that this was really quite wild, but it was great fun. There was much mirth and merriment, and it reminded us all of being young, of when we were first learning to fly on the currents.

But it proved to be a long journey.

And although the early excitement wore off, we held together. We persisted until at last the screamer got excited because it was nearly home.

We drew near to a world, a gas giant with moons, and in the

---

175 I recognize that feeling today. The feeling of trying to duck the spotlight when fate shines it on you, the "oh crikey" of not feeling adequate; and never was a truer word said than "a problem shared is a problem halved."

dimensional frequency on which we were approaching, the world appeared green and beige, flushing magenta at the poles. An orange-hued atmosphere wrapped around it like a glow.

We began circling the world, and we waited to be told what to do.

As we circled around we were told by the screamer that we needed to give it to its guardian beings.

But where were they?

Were they even still here?

When we'd begun to fear that the guardians were no more, we saw them coming out of the world and rising up toward us. They were beings of higher-dimensional light, and they reached out gladly to receive the screamer, a crystalline configuration formed from the same substance.

They sincerely thanked us for returning it to them.

But that was not enough … We needed more.

We pressed them for the answers that had brought us so far, and in such an unconventional manner for our species.

"You must tell us, what is this about? Why did we need to bring it back? Why was it distressed? Why did it go?" We asked and we asked.

The light beings communicated that it had been stolen by forces that wished to destroy their world.

We considered this.

We wanted to know if it was the only one of its kind. The answer was a resounding, "Oh, no, but it is one of the few remaining."

We pressed to know more.

Now we dragons, being purely energy beings, were not beings who really took much notice of the denser vibrations of matter (those which humans are familiar with). But it was explained that long ago there had been counterparts to the crystalline configurations of light energy that were composed of much denser material, 3D matter, and also counterparts at the levels of the finer etheric energies that bridged the frequencies between gross matter and higher light. But the 3D counterparts were long gone, and those on the etheric levels had perished due to energy decay. Their loss had stopped evolution unfolding any further on the world, and it had begun to deteriorate and to devolve. It had become less and less habitable for beings of any form. And so the beings had begun to leave and the planet had begun to rot, just as a tooth rots, when there may still be a physical husk of tooth enamel to be seen—but the nerve is dead and all the inside is rotten.

The planet had to rely on its last few crystals of light to keep it in contact with the Creator and the higher beings of the universe, and when they went, the world would die. It would be ripe for collision with asteroids … it could implode in on itself … and there were many ways it could be reduced to planetary shards and fragments.

At that the dragons understood.

They realized why the crystal was so distressed. Its home's future and very existence depended on its safe return, and if it had been too long in the returning there may well have been no "back" left to return to. Satisfied, they left.

* * *

I like to think that the dragon people shared this knowledge with others of their kind, and that as they sift about, busy in the gas clouds of the universe they still keep a weather eye out for any crystalline skulls in distress on any world. For that was what the screamer was, it was one of Jupiter's equivalents to our crystal skulls of light. The life-forms there were more amorphous than on Earth, and the roundish, blob-like shape of the crystal of light reflected the form of the beings on the gaseous world; less a skull more a body, as their seat of consciousness was not one of skulls, or bones at all.

The inner guides told me we are the guardians of our solid 3D crystal skulls, and if we take good care of the ones we have left we will not have to worry about those on the higher levels of ether and light. They will be securely anchored through the solid crystal ones, and the energies of unfoldment will be able to continue flowing down from the Creator to assist the Earth in her development.

Earth is fortunate in that she still has a lot of her crystal skulls left, and so we have the chance to get it right. And I was reminded that there are those which are lost, but still function in a muffled fashion beneath the seas. They still contribute something; they still help to maintain the energy grid.

* * *

It was time to return through the first door, and prepare to enter the second. This had a high-gloss red finish.[176] It swung open easily enough, and bracing myself to meet the unknown, I visualized stepping through.

Other life recall 2

Everything in the sleeping pod was pink.

Resting in there was like wallowing in a sea of soft, pink marshmallows. It was easy to get comfortable because we simply burrowed into the pink mounds of soft, round, cushioning modules that were heaped up on high and scattered everywhere; the pod was so full of them that some had spilled out into the corridor.

My sleep period had finished and it was time to resume my duties.

I made for the pod's entrance and stepped out into the corridor, picking my way past stray modules that had escaped. Once in the corridor—and more fully awake—I felt a familiar numbness descend like a gray fog. I paused, and realized it was only the dull blandness of my life that numbed me.

Veronica asks me to describe my body.

I become aware that my body is that of an insect, and that I resemble a giant praying mantis. I look ahead of me, down a wide and very straight but gently illumined corridor, and I can see that it slopes down toward the area where we have plants and where we farm the caterpillars for our food.

At this point in the recall I feel as though I am inhabiting a moment crystallized in time, like a photograph in an album—but I am also in possession of the expanded awareness that comes with the session and that brings me more information. I know that the growing area is but one of many designated zones on board our

176   Looking back, I can see how appropriate this was. Red relates to the base chakra, where issues of physical survival have their focus.

craft, and that this is where I work.

In our craft, we cruise the stars as though on board a small flying world. And this is where I live ... and all I've ever known.

We cruise between worlds and visit them for supplies, but this is our only home. Our species have many such homes cruising the stars, and what is left of us live in the flying worlds. It is understood that we originated on a planet; that we had indeed had a home world long ago. And we know we had already developed this off-world way to travel before something terrible happened at home.

Suddenly it was no longer there.

All that was left of our species were those in the flying worlds—so we could never go back. We could never go home because home had gone. All we could do was continue as we were in our little flying worlds, stopping off here and there to refuel with whatever we ran out of.

And why did it happen? Veronica asks.

We did not understand the importance of the stewardship of our planet. We were like the ants and termites on Earth, who just go on expanding their colonies without considering the bigger picture, and we were like the humans of Earth who spread like a consuming cancer across their world—and so we understand how easy it is to do that until it is too late.

But it is not just us who have brought this fate upon ourselves ... oh, no, it is not just us, and we are but one of many species monitoring the Earth today who are all in the same position. It is a common pattern in the universe. Most of us are trying to help educate humanity in subliminal and subtle ways, in an attempt to arrest the pattern before it repeats again, before it is too late.[177] It is so frighteningly easy to lose your true home, and once it has gone, existence is hollow.

Ours has been gone a long time now, long before me. All I

177 Through interaction in sleep states and through what may be termed "alien abduction." Abduction contact is a big topic. There is not room for a serious consideration of it here, but there is more about it in book 3, *Divine Fire*—and I recommend anyone wanting to look into it to begin with John E. Mack's book, *Abduction: Human Encounters with Aliens*. It was written while Dr. Mack was a professor of psychiatry at Harvard Medical School. He could tell the difference between delusional states and the aftermath of a traumatic experience.

know is what they say. Nobody likes to talk about it, but there are times when we gather together to hold an observance to remember home, and we say a prayer for what was our mother world. It is at times like these we vent our grief while pictures of what was our home planet are projected around us to intensify the experience and remind us of what we have lost.

We do this because we need to connect to each other, because we connect through vibration, with what's best described as a hum frequency. When the hum sinks too low (think of the hum of a beehive), it does not maintain the health of our internal organs, and then we know we need a grief-letting. So we come together to pool our grief, to let it out, and then the vibration will begin to rise again and we will all feel a little better … and then we can go on.

* * *

Dipping into this existence I learned of the unutterable sadness caused when a world is destroyed, and that this grief is carried like a crushing weight by the beings left behind. This is a warning to the people of Earth, to help them realize what a treasure they have and how easily they can lose it.

Other life recall 3

I had to face the last of the three doors. This was the largest and looked quite daunting. I'd glimpsed it before in earlier sessions and it had inspired fear in me. It was a big black door, but as I got closer to it I could see that it was not solid at all but made up of a pulsating cloud of tiny black flying insects. These were "guardian insects," the guides said, "there to hold the threshold, to stop things coming through from either side."

Reassured, I passed through the cloud and stepped into night.

I found myself standing on the edge of raised land, looking down toward the entrance to caves. In the darkness, I could discern that the ground was deeply ridged; what little starlight there was caught on the crests of the ridges, and it almost looked as though the land had been plowed. But this was a cruel irony. The land was hard and parched, the patterns carved into the landscape by ancient winds. This land would never again receive seeds and awaken with life.

I stand and consider.

I am filled with the sadness and desolation of the land, and I am alone. I've traveled patiently on foot to visit my friends who live in this set of caves, and I feel weary, but my love for them gives me the strength to go on.

This is Mars.

This is the world we inherited from our forefathers.

Life here is not impossible, but it is very difficult. We know from the legends that it used to be so different ... long ago. We are still here, oh, yes, we are still here, but there wasn't this wind and there was water and plant life on the surface, and things weren't so harsh or so barren ... We do what we can in the caves, we hang on to life, but it is an austere life that has been robbed of much of its beauty.

Everything is just so difficult and we grow weary of spirit ... as people do on Earth when they watch the deserts come to take their land. Then they can no longer grow their food and the rain no longer falls.[178] But it's just like that over our whole world. And we hang on, but we wonder why. We wonder what we hang on for, and yet we do. And in the face of all that aridity there's still the spirit, the community, the love you have for other beings, and that's why we go on. And we don't remember how it came to this, because it's been so long.

* * *

---

[178] It's not that the Martian being was familiar with Earth, but that I knew that, within the expanded awareness of the session.

And interestingly enough, a BBC news item on December 16, 2014, has bolstered the fact that there is, or has been, life on Mars. Methane, a gaseous product of life, has long been observed in the Martian atmosphere (by orbiting spacecraft at Mars and by telescopes at Earth), but NASA's Curiosity rover—**which was actually exploring the surface *on* Mars at the time**—had just monitored a number of short-lived spikes ten times higher than the low-level amounts constantly in the Martian background ... *Something* was giving rise to the plumes of methane rising from the land beneath the rover.

This recall, like the last, was only a fragment of a life. I hadn't needed to see more because it was enough to give me the message. My inner guides told me I had been shown this because I needed to understand how difficult it is to live on a world that's lost a lot of its skulls. The physical, three-dimensional ones of Mars are long gone and so the physical level of that world has degraded. There are still higher-level ones left, but as the pattern has been broken with so many missing, the energies can't flow properly anymore.

At this time, there are still sufficient energies of light and ether trickling down through what is left of the skulls on those levels to maintain a certain number of life-forms on the planet, but if more of the higher-dimensional skulls go, the number of life-forms will dwindle until there comes a point when the life-forms will eventually give up altogether. Their spirits will go out, like candles in a wind, and they will leave behind an empty world. They might incarnate elsewhere, but never again on the red planet.

And yet Mars still has a planetary heartbeat, it's a world that still lives. It's going through a winter, sort of dreaming within, with not much life to be seen on the surface, although there is some in the extensive system of caves. But the spring may never come because the skulls don't come back. They were forfeited by the actions of life-forms, not by the innocent animals and plants who suffered, but by the dominant life-forms—those with the power to change things, those whose decisions affected their world, and whose stewardship the world should have been in. Their bad decisions and wrong actions forfeited their skulls, and with the physical ones gone they could no longer anchor the higher-energy ones. And so it was much easier for them to go too, easier to be stolen, easier to drift, to just decay and disintegrate, their energy patterns dissolving … gone. It was all too easy.

I learned that it's not too late for Earth, yet, although we're beginning to see changes that are not for the benefit of the world or its life-forms.

The Earth is the last hope for the solar system. She has been slow to develop, and so she's been slower to decay, and slower to lose her skulls. We are the children of the solar system, and we need to learn from the mistakes of our older brothers and sisters on the other worlds.

The other striking thing from this life was the importance of love, as that was what had brought me to visit my friends. There was so much desolation and such a deep heart and soul ache for what they'd lost, and yet they still clung to life. But it doesn't have to be like that for us, it doesn't have to be so hard.

* * *

This session had been very difficult.

It wasn't the strangeness of the beings that made it so, but the level of soul ache. Veronica is gifted with second sight and sometimes sees otherworldly energies when we work. She said that a comforting white mist had formed around me during the session, and that its purpose was to support me through the recall. My word, when it came to recalls 2 and 3, I had really needed it.

This wouldn't be the only time we'd encounter the mist.

My next task was working on *Divine Fire*, and as the research sessions began to mount up there were other harrowing recalls. *Divine Fire* is about the future, and our future is in flux. Everything hangs on the choices we are making now. What we do, and sometimes more importantly, what we fail to do, makes a difference.

Just as you travel into the past during a regression session, you can enter the future too, because progression is no more difficult than regression—but the future is not as fixed as the past—the past is solid. You access the *possibilities*, with the future, and which will manifest is up to us now.

The time lines certainly warranted looking at.

And some futures certainly warranted the mist.

Particularly the extinction event.

But nothing is fixed, yet.

As it says beneath the Sphinx, it's no good leaving it to our leaders, it's the goodness in the hearts of ordinary people and their common sense that will save us, if we are to be saved.

And we do still have the skulls ...

Chapter 15

Skulls in the Present Day

Most important of all, the skulls are still with us, still potent catalysts for change and spiritual evolution. They are not just footnotes in a history book, belonging to the past. They have come from the past, but they have a place in our future. And if we let them, they can help us in the present. We can go visit them! Americans are lucky because most of the Crystal Skulls were taken to their country, and that's where they are today. But here in Britain we have at least one.[179]

RA NAN SA: Visit 3

It was one of those times when I'd thought the book was finished. I'd come to the end of a redraft, it was summer, and I found myself unexpectedly in London. I thought I'd pay Ra Nan Sa another visit.

He was still "available to the many in a temple of learning," as he had so quaintly put it to me the first time I went to see him. The "temple of learning" in question is the beautiful and imposing British Museum in London, a storehouse for ancient treasure. It suits him to be there, available to be consulted by those in need, just as he had been so long ago in far-off Atlantis, and at the Temple of the Sun at Teotihuacán.

The glass display case makes scrying difficult and you can't touch the skull, but when you are sitting quietly on the benches

---

179   Merlin's skulls were buried with him but I sensed they were later reclaimed by those who knew he had them, and that they returned to the Druids. They belonged to what amounted to a secret society. I'm sure the skulls still exist. They may be sleeping in a china cabinet somewhere (probably in Wales or Scotland).

beside him in room 24 it is easy to tune in and hear his silent voice in your mind—that is, if you prepare yourself as you would for a simple meditation; relax and quiet your mind. The museum officially regards him as "fake" because they no longer believe him to be of Aztec manufacture. Indeed, he isn't Aztec, but he's happy with being described as "fake" because it keeps him safe. There is a photo displayed showing cutting marks, but as I said in chapter 1 there is no way of telling when these were put on. He has belonged to the museum for over 120 years now so they have had ample time to polish the skull up for display with twentieth-century materials and techniques. They must have examined it closely before they bought it, and been satisfied it was genuine then, even though it may not suit them now.

When I arrived, he was surrounded by children and was busily being photographed from every angle.

I went up and silently introduced myself by thought. And as I began tuning into Ra, I admired the crystal. There are glorious patterns in the upper part, but the jaw itself is as clear as glass. "Ascension crystal" is what they call this flawless quartz when they sell replica skulls today.

As people moved away, I sat down on a bench. My head was buzzing and my eyes wanted to close. I got out pen and paper. I pictured God's light around me, asked the archangels for help, and specifically requested Uriel's guidance so truth would imbue my experience.

Immediately, thought impulses began flowing into my mind and the nearest appropriate words in my vocabulary began coalescing around them. My eyes were dreamily relaxed and only half open as I wrote down this message:

"I foresee a coming together of the races of Mankind, united in a single cause—to overthrow the yoke of tyranny wheresoever it oppresses the human spirit. My children are awakening from the slumber of the ages where they lay lost in the dreams of matter, imagining themselves no more than part of the material world, deeming too precious the illusions of matter, and blind to their own spiritual heritage—their birthright of spirit with eternity as their playground.

But now is the start of the awakening into joy. For now is the time come to begin again that which was started long ago. The cycles return and urge you to transcendence. Uplift your minds to joyful pursuits and kind and loving thoughts. Create your ideal future with your own minds, when they are firmly focused on that which is truly important—life, love, and joy—for gloomy thoughts will not save Mankind, but joy and loving brotherhood will. Let the sisters of the world take their place in the positions of power, and let the new energies streaming to your planet from the cosmos lift you all into the next way of being—being in the world, but not being consumed by it, nor consuming it in the endless search for meaning through consumption. There is no meaning in consumption, and unchallenged it has the capacity to consume your very soul, dissolving away your spiritual strengths and previous achievements, leaving the soul diminished.

Know you are not your bodies, but that you are so much more—shining spirit, divine gold, born from the mind of God, the Great Creator of the heavens and all that is. Be at peace. Enjoy your birthright as shining, golden, spirit beings of love and bliss. The rest is shadows of misery, and illusions that can trick the unwary into blindness of their true nature. Let no one take your birthright from you."

That was it. The audience was short. It terminated sharp at noon on the dot, but I was told to return after lunch and the discourse was resumed in the afternoon. I had questions to ask about the book … but at the end of it all I was given this:

"Be nice to your friends for they are more precious than jewels. They are the jewels in your life. Take care of them. Do not let them go or lose them by being careless."

I really like the image of our friends as jewels, it helps me to see how important they are, and how important it is to make time for them, and I shall treasure this.

But despite the crowds, I had persisted in my fruitless

attempts at scrying, only to get more and more frustrated. It was the school holidays, and the *Indiana Jones* film has made Ra an international star! As the afternoon wore on there were more people than ever clustering round him, and I was becoming irritated by all the children and the photographing. It is one thing to sit unobtrusively writing on a bench, but quite another to be standing up staring into the crystal, and they made me feel very self-conscious. I wished they'd all go away. This had the effect of locking me into the beta level of everyday consciousness, and it denied me access to alpha. The young people were certainly responding to Ra, and although I wished they weren't there, Ra Nan Sa's response was very different. He said:

"Be glad for the young ones who flock around me. I draw them like a magnet because they sense me and our communal purpose. For so it is. Destiny calls. Listen. Follow. And we will have the golden road to the future of our dreams."

I was being selfish. After all, there was nothing particular I needed to see, and after I'd given up all hope of scrying I sat down and was told I was trying too hard! And that I should lighten up and rejoice!

On the train home, I couldn't help but marvel at how miraculous it is that we still have the skull, and that it is so readily accessible for us all today. It is even easier to see it now than when it was in Atlanta, or later, at Teotihuacán.[180] Never mind having to make appointments with priests, undertake treks that took years, or make pilgrimages—three hours later I was back in Newcastle and getting the Metro home to Whitley Bay, after what had been a nice day out.

* * *

The controversy over the origin of the skulls is dealt with in chapter 1. That is where you will find the facts to defeat the deliberate

---

180 As Wama-marma (chapter 2), I'd consulted this skull in the Great Temple of Atlanta, and as Moves Like The Clouds (chapter 8) I'd visited Teotihuacán and seen it flanking the chief skull.

misinformation that abounds, put about by people for various reasons. For example, it makes a cheap cable TV program if you're quite happy to willfully ignore facts and misrepresent people by dodgy editing in favor of your own biased agenda. It might make a quick buck for these people but it does no service to truth. And apart from anything else this sort of **misinformation and fake news is very disrespectful to Native elders who are skull guardians.** Haven't Native Americans suffered enough without having their sacred skulls maligned?

Never mind tool marks and pointless speculation over when any particular museum skull was made—something that can never be scientifically determined because you can't date crystal nor ascertain when an object's surface received the marks—the only thing that matters is <u>do they function?</u>—can they answer our questions? And from my own experience with the ancient skull Sha Na Ra and the British Museum's Ra Nan Sa I know they can. **But will we ask the right questions? And will we heed the answers when they come? There hangs the future.**

Years ago when Native Americans were being driven from their tribal lands, and the herds of buffalo slaughtered, their elders saw the future. They asked their crystal skulls what was coming and the answers that came back became their prophecies. They warned us then. They told us that when we've poisoned the last fish we can't eat money. But no one listened. Today the amount of plastic in the seas is a scandal and it's been in the news that plastic particles contaminate a lot of the fish we eat. The oceans are choking on plastic and the hormone disrupting synthetic estrogens that are a part of plastic leach out and accumulate in our body tissues … changing us from the inside, affecting fertility.

According to a recent study cited by Greenpeace there will be more plastic in the seas than fish by 2050! The years have seen their prophecies come to pass. Iron snakes now really do cross the land. We call them trains and rails. Few prophecies remain to be fulfilled.

The prophecies are a topic for *Divine Fire*, the next book. But I mention them here because **I think we *are* ready to listen now.**

Native elders have presented their crystal skulls at the United Nations.

On December 22 and 23, 2010, crystal skulls were introduced to the United Nations by Hunbatz Men, a Mayan Daykeeper, Don Pedro Chuc Pech, member of the Mayan Council of Elders, and Don Alejandro Cirilo Perez Oxlaj, Grand Elder of the living Maya.

At last they are emerging on the world stage, and with the wonders of the Internet anybody can watch it on YouTube. Just put in: 2010 crystal skulls at the United Nations.

And never mind what others think, I advise you to visit skulls like Ra Nan Sa if you get the chance, and make your own mind up. If you are interested in receiving healing, chapter 3 explains how to utilize the skulls' healing properties. Take some crystal marinated water with you and drink it there.

May God bless you.

* * *

November 22 (23), 2014, saw the first of the annual **Crystal Skull World Days**, where meditations for peace and harmony are synchronised across the globe. They have happened every year since and anyone can take part.[181] And while I would dearly love to see a skull gathering held at Stonehenge, uniting our minds in this way may be more important now than any physical reuniting of any particular thirteen skulls. Perhaps it really is that simple! That remembering about them, and acting on that remembrance, is the key to accessing our deepest wisdom—the key to creating the future we want, thus avoiding a disaster. Nothing is inevitable, yet. The alarm clock is ringing. The more of us who wake up, the better our chance of entering a Golden Age. Give this book to a friend.

Because we could create heaven on Earth.
We really could!

---

181 Find these events and more on www.crystalskulls.com website.

Meditation and Prayer for Healing the Past

Deliver me now from the sins of the past and the wounds of the world. Cleanse my spirit and my soul. Renew me. Renew me with the Creator's light and fill me now with boundless energy. Wash me in light, make me whole, and may I be blessed, and an instrument in thy service, to bring about the healing of the world and myself.

Visualize divine light flowing down to you from God, flowing into your crown and all around you, dissolving any darkness and shadows of pain within you. Breathe in the light until you are filled, and then continue for a little while longer as you visualize the light still flowing down from God to you, becoming a fountain now, that flows out to bathe our cities and our lands with light. Nourishing and strengthening, bringing healing and cleansing, you and the Earth washed and made new with light.

And when you have done as much or as little as you have time for, finish with:

**I accept that it is done.
I thank you.**

(Doing it in silence is fine, but the spoken word carries more power.)

(Relates to Chapter 7)

Battle Hymn of Merlin's Children: *PEACE, HARMONY, HEALTH*

Meditation

Make yourself comfortable, switch off your phone, close your
eyes.
Visualize light flowing down all around you, keeping you safe.
Hold a crystal skull in your hand (or a crystal you love).
Visualize Stonehenge.
Visualize yourself there.
Greet the site guardians (sometimes you may see them) and declare
your purpose.
Enter.
Visualize putting your crystal or skull down. Sing as you watch it
grow until it fills the circle, and goes on growing until it holds the
circle within it. Sing your heart out!
As you sing visualize the crystals in the stones waking and dancing
and the rocks below vibrating and zinging, see the energy flowing
round and round the site and down the ley lines and out round the
world. Have fun! Singing is good for every cell in your body, never
mind the good you are doing the world. Use the power of your
mind.
Switch yourself on and you will switch on the crystals.

When you have done all you want, reduce your singing, quieter
and quieter
and shrink your crystal back to its original size.
Pick it up. Thank the site guardians, take leave of them and return.
Open your eyes.

Welcome back!

*The spoken word has more power than a silent thought—but that
also works! You can sing anything you feel comfortable with—*

*it is the intention and the vibration that counts. I suggest **Peace, Harmony, Health.** Sing it high and sing it low, really rumble Health down into the stones sometimes.*

In the northern hemisphere send the energy round clockwise, in the southern hemisphere send the energy round counterclockwise. (The same way water spins down a plughole, going with Earth's natural flow.)

In addition to the light you can ask your guides and angels for protection before you start. (If you have read *Spiritual Gold*, you will know that before any inner work I like to ask in the Archangels Michael, Uriel, Gabriel, and Raphael.)

(Relates to chapter 11)

Bibliography

Archeology Magazine. Published in the United States.

Castaneda, Carlos. *The Teachings of Don Juan Juan.* Berkeley: University of California Press, 1968. Published by Penguin Books 1970; rptd. 1972, 1973, 1974, 1975, 1976, 1978, 1979, 1981, 1982.

Cayce, Edgar Evans. *Edgar Cayce on Atlantis.* New York: Warner Books, 1988.

Churchwood, Col. James. *Cosmic Forces of Mu,* Volume 2. Albuquerque, NM/Saffron Waldon, England: A BE, Books/The C. W. Daniel Company Ltd. Co-Publication, 1992.

Cope, Julian. *The Modern Antiquarian,* includes a Gazetteer to over 300 Prehistoric Sites and photos of stone circles and dolmens. London: Thorsons (HarperCollins), 1998.

Icke, David. *Human Race, Get Off Your Knees.* Ryde, UK: David Icke Books, 2010.

Menzies, Gavin. *The Lost Empire of Atlantis.* London: Swordfish (Orion, a Hachette UK Company), 2011.

Morton, Chris, and Ceri Louise Thomas. *The Mystery of the Crystal Skulls: Unlocking the Secrets of the Past, Present, and Future.* London: Thorsons, an imprint of Harper Collins, 1997.

Muck, Otto. *The Secret of Atlantis.* (Germany 1976). Great Britain: William Collins Sons & Co., 1978.

Murray, Kathleen. *Divine Spark of Creation: The Crystal Skull Speaks.* Huntley, UK: Galactic Publications, 1998.

Newberg, Andrew B., MD. *Born to Believe: God, Science, and the Origin of Ordinary and Extraordinary Beliefs.* New York: Free Press, 2007.

Newberg, Andrew B., MD. *Principles of Neurotheology.* London: Routledge, 2010.

Newberg, Andrew B., MD. *Why God Won't Go Away: Brain Science and the Biology of Belief.* New York: Ballantine Books, 2002.

Physical Review Letters. Journal. America.

Randall, Lisa. *Warped Passages: Unravelling the Mysteries of the Universe's Hidden Dimensions.* New York: HarperCollins, 2009.

Rossetti, Francesca. *Psycho-Regression: A New System for Healing and Personal Growth.* London: Judy Piatkus, 1992.

Science. Journal. America.

Steinbrecher, Edwin C. *The Inner Guide Meditation: A Transformational Journey to Enlightenment and Awareness.* Wellingborough, Northamptonshire: Aquarian Press, 1982; rptd. 1983, 1985.

Thomas, Andy. *The Truth Agenda.* Lewes, UK: Vital Signs Publishing, 2009.

Watkins, Alfred. *The Old Straight Track.* (1925). London: Abacus edition published by Sphere Books, 1977.

Webster, Graham. *The Cornovii.* (The area of Cornovian hill forts in Figure 4, p. 8, corresponds to my memories of the Welsh Marches at the time of Johannes, covering a more extensive area than might be thought today.)

Yogananda, Paramahansa. *Autobiography of a Yogi.* (1946). Los

Angeles: Self-Realization Fellowship, 1979.

About the Author

Paulinne Delcour-Min is a regression therapist, artist and teacher. Over the years she has helped many people review and learn from their past lives in order to benefit their present one. Her passion for understanding her own previous life times has led to an extraordinary journey which she shares with us through her books.

After raising her family, she now lives by the sea in the North East of England with her husband, who is also a writer and therapist. She would love to hear from you and can be contacted through her website.

www.paulinnedelcour-min.com

If you liked this book, you might also like:

Joys of A Guardian Angel
by Annie Stillwater Gray
The Power of Giving and Gratitude
by Anthony DeNino
Little Steps
by James Ream Adams
Divine Gifts of Healing
by Cat Baldwin
Atlantis and the New Consciousness
by Joanne Prentis and Stuart Wilson
The Old is New
by L.R Sumpter
Tales from the trance
by Jill Thomas

For more information about any of the above titles, soon to be released titles,
or other items in our catalog, write, phone or visit our website:
Ozark Mountain Publishing, LLC
PO Box 754, Huntsville, AR 72740
479-738-2348
www.ozarkmt.com